$15.79

Reflections on Affirmative Action in Construction

Paul King shares platform with Mayor Richard J. Daley, as host of the 1973 National Association of Minority Contractors Convention in Chicago.

by
Paul King

authorHOUSE®

AuthorHouse™
1663 Liberty Drive
Bloomington, IN 47403
www.authorhouse.com
Phone: 1-800-839-8640

First published by AuthorHouse 9/2/2009

ISBN: 978-1-4389-9564-9 (sc)
ISBN: 978-1-4389-9565-6 (hc)
ISBN: 978-1-4389-9566-3 (e)

Library of Congress Control Number: 2009909096

Printed in the United States of America
Bloomington, Indiana

This book is printed on acid-free paper.

This book is dedicated to all of the unselfish pioneers who were inspired to take action to create change in the construction industry with the hope that future generations take advantage of the opportunities they created and follow their example in fighting for justice.

TABLE OF CONTENTS

Conclusion

Epilogue

About the Author

Acknowledgements

The journey contained herein was inspired, assisted, and encouraged by too many to name, but some must be.

Rev. C. T. Vivian, for his guidance in the 1969 demonstration; and the other eleven individuals/groups who comprised the coalition that called for action and mobilized the participants.

Parren Mitchell stands like a giant over other elected officials in creating the link between Black business and national policy.

Ray Dones and Joe Debro, who hosted the first NAMC Conventions and invited Tyree Scott and Jim Takisaki to become directors.

Art Fletcher, assistant secretary of labor, and John Wilks, director of OFCC [Office of Federal Contract Compliance], became my mentors and inside government supporters.

Congressional staff leaders, Beverly King and Clarence Bishop guided us in the workings of Congress.

Compliance officers at the national, state, and local level who monitored the enforcement of the laws.

Hilton Smith with Turner Construction and Art Queen who continue to lead NAMC in its 38th year.

None of this would have been possible without the patience and professionalism of Dr. Gwendolyn Keita Robinson. Gwen is an historian and archivist in her own right, but has willingly collaborated with me on projects such as this.

To Sham Dabadghao and Sandra Dixon, my partners at UBM, which provided the forum to do much of what was accomplished after 1975.

To C.C. Turner and the founders of the West Side Builders Association where it all started, and to Garland Guice and Brenetta Howell Barrett of CEDCO for assisting in getting funding for the organization. To the late Rufus Taylor and James Martin, who led the United Builders, and to Glen

Harston and Taylor Cotton who continued the struggle until the advent of BCU [Black Contractors United], where my son, Paul III, served as executive director for a time.

Local aldermen, Ed Smith, Toni Preckwinkle, and Bill Beavers are examples at the local level, as was president John Stroger at the county level.

Mayors Harold Washington, Eugene Sawyer, and Chicago Corporate Counsel Jim Montgomery, created the ordinances that became law under Richard M. Daley.

Special thanks to Hermene Hartman and **N'Digo,** for providing the space for me to keep a spotlight on Affirmative Action in construction.

Finally, and most importantly, my family—my wife Loann, and my sons, Paul III and Timothy, whose tolerance and support encouraged and allowed this journey to be taken.

FOREWORD

REFLECTIONS IS A book that chronicles the public life and work of Paul King and his ideas, analysis, and role as a leader in a movement to bring African Americans into the construction industry. The objectives of that movement were to increase the black labor pool by providing access to training programs, and to develop a cadre of general and specialty subcontractors with the capacity to build substantial commercial and public sector projects. Like all good leaders, Paul had spent a period of preparation as a chemist and small-scale painting contractor before the turning point for both the man and the movement came on July 23, 1969. On that day, a number of local organizations, including the "teen nations" AKA "street gangs" who struck peace accords in order to participate, assembled at a federal construction project in Chicago's black community, and **shut the job down!** Despite the presence of local citizens who knew "how to rumble," they operated in the spirit of nonviolent direct action under the leadership of Rev. C. T. Vivian, one of Dr. Martin Luther King, Jr.'s well-known lieutenants, who was a veteran of such memorable civil rights campaigns as the battle of Birmingham.

The 1969 Chicago movement came on the heels of a number of progressive changes in the law. It was the final year of a decade that had brought significant reforms to American society, including the effort to dismantle segregation; establish the principle of equal opportunity through passage of the 1964 Civil Rights Act (in the spirit of the 14th amendment); and secure the right to vote for African Americans in the South, as the 15th amendment had articulated almost a hundred years earlier. It was the era of the **Second Reconstruction**, ushered in not by a Civil War, but by a **civil rights** movement that mobilized hundreds of thousands of African Americans, joined by white citizens of conscience, who decided that the promise of the Constitution and the Declaration of Independence should apply to **all** members of the body politic.

Change did not come easily. Although the path of nonviolence was taken by Dr. King and his legions of followers—the road to freedom was marked by the sacrifices of such leaders as Fannie Lou Hamer, and watered by the blood of martyrs, including that of our beloved leader, Dr. King himself.

But as a consequence of their patriotic efforts, much was accomplished, not the least of which was a marked increase in black voters and elected officials. **Still there was a fundamental piece missing from this puzzle of progress, and that was an economic agenda.**

Perhaps not coincidentally, that same piece had also been missing from the first Reconstruction—an economic component that could provide a basis for full participation in American society as "first-class citizens," by guaranteeing an equal opportunity to "pursue happiness." After the Civil War, there was no bequest of "40 acres and a mule" for the former slaves, whose labor and personal **value as property** created the wealth that fueled the industrialization process domestically, and established the United States as a leading exporter [cotton] internationally. Even foreign immigrants were given land through the various homestead programs of the late 19th century, but the slaves, whose backs had supported the development of the American economy for centuries, received virtually nothing; and were legally excluded from almost everything as the nation moved towards a system of apartheid after the Plessy v. Ferguson Supreme Court Decision in 1896.

The movement to bring African Americans into construction—one of the nation's largest industries and a primary indicator of the health of the economy, must be seen in this historical light. The principle of **Affirmative Action** emerged during the civil rights movement when President Lyndon Johnson issued Executive Order 11246 in 1965, which asserted that government contracts should be carried out with a labor force that reflected the demographic profile of the local community. In other words, public funds must provide the opportunity for fair distribution by taking into account the racial characteristics of the population in which the work was being performed. The **white majority resisted this principle** from the very beginning even though it was clearly equitable. They basically saw themselves as the **owners** of the American economy, and African Americans as their *minions*.

It is noteworthy that during the first Reconstruction, most African Americans wanted to **own** something, **land** in particular; but one hundred years later, most African Americans were looking for **jobs—in the land of capitalism that we had helped to create, we had lost our ownership consciousness.** But not Paul King. Back in the day, when many "movement people" wore dashikis and blue jeans, Paul King, as I often thought of him, was "the brother with the suit on." **He always meant business— mainly because he knew what business meant.** He was the son of an entrepreneur—his father, Paul Sr. was the first man to bring fresh southern produce, "greens" into Chicago supermarkets during the Great Depression. Paul grew up seeing his father rise at 3 A.M. in the morning to greet a long day of work that began at the South Water Markets. His vision of the future was different from many of his comrades in 1969 because his past was different. Some white business owners responded to government and community pressure by employing more African Americans, which was one of the objectives. But Paul King had his eye on a different prize that most white business owners did not welcome. He didn't want a job. What he wanted was the opportunity to develop black-owned businesses with the requisite management, technical, bonding, and financial assistance that would make them successful enough to **provide jobs** to others in the community. In the absence of such firms, Paul and his partners established **UBM, Inc.** five years later in 1974, and the company grew to eventually become the largest African American-owned construction firm in the state of Illinois [another way of saying that they were the biggest and best in Illinois history], with a spot on **Black Enterprise** magazine's list of the **top 100 African American businesses** in the nation.

It should be noted that Paul had begun to study, reflect, and write about the importance of black entrepreneurship and the role that it could and should play in the overall framework of community economic development and beyond well before UBM was launched, not after. But business was not the only thing that he studied--in fact, I met Paul in a graduate course on African history at Roosevelt University. In a society where many people scarcely watch the evening news on television, Paul read the New York **Times** and the **Wall Street Journal** *daily*, as well both classic *and* current scholarly works about African Americans. He was *always* well informed; well rounded [a *blues/opera/theater aficionado*]; reflective, and committed to the education and social development of young black men, as displayed through his work with his fraternity, Alpha Phi Alpha; UBM's corporate citizenship programs; and his son Timothy's Urban Prep Academy. Thus, this record of his writings not only documents a vital part of the evolution of African Americans in the construction industry—indeed, **his story** encompasses much of the **history** of that process; it also represents *his prescription for racial progress*.

There are not many people who get to see their ideas come to fruition, or their lifetime struggles rewarded—Paul King is one of those people, although he would be the first to say, *a luta continua*—the struggle continues.

This book chronicles his journey, and shares his wisdom and experience. Although it reflects times past, it is also appropriate for this moment because it reminds us of the ***unfinished business*** that remains as we contemplate the next steps in this long battle for economic justice and "first-class" citizenship. Therefore, we can all profit from reading Paul King's saga about his life and work in a major industry that affects us all.

Gwendolyn Keita Robinson, Ph.D.

Chicago, 2009

INTRODUCTION

Reflections is a collection of various articles and speeches that I've written over the years in defense of and support for Affirmative Action in the construction industry. It documents a struggle for economic justice that began on July 23, 1969 when various community groups assembled in Chicago to demand equal participation in local federal construction projects. There is much more to be said about this subject, but here we hope to provide examples to those seeking to create change in their own particular sphere.

The book emphasizes four main areas of concern with respect to the construction industry:

1. The employment of Affirmative Action as a tool to break the discriminatory pattern of exclusion by construction trade unions, including their collaboration with the Chicago Board of Education's apprenticeship programs that prevented the training of black tradesmen.

2. To demonstrate that organizations focused on issues of discrimination, such as those we confronted in 1969 federal construction contract shutdowns, can create positive **change** locally that reverberates nationally. These organizations must be led by individuals who can sublimate their egos in favor of a common goal by being prepared, committed, persistent, and never giving up.

3. To promote the expansion of Black tradesmen across the trades as a vehicle for promoting an increase in the number of Black subcontractors, and eventually creating a larger body of substantial Black general contractors.

4. The development of viable black construction firms: I co-founded UBM, Inc. in 1974, which by 2004, was the largest Black general contractor in the state of Illinois. UBM accomplished everything I sought to prove as a black business with the capacity to create positive solutions to problems that besiege our community. As a Black business we:

   • **mentored** students each summer;

- hired and trained recently incarcerated **ex-offenders** without recidivism
- built construction projects with a **100% Black workforce**; and
- completed projects with **70% Black subcontractor participation** while **creating 120 Black jobs for community residents**;
- funded **scholarships** at the community colleges for Black students at a time when less than 5% of Black male students from Chicago Public Schools were graduating from college
- **funded special courses for black job recruits** seeking to enter the world of construction work;
- **hired Black college graduates with little or no construction experience**, and successfully trained them. Some went on to start their own businesses, and others became executives with large majority firms.

Parren Mitchell (D-MD), elected as Maryland's first Black congressman in 1971, was the first and foremost example of a Black elected official being effective in the minority construction industry. He invited me to be one of the first members of his Congressional Black Caucus Business Braintrust, and out of this relationship came the first national legislation requiring mandatory Minority Business Enterprise [MBE] utilization. This book demonstrates how Black businesses and individual leaders can address problems in its community; educate elected officials on issues that benefit their constituents, and hold them accountable. It's not a manual, but there are many lessons provided herein that can serve as a guide to community redemption and progress—all learned by me while fighting for change in the construction industry.

Purpose of Book

The purpose of this book is to describe the path traced by a small group of Black construction contractors who recognized that through unity, there were possibilities of strength. It is not so much a success story as it is one of hope, determination, and conviction of purpose. We believe that this manual might provide a model for minority contractors around the nation. Hopefully, there are items herein which can transcend state lines and through regional alteration, help our brothers in construction to fashion an existence in this industry which will give them their fair share of the economic activity in the building business. To improve upon our victories, to avoid our mistakes, to commend those who help us, and to share in our commitment is the wish extended to all minority contractors. We believe that it is our solemn responsibility to develop ourselves into viable construction employers so that we may be able to employ our unemployed and underemployed brothers in this, our nation's largest industry. We must grow into functional business entities so that we may support, in a financial way, those institutions relevant to the needs of our people. It is our firm conviction that our goals, if achieved, will enable us to build a real Black community, a better Chicago, and a great America.

Pictured left and above: 1969 protest demonstration of Chicago construction project shutdown

1

Executive Director's Message, 1972
by Paul King

Paul King, Executive Director, UBAC

Ours is a polarized nation; this is not an indictment, but a recognition of a situation for which none of us are totally responsible, but surely will be judged as to our part in continuing it. Because of this awareness, my remarks are directed at specific groupings which do, or should, affect our industry.

To white building trade unionists, I would ask you to reflect on just how long you expect to flaunt the law and disrespect Black people. Would it not be better to use your strengths and energies to secure a better life style for your membership than to continually wonder if the Federal government or Black communities will close your jobs and put your workers in a daily trepidation over loss of time? It is clear that American cities are to be rebuilt, and Black people will be the majority in these urban centers. What manner of men are you that you would destroy your organizations rather than share the advantages of trade unionism with others? No person aware of construction believes the worn out, shallow excuses you give for your acts. Black people denied now have only but to wait a short time longer, for if you do not respond to the mild urgings of communities and government presented thus far, there will come a socio-politico-economic flood governed by cosmic forces that will blow you away.

To white contractors, especially those, of you who just want to be profitable businessmen, I ask you what has become of your manhood? You're damned if you do, and damned if you don't. Bound to deal with racist unions in agreements that force you to discriminate through association, you are the one who really loses big. The demonstrations close your jobs, disrupt your completion dates, and cause you substantial losses. The Federal government cites you in violation of the law, suspends your funds, and prevents you from working on other projects. You can alleviate some of the pressure by continuing to work with Black contractors. Regardless of agreements, you are the entity that does the hiring. Thus, where a racial imbalance occurs, you are the one who is directly responsible. The Chicago Plan embarrasses you, and surely it should. Seize the opportunity to create, develop, and use Black contractors, and we will become your partners in compliance. Require joint ventures of your mechanical subs, and others. Further development of Black specialty firms will result in greater competition for your work, and surely we will bring minority workers on the job. After you've caused a joint venture to occur, monitor it to insure real growth for the Black contractor. To have a Black face fronting for a white operator serves no purpose but to continue exclusion.

To the Federal government, we can only suggest that you continue the positive efforts you have displayed. But recognize that without continued surveillance and cooperation with the Black community, your stated goals will not be reached.

To Black community organization leaders and Black elected officials, I would ask that you educate yourselves to the dynamics of this construction industry. The unemployment problems, economic development, educational, and housing problems you spoke of prior to assuming your offices can be dealt with in the construction arena. Black workers are your constituents, get them jobs and they will be your supporters. Black contractors can be prosperous businessmen capable of supporting your efforts in a financial way. Help them develop. If you fail to heed this request, we shall be forced to question your legitimacy as our representatives.

To the Black construction job seekers, you must assume an active role in pursuing this issue. In Seattle, Denver and elsewhere, the leadership in this struggle has transferred to those Blacks who are involved, or want to be involved, in construction. No longer can Civil Rights groups, community leaders, and ministers lead the fight. It is for those of us desirous of jobs, desirous of contracts who must continue to help government enforce the laws that apply to hiring *us*. We need the support of Black leaders, ministers, and community groups, but it is our responsibility to provide the sustained effort in changing the felonious practices currently occurring in construction.

To the Black contractors, whether you agree with UBAC or not, you must recognize the need to abandon the individualist theory which has kept you weak. Identify with the community; help leaders and organizations whose group strength can give muscle to your development. We have been training Black workers, free of charge, for decades. Now is the time to realize that it is not just a Black contractor problem and Black worker problem; it is a Black problem in construction. The day of one-man operations is over. We must develop firms with the necessary competent parts to insure a viable operation. It is our duty to develop ourselves, for in doing so, we can, in fact hire our people, support our institutions, and build a real Black community.

PHOTO/ GRAPHIC HISTORY:

1969 PROTEST DEMONSTRATIONS

News Clippings from 1969 construction protest demonstrations.

Coalition leader C.T. Vivian being prevented entry to Government hearings by angry mob.

Ass't. Secretary of Labor Fletcher facing union members who forced cancellation of Committee investigation.

Conservative Vice Lords and other teen nations at demonstration.

Black being told point blank
Stop, we don't want you!

The Silent Majority becomes
the Violent Majority.

Out of all the white violence, a Black
gets arrested.

Teen Nations arrive at Shut-downs.

Troops stand at peaceful parade rest.

Rev. Jesse Jackson lends his energies
to the struggle.

Coalition gathers community support
in massive rally.

Negotiations...meetings...press
conferences...negotiations...meetings
...press conferences...and so on.

Finally! The Chicago Plan is signed.
Mayor Richard Daley joins Thomas

Murray of the union, and Dave Reed
representing the Coalition.

THE UNITED BUILDERS
ASSOCIATION OF CHICAGO

November 1971

Original EDITORS NOTE: *Paul King, a painting contractor, is the Executive Director of the United Builders Association of Chicago, and Labor Chairman of the National Association of Minority Contractors. As a member of the Coalition for United Community Actions Negotiating Team in the Chicago Plan, he has been close to the Black sub-contractor problem to which reference was made in an article appearing in the June 1971 issue of the CHICAGO LOCAL CON STRUCTION magazine. However, Mr. King feels that some of the conclusions drawn in that article are not applicable to a well-planned, honest approach to the usage of Black subcontractors. In the following article Mr. King presents a graphic picture of the problems that confront a minority sub-contractor in his dealing with large general contractors.*

Over the past two years, the awareness of the minority contractor has grown within the Chicago construction community. In July of 1969, it was a small group of contractors from the West Side Builders Association (now The United Builders Association of Chicago) who participated with community organizations in closing down projects in their community on the west side of the city.

Since that time, many minority contractors have benefited from this effort. In certain parts of the city, we have signs listing as many as 8 or 10 Black subs: A dramatic comparison to the zero at work at the west side site focused on in 1969. Whereas the attention has increased, the effective positive usage of the minority contractor is still not a reality.

Dick Pepper of Pepper Construction Company has cited many views on the subject of minority contractors (Chicago Local Construction, June 1971). To a large extent, he is experienced enough to elicit strong evidence in stating the minority contractors plight. Unfortunately, he was forced into a reactionary position in his firm's major encounter with Black subs. Instead of having the benefit of predecessor's experience, Pepper Construction Company had to react to tremendous local and national pressure.

Of the several Black subs that worked the two projects with which I am most familiar, only one has not shown significant growth and development. Hence, the Pepper firm had to absorb a crash Black sub training experience. Thus, in one way, many other white general contractors are indebted to Pepper because they will not face the same problem. There are, however, certain elements that, as Black contractors, we need to add if Peppers analysis is to be helpful.

Many minority contractors do not have the ability to estimate jobs within the time they are informed of the job. Hence, at the very outset, he is at a disadvantage. Not having an estimator in his own shop or access to an estimator, he often misses the due date or renders a hurried erroneous estimate.

Some possible solutions to this estimating problem have been established between United Builders Association, the University of Illinois and the Builders Association of Chicago. These range from:

- Providing quantity take-offs and allowing a sub to convert these into his actual costs.
- Providing a general contractor estimator to assist in the quantity take-off where blue print reading ability is limited.
- Providing special programs for bid preparations, as was done between the Builders Association of Chicago, the University of Illinois and the United Builders Association of Chicago last year.

It becomes incumbent upon general contract ors to recognize the need to "develop" Black subs which, necessarily requires "negotiation" as opposed to competition." It is true that minority contractors do not have proper working capital. We do not have the track record, friends, relatives or old family ties which gives us access to the money that white contractors can get.

On the other hand, minority contractors should not be forced to finance the general contractors operation. Oftentimes its 75-90 days after work commences that we receive a payout. A serious boost to our financial viability could be seen if general contractors would pay for 90% of the work completed in the first two weeks of work within a few days of the particular interval required.

The 10% retention is an unbearable hardship especially on the trades who start in the early stages of the job commencement. A guarantee from the sub with a nominal amount left up for a given period should suffice. Ten percent (which is a lucky mans profit) being held at no interest for a year or more is harmful to the minority con tractors growth and continued operation.

An immediate reaction by general contractors to these comments is: That's the way they get paid from the owner or the government, and therefore required to impose the constraints on the subs. Perhaps general contractor and Black sub coalitions, on these issues ought to face owners and government agencies. The same government urging the use of Black subs should be made to understand the working capital problem.

General contractors associations need to have greater control over their members. Many generals are doing smaller jobs that suit the production capacity of many minority contractors.

Joint ventures need to be established on jobs of all types. True joint ventures should be supported and monitored. This is especially true in the mechanical trades. One sure way to train minority firms is to create learn while you earn situations.

Supervision is the principal malady of the minority sub. This problem ought to be attacked by general contractors and the subs together. Perhaps stipulations ought to be included in contracts, so that if work is bogged down or mismanaged, a superintendent will be placed on the subs payroll for so many hours per week as a resource person or troubleshooter. This is a cost that could be entered as a line item job expense and go to the general contractor for the minority contractor. The objective is not to subsidize errors, but to subsidize minority sub development by having certain funds available to offset mistakes. One problem we find is that mistakes can be discerned early in the job, they only become disasters when they are allowed to persist. Technical assistance funds for this purpose can be helpful.

There need to be some training sessions given to the project managers and field supervision of the general contractor as well. A major contribution to the failures we have seen has to do with the super being expert in getting a building up, but profoundly stupid in relating to people and interpreting the new set of parameters brought on the job in the form of developing Black subs. Many hours and dollars could have been saved if contracts were prepared, thoroughly explained, project meetings held, and a new attitude geared toward development rather than the traditional sub exploitation.

The fact that over 72 contractors attended the seminars sponsored by UBAC, BAC and University of Illinois is indication enough that minority sub contractors want to improve their conditions. What United Builders Association is moving to ward now is an extension of this relationship to increase the education and on-the-job experience of these contractors.

Funds need to be injected into the minority contractor milieu. Not to the general contractor, but to the Black sub in connection with general in such a manner so as to insure the job's successful completion, offer a profit to the sub, and provide to both parties a learning experience which will offer Black and other minority contractors a fair share of the construction activity.

THE **BLACK**SCHOLAR

FEBRUARY, 1972 $1.25

THE BLACK COLONY, U.S.A.

ROBERT ALLEN

ANGELA BLACKWELL

CHARLES C. DIGGS, JR.

PAUL KING

IMARI ABUBAKARI OBADELE

LINDA N. RIGGINS

SIDNEY WALTON, JR.

THE ROLE OF BLACK BUSINESS: DELIRIUM OR IMPERIUM?

Part I

by PAUL KING

DURING THE 1960'S, the unique combination of classical rhetoric, a massive, resurrected consciousness--buried since the heyday of Marcus Garvey--and the rise and demise of our finest spokesman brought masses of Black people to a fever pitch. We recognized white institutions as racist and dysfunctional, we came to learn of our history, we defined a new beauty value, our hair grew, our anger grew...but, our people were **never told what to do next**. Our revolutionaries were killed or jailed and other than the immediate rebellions after Martin Luther King's death (outside of Memphis), even these events had no visible effect on the masses of Black people save to reinforce the belief that white society is repressive. There has been no move within our communities to develop sanctuaries for our recognized freedom fighters or those who so consider themselves. As a matter of fact, in some quarters, the more Black youth and other activists were jailed or killed, the more Negroes were convinced that they deserved to be eliminated. This was due in part to never having understood the policies of certain Black groups, or to fear of vocalizing even lukewarm support. I suspect that Peter's triple denial of Christ was not too different.

Intellectuals do a fine job of researching problems and writing in scholarly journals for their own benefit, but what they do, based on their conclusions, to proselytize among the people is still another matter.

I RECALL THE EARLY SUMMER of 1969--a group of eleven other dedicated persons and myself (representing over 60 other organizations) embarked upon the struggle of getting more Blacks into the construction unions. A like effort had been in process by the NAACP, Urban League and other groups for some years. But ours was special, for we took enough people onto construction sites to physically intimidate white workers into leaving the job with our mere presence—non-violently.

15

Our major advantage was surprise attack. We shut down work in the Black-occupied areas and we had the peaceful presence of large numbers of Black organizations such as the Black P. Stone Nation, Disciples, and the Conservative Vice Lords who had gained great notoriety for their alleged violence. This was the first demonstration that led to negotiations with the major construction contractors, union representatives, and city officials, including Erwin France and Mayor Richard Daley. Our victories or defeats would undoubtedly influence the outcome of negotiations in other cities where shut downs had commenced shortly after the Chicago effort.

Black intellectuals in the city--who had researched such questions as the European ethnic make-up of city and state government, the board of education, and the judiciary--did not offer the fruits of their efforts to aid in identifying pressure points as our drive continued. Black lawyers, knowledgeable about the legal ramifications of our pursuits, were in the shadows if present at all. Black political scientists and social theoreticians who were discussing daily such books as Banfield's **Political Influence**, didn't care or didn't perceive the opportunity to translate the knowledge gained in reading about Chicago family connections, labor ties, and political maneuvering into the practical application needed within the atmosphere we created. Certainly no one group is to blame for the failure of our attempts to result in greater success. Obviously, we approached the disruption of institutional racism in an atmosphere that provided the greatest shelter for racist unions. This experience certainly points up the need for Black groups to stop operating in a contemptuous or envious professional elitist vacuum.

It is absurd to have a cadre of intellectuals, knowing facts and special features of a problem, allowing activists to blunder through negotiations reached via confrontation. Far be it from me to harp on intellectuals too much, considering Harold Cruses contribution on the subject. Conceivably, that could be a bad name to bandy about at a Black Scholar-sponsored gathering-- yet, I understand the Cruse Abuse sent Brothers Hare and Chrisman crying all the way to the bank. Suffice it to say it is my sincerest hope that this conference will favor the question of intellectual responsibility with some of its valued consideration.

It is widely known that Ossie Davis, speaking at the Congressional Black Caucus dinner, said it's not the man, it's the plan. He said something else in that same context which, it seems to me, is infinitely more important: in essence, after the plan was laid out in the face of resistance to the strategy, Black people were all exterminated save two of us a little Black boy and a Black girl, in hiding and the small child says to his mate, what's the rest of the plan Sister?

Two things are inescapably clear and necessary in this all too real eventuality are that a plan existed which was known and accepted by the people, and provisions were made for the young to understand its relationship to each of us. Who among us is so foolish as to expect any one person or special interest group to conjure up a strategy, print it, distribute it, and then have it executed? The facts suggest that we must have *an ideology developed and legitimatized by new institutional forms.* This ideology must be *understood and accepted by as many Blacks as possible*, and must contain attitudes and courses of action toward those who do not subscribe to it.

We need a plan that will move toward these ends. Widely agreed upon goals, timetables, and methodology are now in no ones pos session, to my knowledge; and if they were, the repression we face would not make it safe to enunciate them for mass exposure.

THERE ARE SOME initial steps we must take in any case. Let me discuss a few of them, as I see it: during the sixties, many of us who acknowledged that we were Black rather than Negro, spent our time (1) studying about ourselves and our history, and (2) identifying the enemy within the white system, and attempting to attack him. In this decade, we must reverse the emphasis. We must in crease our knowledge of white systems, especially since the previous decade has created a different perspective from which to accomplish this investigation. Then, it becomes incumbent upon us to recognize the evil, the dysfunctional, and the weak within the Black populace. We must, at this point, turn inward and develop a method for dealing with the elements within our own ranks which, ignoring current white action, tend to cancel out the effectiveness of our too few productive acts. Hence, there must be a plan aimed toward establishing a methodology rather than a plan of action as a first step. A plan of action without agreed goals and methodology seems awkward.

One must appreciate, for example, the function of scandal on the Western European mentality. It was a whore's testimony in the Profumo case that caused harsh rumblings of "immorality," thus creating a change in England's ruling party. The prostitute, managed by a Black pimp, named several high-level ministry officials in this moral decadence. It was Mary Jo Kopechne's drowning at Chappaquiddick and the immoral undertones connected with it that caused Edward Kennedy his greatest political setback. It is almost amazing to recognize the weird hypocrisy whites manifest in this regard. The public sympathy for him after losing, through assassination, two brothers--one a president, and the other a presidential candidate the magic and money of the Kennedy name all succumbed to the scandal for a given period. (Can you imagine what leverage Black maids, chauffeurs, and secretaries could have if they knew how to use this knowledge gained by being privy to the personal actions of important whites?) Whether the damage born of scandal was permanent is one question, but its import when scandal struck is without question.

Abe Fortas resignation from the Supreme Court is another case, as is that of current Secretary of State of Illinois who declined to run for reelection due to disclosures about his ownership of racetrack stock. Cook County States Attorney Edward Hanrahan's fate as an elected official will be interesting to observe in this con text. His involvement in the deaths of Black Panther Party leaders Fred Hampton and Mark Clark, which resulted in an indictment placed against him, should make a difference in the political heights to which he can ascend.

This country, seeking always to be number one, is constantly fighting to protect its international image as a world power. It is the influence of current world opinion, pro-American and anti-American, which provides a built-in system of checks and balances and which can be an invaluable tool in developing the plan. A white British leader once wrote that England was forced to either grant its African colonies independence or kill them all, and world opinion would not allow the latter. The entry of China into the United Nations, increasingly vocal African nations, and other countries that (for their own selfish reasons) are friendly toward Blacks, provide a key dimension in the internationalization of the Black Plan.

THE WAY INFLUENCE is used to achieve the ends of special interest groups, as Banfield points out in the relationship of organized crime and the Godfather syndrome, is important to us. Most important, however, is the need for us to recognize the powers that wield the greatest influence in this country:

1. The few super-wealthy families
2. The top 200 corporations
3. The Pentagon and its military-industrial complex
4. The Federal and state governing apparatus
5. The Federal legislative apparatus
6. The organized labor establishment

Such facts should have wide exposure in layman's language. As I see it, we cannot move too far without understanding the workings of these entities. We must recognize the points at which they disagree among themselves, one group against the other, and where our support for either can merit us the greatest advantage. We must recognize our mutual interests, seize opportunities for our people, and plan. Needless to say, there is no inherently common interest in Black peoples quest for freedom among any of the six elements listed. However, parallel lines are the only ones that never meet and I am simply saying that at various times, limited though its magnitude and direction may be, the Black vector will cross the lines of force of this nations super powers. There is something to be gained for us in the proper exploitation of these points of common occupancy.

Organized labor is a good example of this tactic. Its spokesmen say their concern for Black folk is manifest when they lobby against the appointment of a Carswell or a Haynesworth to the Supreme Court. At that point, they are pro-Black; but their direction is 179 degrees from ours when we enter the quadrant encompassing the quest for Black entry into their construction trade unions.

As we focus on Intra-Black considerations, an entirely new ethic must come to the fore. I am convinced that without dealing honestly and realistically with the negative actions of Black people relative to other Blacks, their causes and meaningful solutions, we can forget liberation (regardless of definitions). No one needs to tell any of us *why* certain problems exist in our intra-group relationships yet, all of us need to hear and discuss what we shall do about them.

ALLOW ME TO play the 20 questions game:

1. What must we do to change the perilous relationship between Black men and Black women? The one in which the man gains the woman's trust and affection and then disrespects her by boasting to others how he exploits that "bitch"--or conversely, the one in which the Black woman accepts the sincere efforts of a well-intentioned man who wishes only to give her attention and respect, and she, in turn, flaunts her acquisition with such words as, "I've got this fool's nose open." This unnecessary contest has deleterious lineal effects on our children with negative psychological dimensions far greater than those of hair texture, nose breadth, or skin complexion.

2. What must we do about the senseless maltreatment of Blacks

rendered by other Blacks?

3. What must we do to define the role of religion in the Black revolution? Black Hebrew Israelites going to set up a nation in Israel, Muslims operating in a closed sect even to other Blacks, Black Catholics organizing with the hope of gaining legitimacy from the Pope?

4. What must we do to bring about a modern perspective on Africa? Are the Egyptians Black? Pan-Africanism, Africans true feelings toward Blacks in America, etc.?

5. What must we do in America to influence change in South Africa? Witness the employees of Polaroid in the U. S. pressuring that company to change hiring and advancement policies in South Africa.

6. What must we do to alleviate the loneliness and helplessness of the Black unwed mother or the separated or divorced Black woman?

7. What must we do to assist Black youths in the passage from childhood into Black manhood and Black womanhood? Is it enough for them to be termed adult after a certain age and set into this world without some preparation and close relationship with older concerned Blacks?

8. What must we do to develop an effective alternative to the current educational process defining as a goal the ability to emerge as productive Black men and women able to survive this racist society?

9. What methods can we devise to gain some productivity from the masses of Black people at whatever level we find them?

10. What steps can we take to eliminate the Messiah complex?

11. What assistance can we provide for those Blacks who have developed a positive consciousness, but who sense no direction in which to move?

12. What methods can we use to expose, judge and punish counterproductive Blacks by Blacks--specifically, those who rip off for personal gain and create new spheres of misery for our people by their acts?

13. What can we do to create a forum in which to openly debate differing points of view between Blacks, while ignoring the foolish notion that intragroup criticism displays lack of unity to the white world? (Did Dubois' and Garvey's importance to us diminish because their views differed?)

14. What must we do toward defining the roles, responsibilities and accountability of Black political officials?

15. What must we do toward defining the responsibility of Black educators to teach all that is necessary for our survival?

16. What is to be the role of the Black businessman or woman?

17. What must we do to resolve the apparent inconsistency in the actions of the Nation of Islam whereas its representatives refuse to discuss common problems with other Black groups, and use white builders in its new construction projects?

18. What must we do toward the creation of a national Black lobby in Washington reflecting the broad interests of Blacks?

19. What must we do to eliminate drug abuse?

20. What must we do to evaluate and educate our people to the importance of the Congressional Black Caucus? And how are we to support it if we find it worthy?

Let me expand on one of the questions further.

In some public schools, the stated objectives of the '60s have been realized--a Black principal, Black department heads, and certain curriculum changes. Moving into the second phase, the precious few truly concerned Black teachers began to implement a thrust to help students learn. It was felt that most teachers (Blacks included) simply were not teaching. Recognizing that the weak spot of some Negro educators is to have their professional abilities challenged, a comprehensive exam was prepared for all classes of a given department. This was done in cooperation with counselors, department representatives, etc., so as to be fairly administered and reflect the variances in different classes. Assume that now, it has been ascertained that some teachers (Blacks included) simply aren't teaching. When statistics, facts, and student testimony identify these professional educational pimps, the group of reformists takes the evidence to the Black principal. *The principal refuses to act on this crucial question. Black teachers not teaching Black students?* Whether it is for reasons of faculty harmony, peer approval, upper echelon pressure, or simple fear that the principal resorts to inaction, the students education is the question, and Black disinterest in Blacks is the issue.

QUITE CLEARLY, IF my twenty questions are to be answered, the answers, in varying degrees, will emerge from that ideology called for earlier, Where, if not in the school, should the young acquire the tools and become inculcated with the spirit and feeling for the ideology, and thereby, for knowing and executing the program that will produce The Plan?

Sutton Griggs made a significant literary contribution to America in 1899, entitled **Imperium in Imperio**. Perhaps a short look at it might provide food for our modern day thought.

The story centers around two young Blacks who, as children, developed a fierce competition between themselves over academic achievement in an inadequate Southern Negro school in the last half of the 19th century. **Bernard Belgrave**, by virtue of an influential white father, was catapulted from the humble elementary school through the finest college, and finally into membership in the House of Representatives. He suffered a tragic love experience wherein the Black girl he loved committed suicide. She did this because she loved him, yet, because of his white blood, feared having children (as it would add to the demise of the Black race). Hence, she killed herself. Her untimely death, coupled with a letter of explanation, brought him to a point of deep analysis as to his life's mission. This frustration was all the more intense when heaped on to his own undying love for his people.

Belton Piedmont, our other hero, proceeded through a Negro college as the result of a white benefactor. He chose to teach after his studies concluded. His life was stunned by the fact that his wife bore a child that appeared so white, that he assumed her to have been unfaithful. The child got dark enough with age so as to relieve him of this hurt, He left without any violence toward her and proceeded to engage in a series of experiences which heightened his recognition of the racism in the land.

Both men became committed to a programmatic action toward racial uplift although being out of touch and operating in different arenas. Piedmont became obsessed with the inconsistency of the Federal government in that it could tax the Negro, commend the Negro to war, etc., yet would not exercise its sovereignty in protecting Blacks from local mob violence and other abuses. Hence, Belton joined an organization structured to serve as a government for Negroes ***within*** the U. S. government. Its initial finances came from the secret contributions and participation of a reputable Negro scientist; others, of his caliber of achievement, participated also. The Imperium objectives were (1) for free Negroes to gain rights and privileges, as men, according to the teachings of Thomas Jefferson, and (2) to secure freedom for Negroes the world over.

 OME OF THE steps it took were:

1. Organized the special education of individuals as to the meaning of freedom, and those who had sufficient zeal joined to struggle for it;
2. Used the group's collective influence to have its members appointed over Black colleges in the South;
3. After careful scrutiny and a series of different rituals testing his integrity and commitment, elected Belgrave president.

The Imperium settled intra-group differences by its own judiciary, and organized an army of the able-bodied. Its judiciary evaluated each national question on racial matters and compared their findings to those of the U. S. courts. A branch legislature was created in every state. The treasury was built by endowments from wealthy members, individual contributions, and other sources of revenue. The Imperium headquarters was a college-like complex which, among its other functions, developed a secret newspaper distributed to members depicting everything of interest to Blacks. The Imperium chronicled international developments, and considered the ongoing issues of industrial development, civil rights, education, justice in the courts, mob law, and politics. When one of its members was lynched because he had risen to too high a post for a Negro i.e., Post Office clerk- the group's frustration reached a fever pitch. A general meeting was called and the Congress discussed various alternatives as to their course of action: (1) amalgamate with whites, (2) emigrate to Africa, (3) war, (4) a civil rights campaign. War was the unanimous choice until Piedmonts plan (the last alternative) was revealed: this was to educate whites to the existence and sophistication of their organization for a given period of time and, if they met with no success, they would move to Texas.

President Belgrave chose a plan that essentially was a combination of #3 and #4. It called for an eventual takeover of land, combined with foreign help and killing of certain officials. This plan was overwhelmingly accepted by all but Belton Piedmont. It shows here that Piedmont was American first, and Black Imperium member second, and as a result, was forced to resign and face the Imperium death sentence. The Imperium was betrayed by a member who, like Piedmont, could not face the possibility of warring with his country, coupled with what he felt was a potentially great loss of Negro life.

One may well ask what difference there is between this Imperium and the Alpha Phi Alpha Fraternity, or the Black Muslims, or the Moorish Science Temple, save the notion of cosmic intervention. The Black Panther Party or the Black P. Stone Nation would not appear too different except insofar as their political views are too different from the larger society in which they have attempted to openly exist. Obviously, the idea of any secret Black organization is utopian to an extent, given the surveillance and invasion of privacy existing today. Rapid mass communication and transportation make the original Imperium anachronistic now.

BUT THE IMPERIUM Model is worth viewing inasmuch as it spins the theme of an orchestrated movement. Could it exist with a multifaceted movement, open in its goals planning and requiring several layers of insulation between the privacy of decision makers and the eyes and ears of the masses of people.

To promote a coordinated effort on behalf of Black people being free to act as men, facing humane treatment according to the principles of Thomas Jefferson and Patrick Henry combined with the morality of Jesus Christ's teachings would be nothing new. That has happened before. The most recent effort ended in the leader of that movement being killed--and the ***black people of that city where the murder took place did very little***--out of fear or per haps because they knew not what to do. That the Brothers and Sisters in Memphis, Tennessee would react more to the brutal slaying of a young Black this year than to the slaying of Martin Luther King strikes me as being significant since there is possibly a new element in our midst.

Fanon reminds us that it is all too important to keep the populace involved and informed of what a movement is all about. Yusufu Soneboyatta gives rightful attention to attaining the **consent of the people**, as he so adequately expresses the pursuits of the Republic of New Africa. I think it is time we recognize the need to identify "the people." Yes, Black people certainly, but which ones shall we seek to bring into the **Imperium**? What Blacks, on the other hand, must be targets for action? I think one of the biggest games white people have worked on us is to require that we spend our time trying to get all of the Black people to unite over an issue, or that we represent all of the Black teachers in New York, all of the Black contractors in Chicago, or all of the Black farmers in Mississippi. Practically all Black theoreticians call for coalitions on national groupings to implement a given strategy such as to take over land, institutions, or to achieve some other objective. Yet, the composition, method for development, and roles therein are usually left unmapped.

I suggest that we most hurriedly add to our strategies the method of dealing with the dysfunctional, neutral or counterproductive elements, persons, or actions within our own Black family that prevent our moving off dead center in any effort aimed at the larger society local, national, or, international.

Black social workers may unite and attempt to deal with the noble cause of protesting over wrongs in the welfare system; but these same social workers might use their leverage in concert with Black teacher associations as follows: in one school, out of 500 Black parents called, only four attended a meeting to discuss their child's education. If 150 of those called were receiving public assistance and they had been told that their check was dependent on their attendance at Parent Council meetings, the story would have been much different. I don't expect the white society to demand, or even openly approve, such acts, but we must begin to utilize what we have going for us to achieve awareness and possibly cooperation, from broader numbers of our own people. One runs a great risk in making statements bordering on the general, such as I do. Where are our people now and how must we relate to them so as to not have a Black obstacle to our Plan, which is greater than the white one? You cannot escape Hamilton and Carmichael s position on the need to close our ranks before entering the open society.

Why do Black people go to Aqueduct in New York? Washington Park in Chicago, Santa Anita in California, and the Fair Grounds in Louisiana in groups in the tens of thousands, day and night, and wager millions of dollars? In some cities where the crowd is 40% to 50% Black, the average total bet per night per capita is $75 $100. It costs at least $2 to get in. Why is there more faith in going here than to a rally or to some demonstration or making a contribution to some Black cause? We find that there are several reasons:

- Suspicion of Black leaders: Rev. King is just getting rich with all that money, Jesse Jackson is ripping off for himself, etc.

25

- The misconception is that the Black folk fighting for our people must be poor. To be legitimate, some Black people with a distorted sense of values, want us to fight in overalls, go to meetings on public transportation, borrow and beg for a plane ticket, etc.
- The faith that if they win at the track, they will get that money to do what they want with it. Now the track takes 10% of the mutual pool and nobody minds.

We must deal with the stage in which those millions of Blacks attending the track, sporting events, and similar diversions, are.

A SOUTH AFRICAN FREEDOM fighter said it: people fight for things, not theories. He cited that the revolutionaries were giving the "people" things the Portuguese had never made available to them, such as food, cement, or other vital needs. I think it is time we recognize that we must meet our people on whatever level they are and attempt to create a sustained relationship on that level until we can identify and satisfy certain of their needs and gain their support, or at least passive cooperation. There is some thing to the Godfather syndrome being viewed in this context, You cant get 500 Blacks to a rally in the summer at 7 p.m., but political parties in Chicago have Blacks on the corners on election days from 6 a.m. to 6 p.m. in the rain and snow, and I mean '*sho nuff*' hustling. The precinct is organized. Old ladies cook hot lunches for the workers; sons and daughters take off from their regular jobs to help their parents who are regularly employed in this work. I mean schoolteachers take personal leave, upper echelon government workers take vacation time, and the unemployed get a chance to pick up some pocket change or expense money. I am convinced that Black people function in this manner because they have faith in the future of this kind of system to provide what they want. They work and are rewarded with a *job* or some *money*.

Our Plan must include an awareness of the fact that our people are patronage-oriented at this time in history. If we are to even think of a Plan that necessitates the consent of even the smallest community, we must come to grips with how we shall meet the needs of the Black peoples whom we seek to "liberate" so they will understand, cooperate, and hopefully, actively support.

O NE GLARING NEED in my mind is the creation of a "Black private sector" or a "Black economic support group." Again, the difference from other such consortia is in the way the Black private sector plugs into my Imperium Model.

To mention a Black private sector, one must include a careful consideration of the Black businessman, Today's Black businessman has, as I see it, a certain obligation to that Black community which supports him. This reciprocity concept is justified either because Black people continue to be his major consumers, or by virtue of campaigns to "Buy Black"; "Keep money in our community," and a less visible, but equally valid reason: that is, the urban rebellions of the sixties have caused both the public and private powers to seek, as a "remedy" to this disruption, such programmatic butterflies as Black economic development, Black capitalism, minority business opportunity, etc. Many Blacks who had viable businesses when this kind of emphasis hit, received instant benefits, for obviously, it was easier to pay your "Black dues" with those who might succeed in the experiment. Those who got into business due to the newly invented entry mechanisms created by the program probably would never have done so without this kind of special assistance. Hence, an obligation to aid in cures of the social diseases that led to the rebellions which prompted Black economic development falls, in part, on Black business. I contend that how we reciprocate is not the same for each business.

PAUL King is Executive Director of the United Builders Association of Chicago, Chairman of the National Association of Minority Contractor Labor Committee, and owner of a painting contracting firm. He is active in construction affairs involving builders across the nation, and led the first work shutdown on Chicago's West Side in July of 1969. He is also a student, a writer, and lectures in African Studies and Contemporary Black Affairs at Roosevelt University in Chicago. King was one of the eight chairmen at the Congressional Black Caucus subcommittee on Economic Development last month and presented the paper, "Black Political Leaders and the Black Construction Issue."

Courtesy of **The Black Scholar**, February 1972; reprinted with permission.

THE ROLE OF BLACK BUSINESS: DELIRIUM OR IMPERIUM?

Part II: CONCLUSION

by PAUL KING

A BRIEF HISTORICAL SKETCH is in order here for the purpose of recognizing the recurrent themes and problems.

In **The Negro as Businessman**, J. H. Hannon and Carter Woodson bring to our attention how prior to 1865, the economic system of the South allowed only a few blacks to learn business by observation, and practically none by actual participation. Those businesses in which we did engage were associated with hard labor and involved menial service. Serving the needs of the given community, these enterprises functioned until outside white merchants recognized the possibilities of this market and took it over.

This free black began to lose out prior to the Civil War due to inefficiency and the socio-economic handicaps faced while operating in a half-free status. In the North, the black was hardly better off due to the antagonism of the trade unions, the larger urban areas demanding increased sophistication and capital and the war-like tendencies European immigrants manifested toward Negroes. There were blacks who prospered and achieved individual wealth exceeding $860,000 in this period. After 1865, the industrial development of the North left the black far behind. Those efforts served to verify presence in business activity rather than any distinct achievements. Following the example of southern whites after losing the Civil War, some blacks used business as a civil rights effort, while being robbed of political involvement.

It has been questioned often as to whether blacks lack of tradition in business has created today's black management void. Lucrative 1) businesses did come into being, many through the unique ability of the black to observe, while working for whites, certain techniques. Upon improvisation, he added the dimension of his own inventiveness and created his own. Those businesses involved mattress-making, stock brokering; other business lines were jewelry, coal, ice cream factory, and specialized clothing manufacturing. That those businesses passed out of existence is explained partially by the following:

1. The sacrifice to maintain them was not adequate to the solution of the whole problem.
2. Many of these businesses were individual and the black businessman didn't take his relatives into confidence.
3. Similarly, they kept secrets of procedure from their employees.
4. Children were excluded when, in many cases, they displayed extravagant, rather than thrifty tendencies.
5. Children often chose to go into other forms or livelihood.
6. Lack of management and lack of employee sacrifice reduced things to individual effort, giving rise to the above.

Racism, and its far-reaching tentacles, provided the additional strangulation of the business.

The effect of the World War I is importantly stated by Harman, and ought to be carefully recalled as we observe the conclusion of the Viet Nam War today.

These businesses that endured received their greatest stimulation during the conflict of nations. The World War (I) changed conditions to the extent of a revolution in doing things. People in general learned to cooperate and to do the impossible in drives. Negroes therefore learned to appreciate their physical and financial strength while awakening at the same time to see the value of cooperation. If they could do as much as they did to raise funds to carry on the war they could do something for their own good. Race riots like those in Washington and Chicago, moreover, tended to drive the Negroes together for mutual help. These Negroes thus aroused, then became not only racially conscious but economically conscious. From this realization Negroes began to enter business in a larger measure.

These black enterprises became abandoned as normalcy appeared, to the extent that over one-half could not be identified by researchers in 1927.

Abram Harris, in his **Negro as Capitalist** listed as the outstanding obstacles to black business development and/or growth as follows:

1. The difficulty in obtaining capital and credit
2. Low wages, competition for jobs and immigration
3. Mob violence

4. Occupational restrictions
5. Prohibitions against owning certain types of property
6. Denial of the right to sue.
7. Restrictions against settlement in the West
8. Civic and educational handicaps

Enter in this milieu, 1907, Booker T. Washington with his book, **The Negro in Business**. By his own admission, he wrote, "I desire to tell...what number of our more successful men have been able to do in the field of business, with the hope that an increasing number of our young men may be encouraged by these examples to take advantage of the opportunities."

E. Franklin Frazier, in **Black Bourgeoisie**, took the position that Washington institutionalized a social myth in this treatment of Negro business. My good friend Ron Bailey has done us the scholarly service of bringing Frazier's book on this subject into a collection called **Black Business Enterprise**. Here, the validity of Frazier's analysis may be measured against current intellectuals like Harold Cruse, James Boggs, and Robert Browne.

The racial uplift purposes seemed to he caught in the belief that black business would allow the accumulation of wealth which would, in turn, lead to the ability to employ thousands of our people. It was further stated by John Hope that living amongst a conquering type race, such as Anglo-Saxons who were business-oriented, it would be suicidal for blacks to avoid entry into business activity. Emerging at this time was the "double-duty dollar" slogan that is not unlike our current "Buy Black" campaign. The idea in the early 1900s was to purchase from blacks who would be able to prosper, expand and employ more blacks, or if expansion were inherently impossible, contribute to Negro betterment via individual accumulation of wealth. Today, the slogans related to keeping money in the community serve as a modern parallel.

MINORITY-OWNED BUSINESS: 1969

Industry Divisions	# All Firms	All Minorities	(000's) Negro	Speaking Spanish-	Other
All Industries	7,489	322	163	100	59
Contract Construction	856	30	16	10	4
Manufacturers	401	8	3	4	1
Transportation and other Public Utilities	359	24	17	5	B
Wholesale Trade	434	5	1	2	2
Retail Trade	2,046	97	45	33	VT
Finance, Insurance, Real Estate	1,223	22	8	8	6
Selected Services	1,803	101	56	29	16
Other Industries and not Classified	367	35	17	9	9

Ten Most Important Industry Groups of Black-Owned Firms Ranked By Receipts: 1969

Rank	Industry	# Firms	Receipts
1	Automotive dealers and gasoline filling stations	6,380	$631,000,000
2	Food stores	11,268	438,000,000
3	Wholesale trade	1,660	385,000,000
4	Eating and drinking places	14,125	360,000,000
5	Personal services	33,906	288,000,000
6	Special trade contractors	13,447	284,000,000
7	Miscellaneous retail stores	6,412	278,000,000
8	General building contractors	2,359	140,000,000
9	Trucking and warehousing	7,252	134,000,000
10	Insurance carrier	104	133,000,000

BLACK-OWNED FIRMS

All industries: # Firms 163,073   Gross Receipts $3,474,191,000

With Paid Employees: # Firms 38,304   Gross Receipts $3,653,363,000

Average # Employees Per Firm 4   Average Receipts Per Firm $95,000

Without Paid Employees: # Firms 124,769   Gross Receipts $820,828,000

Average Receipts Per Firm $7,000

It takes little research to recognize the failure of these goals. The reasons are obvious to anyone giving serious attention to the question. The U.S. Census Bureau's Department of Commerce gives us the following statistics:

Whereas the low number of blacks employed by current black businesses gives little hope of developing any large influence through employership, such was anticipated and is executed so well by whites. As Andrew Brimmer points out, the break down in segregation and the recognition of the black market by larger white concerns limits the hope of expansion, for the present flock of businesses, to say nothing of new ones emerging in these same types of entrepreneurial activity.

I feel that with the emergence of anti-capitalist ideology being manifest by Third World nations, the United States will try to allow more black businesses to develop or survive, if for no other reason than to give currency to its principles of individual accumulation of wealth--clearly, nothing to rival the 200 major corporations--but at the marginal level we have kept to date appears to be no threat, while serving as good advertising for American ideals.

The task is with us, however, to conceive of how these black businesses might be relevant to our Imperium Model. Obviously, financial contribution and employment are two ways. Yet, save construction, which I shall speak of later, there is little to be expected from existing businesses insofar as employment beyond the aver age of four employees blacks presently maintain. Yet, the built-in positive features they do possess are the black traffic (barber shops, beauty parlors, taverns, pool rooms, restaurants) many maintain, and the influence over other blacks held by a few.

Bear in mind that it would be nothing new for these small businesses to contribute some money to various entities. They do it all the time and get literally nothing for it. Self-employed barbers operating their shops contribute to some union that doesn't serve their real needs. These same barbers are fearful to start work too early or work too late lest the unions take reprisals against them.

Small shop owners will receive a visit from a friendly caller associated, allegedly, with a local district police benevolent foundation. He will contribute to the ad book and obtain a decal indicating his sup port. These black businesses donate or pay, as the case may be, because they have visible proof (or blind faith) that this money does something for them. Whether it is to operate in peace or feel closer to local community authority, the investment seems justified. I see no reason why yearly or monthly donations to the Imperium Foundation could not he made. Yet, it is for those who espouse this to determine what structure can be set up to take in funds, be impeccably honest and discreet in the administration of same, and further do something mundane for the small shop keeper while keeping him well informed of the relationship between his contribution and the advancement of black people. If the message of the week was stapled to every cleaning bag, if tapes of Martin Kings sermons were played in the laundromats, if the Organization of Black American Culture (OBAC) and other black cultural groups were allowed to perform in the various taverns (and receive some of the revenues), we would be touching far more people than we currently do. Business offices that, just once a week, let community groups use their telephones, copying machines, and typewriters could help in this way. What if the various hamburger and chicken joints played speeches of Malcolm, songs of Nina Simone, poems of Don Lee and Nikki Giovanni at their prime business hours of 12 and 3 and 6? Garages and halls and restaurants just making space available to meet for homeless or "vagabond" community groups would serve as significant contributions. Of course, there are numerous other services: stores and distributors donating products and services at cost on occasions, etc. Recall that I am not dealing in the value of judgments of whether capitalism is good or whether blacks can ever be capitalists, I raise only the question of utilizing those phenomena occurring in our midst that might be made productive.

Members of the local Black Panther Party have suggested these ideas might work in that black businesses that gave goods and services to their feeding program, the jail visiting program, or the health care centers could be repaid through free advertising or recognition in the Panther newspaper. This, along with the added promotion and with the distribution of the Panther's free services, should be remembered by the recipients.

Contributions to the Black Imperium Foundation, if the body consisted of blacks representing a wide spectrum of contacts and influences, might help these businesses in cutting red tape, getting loans getting a child in college, or adequate legal assistance in a court situation.

CLEARLY, THERE IS presently the similar type of assistance offered to whites vis-à-vis political, religious, club, or ethnic membership; but there is a deep chasm between blacks and such help. Black political officials assume positions that were seats of power when occupied by whites, and when blacks acquire them, they cease to operate as such. Some black officials claim there are no black vehicles to take advantage of what they can deliver and we, their black constituency, go on being deprived. A serious question exists as to how black ascendants to positions of influence can do things for black people. Similarly, I am convinced that we must he ready to provide black political officials with sanctuaries of support if they attempt to help us.

As to the small businessman, because he is stationary, he is a victim of such abuse to date. Being gouged by salesmen, unions, police, and black and white extortionists for another group to ask him for money might be the straw that breaks the camels back, and drive him out of action. Hence, we lose a politicizing locus, because in eliminating his shop, we lose contact with his traffic in black people. Perhaps we need to organize black youth according to neighborhoods and have the Imperium molders pay the youth who have been trained for this delicate work according to Imperium procedures and objectives to see if the idea might work in strategic locales.

We ought not be overly sympathetic and forget the number of barber shops, taverns, and pool rooms which have served in the past for numbers running, book-making, and other forms of illicit traffic. These businesses could conceivably participate in the legitimate traffic promoting valid black concepts through whatever means best fit their circumstances, If they cannot be educated to the value of it, encouraged by channeling business their way, perhaps positive coercion or the threat of exposing their illicit activity might be reason enough to gain their support.

Obviously, the few black businesses existing as mortgage bankers, real estate, newspapers, insurance, radio stations, cab companies, and black full service banks present fantastic opportunities.

Suppose, in the case of the black parent who would not attend his child's parent Council meeting, that he was told by his landlord that he would have to move if he didn't go to the school to see about his child: suppose the black-owned or man aged stations carried a series of let it all hang out commentaries, along with tell it columns in the black press. Then, the black faculty and principal displaying lethargy toward the crisis of teachers failing to teach black students could be exposed.

My first experience in trying to go from midtown Manhattan to Harlem and being passed by over 13 white-driven cabs who picked up a white person a short distance away has made me a selective taxi rider. I choose a black driver. Any one who has seen "SHAFT," and due to the fantastic efforts of black media experts in Communiplex and Stax Records, this includes most of us I'm sure, can readily see the potential value in transportation companies being plugged into this new model; and it would not be difficult to effect reciprocal benefits.

At Chicago's O'Hare, everyone hustles to get a black passenger, for at worst it's a $6 trip. In my case, and for most south-side residents, it's in excess of $10. I retaliate against the New York bigots by my actions elsewhere. I suspect if a plan addressed to this question alone were invoked and disseminated black transportation companies would undoubtedly prosper and see their interests promoted in the Imperium's program.

BECAUSE I AM speaking of practical actions, it would be remiss on my part to avoid answering the theoretical question of am I not promoting a national Operation Breadbasket model? Jesse Jackson has done a Trojan-like job in assembling different divisions; yet, too many of his followership are just that--his followership do not carry out in everyday life any of the things they applaud on Saturday morning. The lack principal in the school situation mentioned earlier is an avid Breadbasket supporter, but fails to do the proper thing once out of the reach of Jesse Jackson's dynamism and influence. Save Ed Reddick, the research ace, and Richard Thomas, the unknown engineer of the fantastic EXPO, and a few others who must certainly exist, there are not enough people or groupings plugged into the utility of the Breadbasket phenomenon--whether or not they fall under Jacksons charismatic leadership. If there are 9000 black businesses in Chicago, why are there only a few associated with this effort? If 10,000 blacks go 35 miles or better to the racetrack, sit in the cold to watch football, etc., why are there less than 4,000 out of over a million of us in Chicago who go to a meeting on Saturday morning within a black-occupied area. This is neither a defense nor an indictment as to the value or efficacy of Breadbasket. It simply points out to me that the need is not to create more organizations or leaders, but to hook up existing groups, unpublicized thinkers, "toms," super blacks, and others and do a job on getting the peoples consent and support.

I am convinced of the existence of a unique set of political, as well as socioeconomic phenomena that makes construction one of the last frontiers for black people to use in advance of our collective pursuits. The businessman, especially the black contractor, in this area has the potential to enter one of the nations largest industries, and hiring and training more black people than any other black entrepreneur.

In 1970, national construction spending was reported at approximately $100 billion. This involved 870,000 contractors. The total industry employment was 3.3 million. For the sake of clarity, I shall define a contractor as one who assembles labor, material, equipment, insurance, financing, administrative and legal services to perform construction. There are functional components to every well-run contracting firm. The several functions are:

1. obtain the work
2. obtain financing
3. secure insurance and bonding
4. legal and accounting services
5. estimating and bid preparation
6. purchasing
7. expediting
8. supervision of work forces in actual building.
9. labor relations, unions.

These are areas of responsibility given to one person or a staff to take care of. In smaller firms, one individual may assume responsibility for areas touching similar tasks such as the sales and public relations- oriented role in obtaining work, financing, insurance and bonding. This is the general scheme under which the profit-makers (at a rate 5-10%) in the construction industry operate.

Now, consider the black position in this picture:

> Total black firms: 16,235
> Total black firms with paid employees: 3,886 leaving--
> Total of black firms without paid employees: 12,349.

The total receipts reported were $464 million for blacks. (These are 1969 figures, 1970 has not changed them significantly.) Now, statistics for this field are never complete. Large numbers of jobs go unreported. Businesses come and go without going through a recorded process. But, what is obvious from the numbers is that we have a preponderance of negotiating tradesmen-- black fellows who attempt to perform all of the functions listed above by themselves, and also perform the labor! These are guys whose entire inventory is in their cars, and whose books and records are in shopping bags.

ANOTHER POINT WORTH noting is that out of the total 16,235 reported, there are 2,359 firms that don't identify with any special craft. But, of the 13,000 specialty or sub contractors, close to 8,000 are confined to painting (2,700+); masonry and plastering (2,600+); carpentry (2,500+). Yet, there are over 15 other specialty crafts associated with most ' construction jobs. This is no accident, and it is a modern day manifestation of the black businessman's oppression which Harmon and Woodson talked about when they wrote "those businesses (in) which we did engage were associated with hard labor and involved menial service…"The highly technical construction crafts--iron work, elevator construction, electrical, plumbing, sprinkler systems, as well as the elite extension of the three crafts mentioned (i.e., painting installation of elaborate wall covering, carpentry--involving intricate or ornate finish work) involve practically no black contractors.

Recognition of this problem brings us to a big question: the construction labor unions. One major reason we have no con tractors in these fields is due to the racist practices of these unions. Blacks have been, and are still being, denied the union apprentice training in these fields that would allow craftsmen to emerge and subsequently enter the industry.

If one were to read some of the Communist-oriented literature on unions, he might get trapped into that romantic rhetoric of black and white workers uniting. Even my elementary understanding of Marxist thought convinced me of the errors of Marx's predictions as they apply to construction trade unions.

In Chicago, when we were negotiating the black employment issue in 1969, both labor (unions) and management (contractors) refused to meet with black representatives separately. While being the fiercest of opponents during all phases of their on going dealings, these two white dominated forces, traditionally antagonistic toward each other, sat together on the same side of the aisle while dealing against the black community representatives. Clearly, unions now create the economic exploitation of black people as much as any other so-called capitalistic force. As I see it, the ridiculous wage contracts they have been allowed to get away with serve only the interest of the majority of its members who are white, its leadership, who get paid while rank and file members are out of work, and its joint apprentice committees, which are white. They have created a situation wherein union members get from $8 to $10 per hour. When added to the taxes and fringe benefits, it costs the purchaser of these services upwards of $12 per hour. The physical deterioration of our cities due to building abandonment is not unrelated to union abuse: for the influence of construction unions in previous administrations had them literally running the U. S. Department of Labor, so much so that you have as law such pieces as the Davis-Bacon Act, which says workers must be paid the prevailing wage, i.e. union rates of a given region. These wage rates have had users of construction services walk away from even attempting to rehabilitate certain buildings. Hence urbanologists can make predictions that the city of St. Louis will be non-existent in 25 years, and the demise of physically damaged buildings, where blacks live, in various cities indicate the same tendencies.

NOW, I HAVE indicated a kind of ambivalence in the above. On the one hand, I opt for black entry into construction unions, while on the other, I cite the unions as being racist and contributors to economic despair. I want black workers to he given the opportunity to benefit from trade union training and an improved quality of life, as workers, through unions or any other entity that will adequately train them and insure their right to work. Out of that opportunity, I see a cadre of technically sound contractors emerging. Most contractors or non-workers found criticizing the union situation are accused of being capitalistic anti-worker types. But, leaving the question of racism aside for the moment, what good does it do to negotiate into an hourly wage rate that is so high that it limits the total number of hours one works? It is not just the seasonality of the industry that causes many workers to fall way short of 2,000 hours per year; it is the simple statement of the owners' position. We just don't have that much money to pay for the work this year! So the work goes undone and people are laid off. Here racism re-enters unemployed black men who would work for $5 and $6 an hour, a rate which the owners could afford, are not permitted to do it because of union sanctions. Union reps usually jump on this by saying to have blacks working at $5-$6 an hour is just further exploitation of the Negro. Who really believes this? Go into any area in Harlem, Beale Street, Woodlawn, Hough, Bedford-Stuyvesant, Watts, Lawndale and ask black cats if they would rather "rock steady" at $5/hour or stay unemployed or underemployed. Unions, least of all, have any real legitimacy in speaking for blacks. I fear their cordial relations with leaders of civil rights groups have confused many people. Sure, they, annihilated Haynesworth and Carswell "for us," but they attacked Art Fletcher and the Philadelphia Plan with the same gusto.

Most union apprenticeship programs allow for entry of men from 17 to 30. Anyone over that must he considered as a journeyman. Now, suppose you have a black father of a family who is 33 years old, semi-skilled and capable of issuing 75% of the journeyman's productivity. He's too old to be an apprentice, lacks the ability to command top dollar, and cant get hired and upgrade himself because most unions only allow two categories: apprentices and journeymen. There are some definite economic dangers in unions as to how they escalate their wages that are automatically borne by governmental purchasing agencies and commercial residential developers. And who absorbs this? Most certainly, the millions whose wages have not risen in proportion to the wages of union workers.

To a contractor, it matters little what the rate is, there is a fixed overhead and profit added to the basic labor cost, hence the anti-worker charge to a black contractor is spurious. The construction union's anti-black posture is evident, and what seems to be evolving here is the question of whether or not the trade unions in this country, with their present composition and policies, especially construction craft unions, are a greater force than the black population? The answer is clearly yes, at this point, in terms of organization, influence, and structure, but insofar as potential is concerned, perhaps not.

What I am suggesting here is that we have an opportunity to create 80,000 additional black businesses in construction; we have the opportunity to place over 30,000 blacks in the industry; and we have the opportunity-- through the above, to influence them through meeting them at the level where many of our people now find themselves--looking for ***things***.

We have going for us, in this effort executive orders that make our pursuits consistent with Federal law enforcement. To shut down a job having too few or no black workers is to stop a crime. These guidelines exist for conventional as well as the new systems building (industrialized housing). So broad are the Federal guidelines on black opportunity in HUD's Breakthrough projects that they were kept hidden from the blacks in Memphis, Tennessee; Indianapolis; Seattle, and Sacramento.

Also, the fact that construction work is highly accessible to the public, especially at the crucial early stages, makes the threat of stopping any job in our black communities, or wherever we can mass large numbers in the center city, quite real. White contractors, developers, and the financiers would rather deal with black subcontractors and black workers just to insure no disruption and no Federal compliance reprisals.

S O MAGIC IS our lack of capable black contractors and workers that even Dempsey Travis, when developing a high rise complex, couldn't give the job to a black general contractor because there isn't one in Chicago who could build a structure of that size. Black community development corporations have to use white general contractors because blacks can't meet their budgets. Hence, the strong possibility looms that our own areas will be rebuilt (in the North) or developed (in the South) without blacks taking part in the housing, highway, office and subway building boom.

Hence, the task before us, as I see it, is to recognize the possibility of the construction businessman and worker being the vanguard of the economic support group in the Imperium Model. This can be done if the many of us help these few now when they need the collective efforts of all blacks so desperately.

There needs to he a total thrust toward the development of black contractors and workers with a consciousness for who helped them, and from this relationship, a strengthening of the black private sector as well as a gaining of the consent of the added black people who, in fact, want and need jobs.

This objective must be to develop thou sands of black contractors and black workers and will call for specific actions from specific groups:

- Black lawyers must begin to file suits against unions and contractors, as did the Justice Department in San Francisco with the Ironworkers.

- Black educators must begin to include top and middle management jobs like estimators, engineers, and accountants as valued professions.

- Black political officials must assert initiative in gaining our rightful share of this market by using the power of their offices.

- Black community groups must develop a consciousness that threatens any work going on in our neighborhoods with out black contractors or workers.

- Black athletes must realize that after 25 years, they needn't remain silent on racial issues. Airlines and sports stadiums being built without black contractors should be boycotted by Kareem Jabbar, Gale Sayers and Vida Blue.

Only such concerted action may, in fact, determine whether we shall have *delirium* or *imperium*.

PAUL King is Executive Director of the United Builders Association of Chicago, Chairman of the National Association of Minority Contractor Labor Committee, and owner of a painting contracting firm. He is active in construction affairs involving builders across the nation, and led the first work shutdown on Chicago's West Side in July of 1969. He is also a student, a writer, and lectures in African Studies and Contemporary Black Affairs at Roosevelt University in Chicago. King was one of the eight chairmen at the Congressional Black Caucus subcommittee on Economic Development last month and presented the paper, "Black Political Leaders and the Black Construction Issue."

Courtesy of **The Black Scholar**, March 1972; reprinted with permission.

Construction: Green Power For the Black Man?

Executive Director of the United Builders Association of Chicago Spells Out the Possibilities of the Industry

by Paul King

Last year, at the occasion of the first State of the Black Economy Symposium,* Chester McGuire, from the University of California presented an excellent paper which laid out some of the basic facts surrounding the Black condition in the construction industry. Mr. McGuire, referring to 1970, indicated that construction comprised approximately 10% of the U.S. GNP. He outlined further that one dollar out of every $10 spent goes into construction; and further that blacks in construction received approximately one cent out of every dollar spent in construction.

1971 rounded out with total construction in excess of $109 billion. This shows a favorable comparison to the 10 percent activity reported in previous years. It has been forecast that during 1972, our total GNP will be in the area of one trillion, one hundred forty-five billion dollars. Construction predictions, again following close to the 10 percent ratio, come out at over $118 billion. In 1968, it was estimated that the black contractor shared in less than $500 million of the total construction spending. McGuire reported approximately $1 billion total in 1970. I can predict, with relative ease, that black contractors will share in $2 billion of the total construction spending in 1972. However, I can predict, with equal certainty, that their profits for this total activity, if there are any, will be far below the expected 5-10 percent because although opportunity to participate has increased, ability to perform at a profit has not risen proportionately.

While I shall not spend time discussing the elements of the black contractors plight in depth, the elements are:

1. Lack of capitalization

2. Lack of management and technical skills
3. Lack of skilled labor
4. Inability to obtain bonds

These problems have persisted since the discussion of minority contractors became fashionable, and they will be with us until we put certain processes in motion; establish new linkages with other black interest or professional groups; and broaden our perspective insofar as what areas of concentration we should focus on within the industry.

HOUSING

Though housing construction only reports in at approximately 1/3 of the construction spending, black contractors have devoted practically 100 percent of their attention to entry into this area. Practically all of that attention has been devoted to conventional or stick building with relatively little or no attention offered to industrialized building.

By this term "industrialized building," I mean concepts of building structures through repetitive techniques similar to an assembly line; or more simply, that a significant part of the building is factory-produced. According to Marsh Trimble of Cahners Publishing Company, there are three general forms of factory-built housing: Modular housing which consists of structures built from one or more three dimensional, cubical or box-shaped units which are completely factory finished and require only to be connected together at the building site. **Modular** units are normally shipped to the job site on a platform and are hoisted on to the foundation with a crane.

Mobile homes are kinds of modules fabricated on heavy steel under carriages to which axles and wheels are attached for transportation. This steel frame is an integral part of the unit and provides the primary structural support when a unit is lowered onto foundations at the job site.

Panelized housing consists of structures built from a variety of component parts, assemblies or sub-assemblies. The majority of these factory-produced components are assembled at the job site to form at least a major structural element of the building.

A third type of manufactured housing is the **pre-cut or packaged** unit. This is a conventionally built home in which all of the structural parts-- such as roof shingles, windows, doors are cut and assembled in a factory, and then shipped on trucks to the building site where they can be erected into a living unit with considerably less labor and expense than if all work was done at the building site.

All of us recognize the need for housing, especially as it affects black people. Construction has been touted as a growth industry because it produces housing that is much needed. The questions we must consider at this meeting are **WHO** will build the housing? **WHAT FORM** of housing construction best offers black contractors rapid entry and a profitable existence in its production? HUD Secretary George Romney stated in 1970, and repeated last year, that within ten years, 2/3 of the housing of this nation would be of the factory-built variety.

Of the 2, 620,000 units of housing predicted for 1972, the increase in mobile home shipments accounts for 85 percent of the total increase in housing units. I might caution you to be aware of the distinction between new housing units and net housing units, especially as it affects black people concentrated in the inner cities; the rate of demolition and abandonment occurring in our communities suggests that the net housing available to black people could be a negative quantity. If this negativism does exist, the cost of traditional construction, buttressed by the racism and flagrant wage demands of the craft unions, contribute significantly to the fact that it is economically unfeasible to rebuild our deteriorating communities.

I make no claim to be an expert on the subject of industrialized building. I am, however, conscious enough of the history of black people to realize that for too long we have made the error of opting for things, privileges or jobs that become anachronisms by the time we acquire them--such as the right to buy a cup of coffee instead of looking ahead toward management or ownership of the coffee shop.

The indicators toward systems building are favorable insofar as black contractors are concerned:

1. The Federal Government has stated a commitment to this type of building.
2. The economics of industrialized housing favor its usage in these trying times.
3. The major producers in the industrialized housing field are seeking allies to give them support against the white-dominated unions who seek to retard this industry's growth.

I do not consider myself a proponent of systems building, nor do I anticipate a total take-over of this form of construction over the traditional methods of building, but certainly if we are to advance at all in our pursuit of a fair share for the black contractor, we must move into and within those areas most conducive to our growth and development.

AREAS OTHER THAN HOUSING

It seems necessary to direct our interest at other activity in the industry, as well as housing.

For example, in 1971, $10.75 billion went into highways and streets; $25 billion went into shipbuilding and repair. It was anticipated by the FAA that airport development for fiscal '72 would result in $280 million worth of construction; the metro subway system in Washington, D.C. projects $354 million in construction and when the subway system construction in Atlanta commences late next year, it is projected that $1.3 billion will be spent.

One may well ask that if that kind of market exists, especially with public funds being involved, why shouldn't the black contractor share to a larger extent? The simple fact is that there are not enough black contractors, and of those that do exist, they are not structured so as to compete in these "unknown frontiers."

Out of 900,000 contractors in this country, there have only been from 13,000-16,000 blacks recognized. Less than 6,000 of those identified had paid employees. The average number of employees held by these firms is four. It becomes clear, therefore, that our number one priority must be to develop more black contracting firms on a crash basis. It is necessary that we under stand that the reason we have so few black contractors (who, by the way, are practically confined to four specific crafts) is in great measure due to trade union exclusion. Many contractors were at one time craftsmen; hence, inability to get into a craft union results in having no con tractors in that specialty field. It is incumbent for us who would seek to have additional black contractors emerge to recognize the inextricable connection between this effort and the black construction worker struggle going on in so many cities across the country.

There is another innovation or attempt at change in the industry that we must now become aware; I refer here to the concept of **Construction Management [CM]**. The nucleus of this idea is the delivery of a quality project in minimum time within a given budget. A sophisticated, well-coordinated building team is organized under the direction of the construction manager who works under a professional services contract.

Vital contributions made by the construction manager are (1) construction input at the design stage where construction time and cost savings are most effectively achieved, (2) highest possible coordination of the owner, architect, engineers and contractors throughout the design and construction phases. Sophisticated cost and management control systems are expected from the CM.

The U. S. Government (GSA) has already initiated construction activity in the hundreds of millions of dollars using the construction management approach. Under a two-step procedure system, the CM is selected on the basis of quality of services offered and the fee pro posed for these services. Among the nations top 400 contractors, it has been reported that 80 firms provided construction management services in 1971, with more than half where another firm was the prime contractor. Ninety of the country's 500 largest design firms offered some form of CM consulting on about $3 billion worth of construction.

There are some considerations of this new system that ought to be looked at vis à vis the black contractor:

Bonding, which has always been a serious problem takes on a new image in the case of the CM; there is no general contractor in the CM approach. What you have are several prime contractors. If we consider a case where the owner is a public agency Federal (GSA), state or city, then contracts will be issued under those statutes governing the respective political aggregate. Hence, an electrical sub, who under the traditional method could have the bond waived by the general con tractor, is now a "prime." As a prime contractor, bid, payment, and performance bonds will be required. This aspect of the CM approach could work to the detriment of black contractors. On the other hand, two potentially positive features are (1) that in the case of private construction, wherein prime (specialty) contractors are invited to bid, the list of invitees could consist of only black contractors. This is quite feasible in crafts such as painting where you generally find a preponderance of qualified contractors. (2) A second feature lies in an opportunity for black architectural and/or engineering firms to enter the CM picture via joint ventures and other methods. Given the current efforts to increase minority business opportunities by the Federal Government, GSA might favorably consider construction management joint ventures including black firms.

Again, my knowledge of these concepts is woefully inadequate, but there can be no question that we blacks in construction must acquaint ourselves with these changes in the industry that will undoubtedly affect our future, if not our current existence.

COURSE OF ACTION

The first task for us is to heighten the construction consciousness of everyone across the length and breadth of the black community. It must be raised to the point that each of us begins to realize that this may be the only industry in which the black businessman will be able to get a significant part of a growth industry and, with that participation, be able to hire a significant number of black people. A new construction project of 500 housing units create as many as 400 jobs at peak periods. It must be understood that unlike a factory, these are brand new job opportunities not existing before the ground is broken. Only when we have hundreds of black contractors capable of performing these jobs, at a profit, will we be able to guarantee any meaningful employment black people in this industry.

After years of demonstrating and negotiating, I am convinced that plans are useless. What is needed is enforcement of the law. Yet, this enforcement is practically impossible because there are enough compliance officers in country to monitor effectively equal opportunity criteria in Federal Statutes. Hence, a course of action would be to form "community compliance committees" that can monitor every construction site in their domain. If a project has no black workers or subcontractors, it should be closed down. If circumstance do not allow for this kind of action, then the community compliance committee should take their findings to local alderman, councilmen, congressmen, Senators, and appropriate local and federal contract compliance officials. This statement, however, is made with the recognition that, in the past, our politician's responsiveness to the needs of black contractors has left much to be de sired. Note, for example, the 1970 construction activity that went on in these counties wherein the Congressional black caucus members represent approximately 6.5 million black people:

City	County	Total Dollar Volume
BALTIMORE	BALTIMORE	$ 227,330,000
CHICAGO	COOK	1,287,796,000
CLEVELAND	CUYAHOGA	337,422,000
DETROIT	WAYNE	474,415,000
WASHINGTON, D, C.		215,986,000
LOS ANGELES	LOS ANGELES	1,524,743,000
NEW YORK	BRONX	2,034,654,000
NEWARK	KING	
	NASSAU	
	NEW YORK	
	QUEENS-ESSEX	
PHILADELPHIA	PHILADELPHIA	354,885,000
SAN FRANCISCO	SAN FRANCISCO	185,745,000
OAKLAND, CA		
ST. LOUIS	ST. LOUIS	302,451,000

This approximately $7 billion worth of construction activity went on in these areas where there was black representation, while the black constituents were planning their way into the trade unions. Certainly, these politicians could have done more to help the black contractor obtain his fair share of this action.

While addressing the convention of National Association for Community Development, I was appalled at their naïveté; they concerned themselves for at least five hours on *what kind* of housing would be built, but little knowledge as to how they could affect who would build it. This must change!

Indeed, construction and the role of the black contractor is an intriguing arena, but it could hardly attract as much of my attention as it does simply because of the dollar volume, need for its product or other technological innovations. Construction's ability to provide jobs and the black contractors capacity to control the decision-making apparatus on *who* gets those jobs is of the highest importance to me, and should be to us all.

The job future for all U.S. residents is uncertain as we move from an industrial to a service-oriented economy. We need not be historians to know quite well that if the employment future is questionable for the country as a whole, for blacks, we can most certainly apply the term "dismal."

Labor has lost its role as the most important means to expand production and has become expendable as the profits derived from it (labor) have been reinvested in advancing technology. To quote James Boggs, "This technology in turn has made the remaining labor so monotonous and fragmented that it is more worthy of robots than human beings."

The result is that a growing number of people, both in and out of work, are beginning to question the purpose of labor and the validity of the prevailing philosophy that man should live only by the sweat of his brow. In American schools and universities it is becoming increasingly clear that the American system of education, dedicated to the increase of earning power and representing an investment of many billions of dollars and the full time occupation of some fifty million people, is a failure and that the basic purpose of education itself must be redetermined.

Approximately a third of the blacks in the work force are termed operatives (assembly lines, drill press, lift and other machine operators), laborers, and service workers. The scientific and industrial changes have reduced the number of jobs available and produced mass unemployment and permanent work force dislocations. The jobs affected are those where blacks have the greatest concentration. Production has shifted away from plants in the metropolitan centers to more mechanized types in more rural communities away from the black work force.

The auto and steel industries, which are said to be the highest employers of blacks, show a tendency toward an adverse black employment situation. Carl Bloice3 reports that totally automated steel mills are technically feasible and in operation in parts of the Soviet Union. A U. S. based auto company has constructed, in Britain, a parts ware house which requires no personnel to fill and deliver orders--this being accomplished by a computerized system involving unmanned fork lifts.

It is further reported that 40 percent of all television and 90 percent of the radios and tape recorders sold here are imported. Multinational corporations have caused over 60,000 jobs to be lost in the electronic industry alone by moving the manufacturing to other countries in search of cheaper labor. 200,000 jobs have been lost as a result of imported cars. It should be noted that 40 percent of these imported cars were manufactured by U.S. companies.

In 1969, unemployment for blacks between 20 and 24 was over 19 percent. The economic expansion of 1961-69, which generated 1.5 million new jobs each year, appears to be over. One of the nations largest employers, the U. S. Army, which drew more than a million men out of the labor force, has itself cut back; it has declined to the point where the draft is expected to cease in 1973.

I am suggesting that this tragic employment situation, looming over black people, with its deleterious effects, is a phenomenon to which the construction industry can (if it will) most readily address itself. A recent university study reported that motivation was higher among construction workers than those of any other field. The old and rapidly dying white construction workers have not left behind them a mechanism for replacement commensurate with the need. The inner cities in which blacks are the majority in many cases will be rebuilt. These factors alone show a great opportunity for thousands of black people to be employed. But, their employment will only be achieved and protected when black business in the construction industry--yes black con tractors, are viable and sensitive enough to gain a strong position of management and control and, with this, train and develop an equally strong black work force.

Construction: Green Power for the Black Man? Well maybe. Clearly10 percent of the GNP, $118 billion, is enough green. But power ... power for the black man will come only when we can secure and guarantee meaningful jobs for our people as businessmen pursue economic advancement.

---

*Courtesy of the **Black Business Digest**, December 1972. UBAC is sponsored by the Chicago Economic Development Corporation.

Sources:
Paul King, "Black Political Leaders and the Black Construction Issue," presented to the Congressional Black Caucus.
James Boggs, **Racism and Class Struggle**, 1970.
Carl Bloice, from **Political Affairs.**

ABOUT THE UBAC

Chicago, 1967. The scene focuses on the multi-billion dollar construction industry, still carrying on its nationwide tradition of ignoring and discriminating against minority building contractors. But, simultaneously, some of these for gotten building contractors are organizing themselves, armed with the determination to eliminate the existing evils in the trade that will not claim them. Finally, the finished product emerges a nucleus group of four black contractors, incorporated as a not-for-profit organization in February of 1968 under the name West Side Builders Association.

Based on Chicago's west side, the four founding members, Channon C. Turner, Roosevelt Betts, Alonzo Travis, and Woodrow Wilson, under the capable guidance of Brenetta Howell Barrett, then Lawndale Branch Manager for the Chicago Economic Development Corporation, held their first meetings in a basement barber shop, later moving to an office on west Roosevelt Road.

As Woodrow Wilson recalled in a recent interview: "I was one of four black contractors sitting in a basement barber shop reviewing our seemingly hopeless plight which had us being totally overlooked in every phase of local construction activity. We were qualified men who could not obtain job contracts to work even in our own neighborhoods; white contractors had the construction industry all to themselves. We knew that this was wrong. As time went on, we raised a lot of Hell and got people to take note of the situation."

The West Side Builders Associations main objective was to expand employment opportunities for minority contractors located on the west side. Other problems, however, soon came to the fore; as new jobs began to open up for minority contractors, they had to face bonding and financing obstacles, a lack of adequate skilled manpower, and a lack of technical expertise in estimating, supervision, and accounting.

With counseling and assistance from CEDC's Brenetta Barrett and Consuelo Miller, the West Side Builders Association was able to obtain a Technical Assistance Grant through the Economic Development Administration of the U.S. Department of Commerce. This funded program allowed WSBA to become viable enough to tackle the obstacles that challenged their organizations members. As a result of the previously unattainable resources and staff provided through CEDC's firm commitment, WSBA quickly transcended neighborhood boundaries and expanded its membership citywide to include representatives of almost all phases of construction activity--painting, decorating, plastering, carpentry, glazing, masonry contracting, tuck pointing, sandblasting, roofing, remodeling and subsequently changed its name to the **UNITED BUILDERS ASSOCIATION OF CHICAGO** to reflect its quickly acquired de-regionalized status and scope.

DEBT TO CEDC

The United Builders Association of Chicago owes a profound debt of gratitude to the Chicago Economic Development Corporation. It was due to the insight of this organization that the encouragement and continued support for formation provided to UBAC's original members. This early help was miniscule when compared to the on-going assistance provided to the UBAC.

Within their relationship with the Chicago Economic Development Corporation, it was stated at the outset, and consistently concurred with the EDA of the Department of Commerce, that the United Builders Association was to become a self-sustaining, independent organization. All of CEDC's actions have been consistent with this original objective. Hence, UBAC found not only one sensitive ear in Garland Guice, CEDC Executive Director, but an entire organization committed to its growth as successful contractors within a soundly structured organization. CEDC has embraced UBAC as one in a family dedicated to the success of each member. It has provided its organizational sophistication as a standard of excellence to which any group should want to aspire. In times of need, whether it be staff shortages, equipment deficiencies, or facility inadequacies, CEDC has always found a way to help UBAC get the job done. The excellent clerical staff at the central office has never denied UBAC's organization the personal concern which a fledgling group needs as it encounters growing pains. Never skirting the rules, but always willing to interpret and aid in measuring up to the rules has been the modus operandi for Deputy Director Jesse Madison.

Brenetta Howell Barrett, who did not stop when she helped form West Side Builders, has continued to bridge the gap between UBAC and the corporate giants in the city. Illinois Bell, American National Bank, CNA, Continental Bank, and countless others know of the United Builders Association because of her efforts.

The various branch offices continue to aid UBAC members in obtaining SBA loans, while keeping them abreast of construction opportunities in the communities they serve. The CEDC Northside branch now works with UBAC, through the able coordination of Conni Miller, in assisting the Spanish-speaking contractors to establish their own contractors association.

CONTINUING AID

The Federal Government continues to help by means of both contracts and grants. For instance, UBAC received a one-year $125,000 contract to strengthen minority construction contractors and provide management and technical services to upgrade their marketing and performance skills.

In addition, the National Association of Minority Contractors, an education institution, in which UBAC's Paul King serves as Chairman of the Labor committee, recently signed an agreement with Assistant Secretary of Labor Malcolm R. Lovell, Jr. to promote on-the-job training for NAMC member contractors. Under the agreement, the Labor Department will provide $166,144 for the establishment of programs across the country.

It has been a long, hard road for UBAC and for black contractors generally, but as achievement is added to achievement, a powerful edifice of black success will assume its proper stature in the skyline of America's future.

THE PHOTO

GALLERY

King receiving the ENR Award from editor, Gene Wyeneth, recognizing him as one of the "Men Who Made Marks in The Construction Industry," on February 1974.

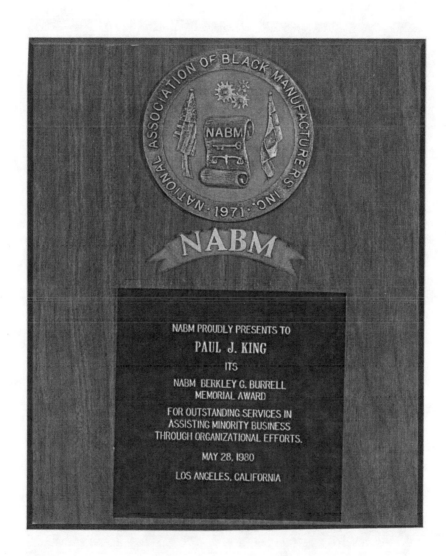

XI LAMBDA CHAPTER
ALPHA PHI ALPHA FRATERNITY, INC.
Presents the
Brother Judge Sidney A. Jones, Jr. Award
to
BROTHER PAUL KING

For dedicated and outstanding services to the Chapter, Alpha
Phi Alpha, Inc. and the community. A pioneer in the affirmative
action movement, still involved in the movement today. A leader
and fighter for full participation for minorities and minority
companies in the construction field. A member of several civil
organizations, an author and a doer. And as a faithful supporter
of all chapter programs and activities of over 45 years.

Given this 3rd Day of September, 2001

W. WAYMAN WARD   ARNDELL RICKS, JR.
Awards Committee Chairman   President

King with Alpha Phi Alpha Fraternity's 32nd
General President, Darryl Matthews.

King and Nelson Mandela at Chicago reception.

With best wishes to Paul King

Jimmy Carter '80

King receives warm greeting from President Jimmy Carter

King with President Bill Clinton

King with Vice President Al Gore

*King with first African American presidential candidate
and U. S. House Rep. (D–NY), Shirley Chisholm;*

King with former Olympic gold medalist and U.S.
House Rep. Ralph Metcalfe (D-IL).

King with first African American woman U.S. Senator, Carol Moseley-Braun (D-IL).

U.S. House Rep. Parren Mitchell (D–MD) with King and his son, Timothy.

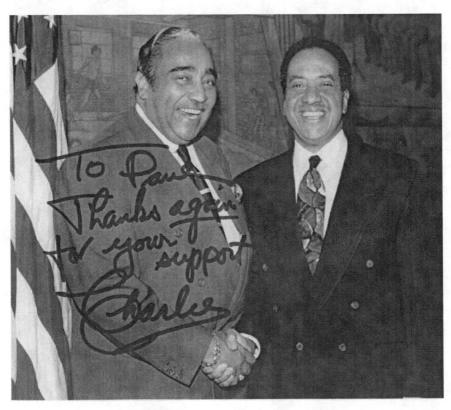

Current House Ways and Means Chairman, Charles Rangel (D-NY) thanks King for his support.

King and Rev. Jesse L. Jackson at Annual Black Contractor Awards Dinner.

King with Congressman Bobby Rush (D-IL).

King with Carter Administration Secretary of Labor, Ray Marshall.

King enjoys a hearty laugh with Chicago's first African American Mayor, Harold Washington.

King with Mayor Washington at City Hall.

King with Mayor Eugene Sawyer.

*This group of black businessmen breakfasting with Mayor Sawyer later
formed the O'HARE DEVELOPMENT GROUP (ODG), which
became the first Black Developers to own/lease and develop land at
O'Hare airport, with King as founder and chairman. From left to right:
Joe Williams, Target Group; Frank Brooks, Brooks Sausage Co.; Paul
King, UBM; Mayor Sawyer; Jerry Jones, Sonicraft Manufacturing;
Odell Hicks, CPA; Mitchell Watkins, management consultant.*

UBAC president Paul King and Mayor Richard J. Daley en route to a session at the National Association of Minority Contractor's (NAMC) 1973 MOVE (Minority Opportunity in a Viable Economy) Convention, hosted by the United Builders Association of Chicago (UBAC).

King with current Chicago Mayor Richard J. Daley

Sharing platform with John H. Stroger, future President
of the Cook County Board of Commissioners.

King attends railroad event outing with Chicago Alderman Ed Burke.

*King receiving a Minority Contractor Award
from Illinois Governor Jim Thompson.*

*King sharing a moment with Illinois State Senate
President Emil Jones and Mayor Daley.*

Black Contractors United presents Mayor Eugene Sawyer (center) with the Parren Mitchell Award: pictured left to right, Rufus Taylor; Paul King; Glenn Hairston; Cong. Parren Mitchell, and Larry Huggins.

Presentation of the Affirmative Action Leader of the Century Award by the Coalition for United Community Action (CUCA). Left to right: Hermene Hartman, N'Digo publisher; honoree, King; Carl Latimer, CUCA president; and contractor, Glenn Hairston.

King with renowned artist, Jacob Lawrence.

Rufus Thomas, King, and Redd Foxx at Wattstax.

The King Family circa 1985: seated, wife, LoAnn; standing left to right: son, Timothy, Paul, and son, Paul III.

BLACK CONSTRUCTION AND ECONOMICS AT A CROSSROAD

by Rae Jones

Something has gone terribly wrong in affirmative action and minority set-aside programs. While fingers can be pointed in many directions, the fact remains those who made the initial efforts and sacrificed the most for Black empowerment in the construction trade, are not the direct beneficiaries of those efforts.

No one is more aware of this fact than Paul J. King. And, his frustration is evident.

Chairman of UBM, Inc., a multi-disciplined construction management consulting agency, a general contractor, and an engineering firm, King was a primary player in efforts 20 years ago, which launched what grew into a local and national Black contractors' movement.

Working under an unusually cooperative agreement with the city's three largest street gangs, and some local community organizations, King helped shut down three housing rehabilitation projects in 1969 on Chicago's Westside. But, before the shutdowns they did their research.

Gangs were used to intimidate workers into walking off the job. They agreed to put aside the individual interests of each gang for the betterment of the entire community. The combined groups strategy was to stop the construction projects to draw attention to the plight of Blacks in construction crafts. Because the projects were valued at millions of dollars, the strategy worked.

Representing a group of 80 Black building contractors, the West Side Builders Association, King and others, sought to force union leaders to the bargaining table where the issue of opening unions to Blacks could be resolved. At the time, the unions were 97 percent white.

"We wanted our fair share of jobs, our piece of the pie," King said. "Blacks would pass construction projects in their neighborhoods and see nothing but white workers. It was a slap in the face a daily insult."

"Our strategy was to initially try to get jobs on a site, then move to being developer and owner of a site, and to gain control over business enterprises, jobs, and all the commerce that interfaces with those enterprises," King explained.

While the short-term strategy worked, the long-term plan didn't. King is frustrated that the early pioneers Black contractors no longer are benefiting from the hard work and energy they put into that movement.

It's a very saddening thing to note that all the proponents, the core, in 1969, were Black. We pivoted off of a Black presence. We pivoted off of a Black commitment. And, we pivoted off of projects going on in Black communities. And, with all of this effort if we look at statistics in employment alone, without even considering development and ownership, we are losing ground everyday.

Noting that the number of minority apprentices has grown from less than 4 percent in 1969, according to U.S. Department of Labor figures, King is quick to caution a careful examination of the numbers. When broken down by race and gender, these numbers, he insists, do not bode well for Blacks.

'It is not that I am against any other ethnic group," King commented. "It is that I believe that there should be a far greater proportion going to the people who started all of this in the first place."

"The people who started Sears and Roebuck have stock willed to their children. Black people who started this struggle and kept it going, ought to have the same kind of stock certificates, redeem able to them at anytime with appreciation based upon the investment that their parents, relatives or contemporaries made."

"When I think of the Black contractor, I am thinking about the Black businessman in the construction industry--an industry that is one of the biggest industries in the United States," King explained.

"At 10 percent of the Gross National Product, the construction industry represents one dime out of every dollar. One out of every seven jobs is some way related to construction. It's a big, big business. So in trying to advance the Black contractor, we're talking about trying to stimulate an agent for the cause of Black economic development. It is part of a process. It is not just trying to make an individual rich. It is a process toward Black economic empowerment."

Unfortunately, that has not happened.

"We're at a crossroad," King says of today's situation.

"What we are experiencing is a total erosion in what we initially meant for set-aside programs."

"The initial activists those most in need, and most deserving are not necessarily receiving full or near adequate benefits. We are being overlooked across the board and it has been justified by a change in the language of set-aside legislation," King said.

He knows what he is talking about. He has lived it and he has watched others suffer as a result of it.

A prominent force behind the local and national push to institutionalize affirmative action set-asides through legislation, King's efforts began early.

As former vice president of the National Association of Minority Contractors, he has traveled 250,000 miles to more than 40 different cities in 24 states, speaking, writing, and having position papers published in various magazines, on the plight of minority contractors. He also has been instrumental in securing government funding for minority contractor assistance programs in Chicago and nationally.

Working with a Black brain trust facilitated through the Congressional Black Caucus, King wrote portions of the Public Works Act of 1976, which relates to a 10 percent Minority Business Enterprises (MBE) provision in construction. Later, in 1978, he testified before Congress on the effectiveness of that provision. The result, the Local Public Works II Program, established a $4 billion program of local public works projects to provide stimulus to the economy, and increase job opportunities and needed public facilities. It contained the unprecedented provision that at least 10 percent of each LPW grant be expended with minority businesses, contractors or suppliers.

Other federal agencies concerned with assisting minority businesses include the Small Business Administration and the Office of Minority Business Enterprise. They also have language to ensure minority participation.

"The situation now is a problem of conjunction," King commented. "We have watched the original language in affirmative action legislation go through various stages. It changed from 'Disadvantaged' to 'Minority' to 'Minority or Women,' then during the Reagan Administration to 'Minority *and* Women.' And, from where I sit, white women are the primary beneficiaries."

King feels there are many reasons for this. When the women's movement caught on in the 1970s, one of the first places they went was where the Black movement already had entrenched preferential treatment. As a result, the word Black disappeared.

"The billions of dollars of construction set-asides that carried minority stipulation, with the whole intent being to have greater development of minority firms so that they would be competitive and be in a position to employ and train other people, hasn't happened as proportionately for Black people as it has for other ethnics."

King does not point fingers for the current conditions in any particular directions. Several elements come into play.

"We had no idea that this would be a lifelong struggle," King commented. "We failed to recognize that opportunities would only be temporarily available to us. We didn't know that what was needed was a continuing effort to defend what you've acquired and to take care not to depend upon the goodwill of others to guard and protect your share."

The situation has proven to be no different locally than nationally. Born and reared in Chicago, King is especially sensitive to what has happened with the Black construction effort here.

While his own company, UBM, Inc., which was started in 1974, has done fairly well, not many others have followed a similar path.

Despite an early agreement for the implementation of employment of minorities in the Chicago building and construction industry, not much ever really happened.

Signed with much fanfare in 1970 by the Chicago and Cook County Building Trade Council, the Building Construction Employers Association of Chicago and the Coalition for United Community Action (an outgrowth of the 1969 Westside construction shutdown), the Chicago Plan committed to provide constructive training and employment opportunities for 1,000 disadvantaged young adults.

"Last October, the minority construction industry celebrated its twentieth anniversary. Over 80 awards were given to those who stood up and made a positive difference." Paul King recognized the past twenty years and projected an Eight-point plan of action for the new decade of the 90s.

A PLAN FOR THE 90S

1. Each new city department/agency head must be educated to Black interests to insure there is no regression. This is particularly true of the new immigrant, that is, new CEOS from other cities.
2. Black economic development must be put on the agenda of every elected official. Jobs, housing, and education are important. But Black business and land ownership are a priority
3. Minority firms outside the Chicago area should not be allowed to fulfill Chicago MBE goals. This may require a local minority business ordinance.
4. Methods on how majority firms are selected to associate with minority firms in meeting MBE requirements need reevaluation. An effective method is to have one or more minority firms present their credentials to the agency and allow the agency to select the minority firm on the bases of bonafides, track record, previous MBE benefits, need for work, etc.
5. Its time for total MBE awards.
6. We need bonafide joint ventures between majority and minority general contractors.
7. We need Black development partner requirements and set-asides for Black developers.
8. It is necessary that reform rhetoric from the public schools cease. We need a new product that will graduate able to participate in the opportunities created in construction. School children should be introduced to the world of construction.

King participated with the Coalition in negotiations to develop the Chicago Plan. Within two years it was clear that the Plan was a dismal failure. A similar plan formulated in 1972, was denounced by the Coalition.

Refusing to sign the 1972 New Chicago Plan, Coalition leaders stated, The Plan we signed has not worked, because there exists no commitment from the various craft unions. It has not worked because the implementation device does not give the minority community proper decision-making power. It does not work because too many of those involved are not sincere.

Only a measure of success was achieved by a handful of minority contractors. UBM, Inc. was one of them.

King attributes his company's success to several factors. His original partners, Sandra Giles and Sham Dabadghao, have been just as committed and dedicated as he, and still play major roles in the company. The continuity has helped.

"I think you must be willing to sacrifice. A successful business takes a lot more time, and a lot more risks than perhaps a job. But, the benefits are enormous--both from a sense of satisfaction and a sense of independence. Just because you don't work for someone else, doesn't mean that you don't work. It's a different attitude. You work harder. You can see and control the results of what you get. We have to associate our young people with a business zeal."

Fortunately for Paul King, and others he has affected, the process started early. His own father was an entrepreneur. He owned a produce company and taught Paul at an early age the value of productivity.

"My father instilled in me a proper mode of conduct, of working long hours. My uncle taught me how to paint and how to work. He taught me how to perform a task. I have had the best of it."

"I was very inspired, but I also was very naive. I thought that when we got through with the construction piece, back in the 60s and 70s, we would get that under control, then we'd go after education. Then we'd go after the police. Then wed straighten out transportation. I had no idea that these struggles were lifelong."

"I never knew that we were operating without an agenda. There's no agenda about Black economic development, Black entrepreneurship, Black land ownership. I don't see anything about communication. When a person does not read, cannot write, cannot communicate, they cannot move outside the small world in which they live each day. You have to be able to communicate in the larger community. That's a form of entrapment. The most depressing aspect is the destruction of the large proportion of the Black family: Children not getting the benefit of a man in the house providing an example; Black women not getting the benefit of proper companionship."

"Black people have survived under the most terrible situations, so I am not truly depressed. I recognize that the little time I spend here on earth is very insignificant in the larger scheme of things. I have to rely in large measure on the proven survivability against the odds of Black people to improve ourselves. But this time history is different because we are being separated from our selves. We're without direction."

"We have to continue to beat the bushes and confront once and for all how we impact the institutions that influence our situation. This is not a new idea. In fact, it so old I hate to say it. We have to be able to support the institutions that are going to be able to influence the health of our people. You cannot tell me we are not able to do it. We don't need a leader or a messiah. We need a collective will. We need some people to leap out here in given areas to be activists and advocates in areas of concern and action. This is especially true for those who have graduated from college."

"But that's the funny thing about Black people. Every time you're ready to throw up your hands, ready to give up, somebody leaps out here with something that will give you some enthusiasm."

And that's also the thing about Paul J. King. Always ready to do something. He always has and he still is doing something to help Black people.

Rae Jones is a public relations practitioner with more than 15 years experience, and is president of the newly established Raediant Communications. She is formerly the assistant press secretary to Mayor Eugene Sawyer, and was director of communications to the late Mayor Harold Washington, Ms. Jones developed communications strategy for Chicago City government, she was the editor of media relations for Allstate Insurance Company, managing editor of a Chicago community newspaper, and a news reporter. Ms. Jones has served as president of the National Association of Media Women, Chicago Chapter, and is currently vice-president of the Black Public Relations Society of Chicago. She holds memberships in the National Association of Black Journalists and the Chicago Association of Black Journalists. She currently sits on the board of the Westside Cultural Arts Council. She has received numerous media awards and is currently writing a book on the historical migration of African-Americans to Chicago's Westside.

In Support of Affirmative Action

Shelby Steele

Review by Paul King

Shelby Steele's recently published *The Content of Our Character* places the author firmly in the ranks of Thomas Sowell, Michael Williams, Stanley Crouch and others — the group of middle class Blacks who are championing the Civil Rights retrograde as progressive. Of the essays found in this collection, "Affirmative Action: The Price of Preference" is particularly representative of this type of thinking.

From the outset, Steele's argument is contradictory. He admits that he will face a "dilemma" regarding his children and their college admittance and poses the following question: Should they, the offspring of a Black middle class college professor "well removed from the kind of deprivation" that would qualify them for the label "disadvantaged," check 'Black on their college applications? Will this designation enhance their chances for admittance, and of greater importance, will the resulting preferential treatment ultimately do more harm than good?

The Content of Our Character Steele claims that on the one hand, his children have been "called names," suffered slights, and experienced racism's impact first hand. Then Steele emphatically states, "they have never experienced racial discrimination and have never been stopped by their race on any path they have chosen to follow." Do not the "slights" and "peculiar malevolence" endured by his children constitute the most insidious racial discrimination facing Blacks? Equally, do not these obstacles obstruct the paths of many Black children, causing problems in self-esteem, confidence and career development?

Steele claims to have been born in Chicago and gone to school in or around the late '40's. Steele was born and raised in a city which inflicted some of the most inhumane treatment on Black people ever experienced by any community in this century. Blacks didn't live, go to school or pray with whites in any substantial numbers. Blacks in Chicago around Steele's time had virtually no political representation, no presence in city government and a negligible influence on business and economic affairs. Steele is old enough to remember this, yet he criticizes with a "peculiar malevolence" the very vehicle, i.e., affirmative action, that led to change.

In young Steele's Chicago, white policemen abused Black elected officials. Affirmative action, racially-oriented hiring and promotion of Black (and later Hispanics and women) police officers, reduced this activity immensely. The redistricting of aldermanic wards with "affirmative representation" for Blacks led to a more evenly integrated city council. Affirmative action led to the election of Chicago's first Black mayor. And it was that mayor, Harold Washington, who issued an affirmative action ordinance requiring that 25% of all city contracts go to Black and other racial minority-owned businesses with 5% to women-owned businesses.

My first experience with affirmative action occurred around 1968 when seeking to bring more Blacks into the construction trade unions. At that time, we relied upon an executive order signed by the United States President. In essence, it says that federal contractors should "not discriminate against" Blacks and other racial minorities in hiring, and should "take Affirmative Action" (i.e., positive steps to ensure employment in these projects that receive federal funding). Now, some twenty years later, we find a Black person from Chicago--one of the most segregated cities in America casting a "negative vote" on this technique used to create fairness in the workplace.

Steele intertwines the concept of affirmative action with "quotas, goals, timetables, set asides and other forms of preferential treatment." I accept all of the associations above but one: *quotas*. Why use that word except to engage and enlist those groups for whom the buzzword is an anathema? I have never seen affirmative action goals or policies state quotas. Affirmative action creates floors companies must at least reach, but not limiting ceilings. Yet, those who embrace Steele's confused position always attempt to make affirmative action synonymous with quotas. And believe me, Steele has become the instant darling of certain white media personalities who, by quoting him extensively, have declared him the Black authority spokesperson of the moment.

Steele claims that affirmative action has contributed to making "Black" the color of preference and has reburdened the society with the very mischief that it sought to eradicate. When did **BLACK** become the "color of preference?" True enough, Black people started the affirmative action effort, but the word "minority" quickly replaced Blacks to include women, Native Americans, Hispanics, Asians and racial groups from the Indian subcontinent, Pakistan and Sri Lanka.

Steele says that racial preferences allow American society to avoid the difficulty of developing Black parity, opting instead for a cosmetic disparity.

Steele argues that racial preference for Blacks implies inferiority that results in demoralization. Steele says the effect of preferential treatment--the lowering of standards to increase Black representation--puts Blacks at war with an expanding realm of debilitating doubt, so that the doubt itself becomes an unrecognized preoccupation that undermines their ability to perform, especially in integrated situations.

I don't think there is any Black construction worker in Chicago who was demoralized when admitted into the union affirmative action. Is there any evidence to support notion that fires have been extinguished "less well" because the fire department contains some Blacks who were admitted due to an affirmative action program? When Georgetown University's law journal made a special appeal for students to contribute, my son felt that the moments be seized to gain experience and further careers. He did not feel demoralized.

Affirmative action affords a Black person the opportunity to work in an area in which there is underrepresentation exclusion. Once on the job, however, discipline and skill must be proven. Affirmative action *does not* guarantee anyone the right to stay on the job if performance is not good. I do not know how Steele gathers his evidence, but I don't know of any Blacks who were helped by affirmative action who view themselves as victims.

Steele goes on to imply that affirmative action leads Blacks to believe that they are owed reparations for slavery and past discrimination and that such reparations are impossible to make. I believe the idea of the government paying Blacks is such a difficult concept, that most whites would prefer to ignore the question altogether.

Strangely, however, the U.S. government agreed to pay reparations to Japanese families (whose freedom and possessions were denied during the World War II) when the issue was raised. The Congress was "educated," the damage was equated to financial terms and finances were quantified, negotiated, authorized and paid, appropriately so.

It is impossible to pay for every Black life lost on the middle passage, sold into slavery or slighted by racism/oppression, but it is not impossible to develop a collective will, to educate the nation and establish a goal to remedy these crimes, as was one of the purposes of affirmative action.

Steele refers to the trap of Black professionals and the so called "glass ceiling." He says, "I don't think racial preferences are a protection against this subtle discrimination; I think they contribute to it."

He says that in any work place, racial preference wilt always create two different tiers. These tiers imply white superiority and Black inferiority and have the effect of stigmatizing the already stigmatized.

Steele is off the mark when he suggests racial preferences contribute to subtle discrimination. Here Steele accuses the remedy of being a part of the original disease. How can this be? Before affirmative action, there were few or no Blacks in certain professional or managerial strata. With governmental enforcement in the late 60's and throughout the 70's, finally, there was entry and advancement into these positions. When affirmative action was assaulted by the Reagan administration and its like-minded Supreme Court appointees, there was a *retrenchment* of Black hiring in these areas.

Without affirmative action, a young average, though hardworking Black graduate of Chicago's public school system, may never have attended college and law school. Today, he is staff director of an international corporation and active in the community. Without affirmative action, a young, average, though hardworking Black graduate of a public high school in Memphis, may never have attended Yale University or Rush Presbyterian Medical School in Chicago. Today she serves a poor Black community as a doctor.

I believe that affirmative action, while no holistic answer, has provided some positive results and offers *hope*. It provides many African Americans with the education necessary to function beyond the realm of athletes and entertainers. Affirmative action has enabled many a Black business to participate in the general market through loan and set-aside programs. These businesses are community-active, supporting Black schools, churches, sororities and fraternities and other non-profit organizations.

The Bakke (medical school), Defunis (law school) and Fullilove & Croson (minority business) decisions, the Bush Justice Department, the Reagan Supreme Court apparatus and Shelby Steele believe this bit of light should be extinguished. I do not!

Paul King is Chairman of UBM, Inc., a Chicago-based construction company that has benefited from minority set-aside programs and City of Chicago mandated minority business plans. He also serves as president of the Chicago Business Council.

bbb

Affirmative Action:
A 25-Year Retrospective View

by
Paul King

THERE IS AN undeserved, but vigorous assault on affirmative action around this country and it started well in advance of Ronald Reagan's election in 1980. This race -based, socio-economic program, targeted by the Civil Rights Division of the Reagan Justice Department has become so significant that college scholarships and other monetary awards are dispensed in accord with it. Supreme Court justices, governors, senators, and presidents are appointed and elected because of their position on affirmative action.

In twenty years, we have gone from seeking to correct the results of discrimination through the courts, to attacks on affirmative action in the courts, via the Bakke, Weber, and DeFunis cases, to the point where what was once universally called affirmative action is now called by some reverse discrimination or a quota system. We even have a crop of persons of African ancestry who find it necessary to rail against affirmative action. And, while other Blacks need speedy victim-relief, some educated Blacks are ashamed to be associated with the term.

I see a similar scenario as that established by Ronald Reagan when he coined the term welfare queen. Obviously, this referred to some Black woman who had inappropriately manipulated a welfare program. Thus, Reagan translated welfare to mean a Black rip-off scheme. Today, we find Blacks, educated through the race-conscious and race-preference era, who say affirmative action is bad. More than a handful of them feel guilt-ridden and stigmatized. Why? Of all the socio-economic phenomena in existence, why is this term being transformed into some hateful, disgusting thing? Racism.

The Experience of Racism

In his book, **Bullwhip Days,** James Mellon states that the dominant theme which threads the Gordian weave of these narratives and lends them so much relevance to contemporary America is racism. We ignore this theme at our peril, for no other social problem has cast so long a shadow over our economic history or cost us so dearly in ruined lives and lost treasures. Indeed, whoever would understand the Black community in America today must seek to understand not only the conditions of slavery into which that community was born, but must also understand the experience of racism.

For it was racism that gave America its most distinctive and enduring character.

Racial prejudice and bias are usually based more on emotion than reason. Prejudicial expressions resulting from mental reflexes rather than conscious convictions wreak havoc upon African-American efforts and aspirations. For while prejudice, alone, cannot be quantified, diagnosed or treated, as science can cope with cancer or diabetes, it does have predictable and explicit symptoms. Regardless of the underlying causes, the manifestations of prejudice in the form of discriminatory acts can be identified and measured. Moreover, they can be treated, and with the required doses of integrity and diligence, they can be cured or excised to grant fair survival chances to the victims. This requires knowledgeable, informed citizenry and advocates.

How Affirmative Action Came About

Affirmative action came about as a result of clear discrimination against Blacks. Although the term first appeared in reference to employment, the quality of Black life in housing, education, and economic advancement was equally dismal. When it became clear that federal judges were willing to require that employers do something about desegregating their work forces, the battleground for equality was clearly economic, and state and federal agencies became advocates for minorities. Executive Order 11246, issued by President Lyndon B. Johnson said, in effect, not only must the federal contractor not discriminate, but the contractor must take affirmative action in recruiting and integrating its work force. Affirmative action plans which applied to construction unions (major culprits at the time) had to use numerical goals for recruiting minority workers, and timetables, with time frames for reaching these goals.

Johnson's directive was designed to make up for past injustices, overcome continuing discrimination and, ultimately, to provide equal job opportunities for Blacks and whites. Unhappily, those aims might seem to contain a painful contradiction. Compensating for past discrimination against some people may appear to dilute opportunities previously guaranteed or expected by others.

When companies hire or promote minority workers, they may be perceived as penalizing white workers. However, there are no known cases of white workers being fired or laid off to provide jobs or Blacks. Affirmative action related to jobs for minorities and women, and its contract procurement counterparts, have been successful efforts.

Statistics prove that before there were affirmative action requirements, the numbers were low for jobs and contracts attained by minorities and females. With the onset of such programs, those numbers rose dramatically. Where there was significant reduction in affirmative action or cessation, as in The City of Richmond versus J .A. Croson Company case finding, minorities lost ground.

Has Affirmative Action Made A Difference?

Have affirmative action programs really made a difference? The answer is a resounding YES! The total of federal, non-procurement, financial expenditures to minority business enterprises (MBEs) increased by 25% from fiscal year 1988 to fiscal year 1989. The totals for subcontract procurement and procurement under grants increased by 14% and 26% respectively in that one-year period. From FY 1979 to FY 1989, federal agencies increased the dollar amount of business with MBEs from $2.4 billion or 2.6% to $8.6 billion or 4.8% of the total procurement dollars spent. During this period, contracts and grants were also awarded to assist in minority business education and training.

In contrast to federal affirmative action efforts, cities and states around the nation, including Philadelphia and Portland (Oregon), New York, New Jersey and California have suspended minority business utilization efforts. Whether by court order or legislation, thousands of MBEs are faltering or failing altogether in this country. In Philadelphia alone, city contracts to minority firms have shrunk from 25% to 3.5% in 1991. The value of contracts awarded to minority companies in open bidding there plummeted to $21.3 million from $65 million in that same period

One of the strongest, intellectual opponents of affirmative action is Nathan Glazer. In 1975, his book, Affirmative Discrimination, launched the current reaction we so often see and hear. He laid out the "its not my fault" route for white America regarding its role in prior Black discrimination. Referring to white ethnics, he proclaimed: these groups were not particularly involved in enslavement of the Negro or the creation of the Jim Crow pattern in the South, the conquest of part of Mexico, or the near extermination of the American Indian. They came to a country that provided them (fewer) benefits than it now provides the protected groups. There is little reason for them to bear the burden of the redress of a past in which they had no or little part, or to assist those who presently receive more assistance than they did. We are indeed a nation of minorities: to enshrine some minorities as deserving of special benefits means not to defend minority against discriminating majority but to favor some of those minorities over others!

Glazer gives a thin shield to those who claim that I didn't enslave anyone. I didn't discriminate against anyone. Why should I have to pay for it? The issue is by what means, on whose backs, at whose expense did the Glazer victims achieve their current position, which they feel is threatened by affirmative action?

The condition of Black people today, compared to the condition of 25 years ago, when affirmative action programs were launched, is quite different. The situation has reached a point where it appears to be out of control. If one accepts the theory promulgated some years ago concerning the destruction of the Black male and the creation of an underclass Black totally alienated from other African-Americans, then things are on target.

African-Americans Are Under Siege!

African-American people are under siege! Forces from without, as well as anti-social behavior in our midst, create daily havoc for many of us. Affirmative action is a tool for helping Blacks in some way. Access to the means of progress, such as entry to jobs, business ownership, professional schools, and other arenas previously denied Black people, is under severe attack.

Some argue against affirmative action because it may benefit affluent Blacks. This argument appears to have little basis, in that affirmative action is not a financial entitlement program. Affirmative action is an opportunity program that takes race into consideration, in the case of Blacks, due to past slavery and discrimination affecting generations of men, women and children of African heritage. Suppose we have a Black student seeking admission into medical school or law school and he/she comes from an educated, middle-income family. Because of the shortage of Black doctors (due to past discrimination) this person is perfectly eligible for affirmative action benefits. He/she may not be entitled to financial scholarships, but certainly to a race-conscious, admissions program. It is a well-known fact that at major prestigious, and numerous, smaller colleges and universities, the children of alumni, athletes, and financial donor offspring are given preferential treatment regarding admissions. This appears to cause no problem. The schools policy, formal or informal, is known and those who apply accept it. However, even equality of education does not automatically provide equality in employment or professional growth opportunities.

These telling points indicate the current mood of the country and suggest that there are no public policy solutions in place for its domestic problems the economy, crime, infrastructure improvement, and drugs. Yet, there is a strong anti-Black attitude coursing through America that is overturning progressive laws and creating regressive ones in their stead. In his book, **Chain Reaction,** Thomas Edsell suggests that as long as Blacks are a central part of the Democratic Party, the Democratic Party will be perceived by whites as obliged to support affirmative action, civil rights and other racially-targeted programs. This, reasons Edsell, is why there has been only one Democratic president in the last 24 years while there has been an overwhelming heavy Democratic majority in the U.S. Congress. This Catch-22 has worked effectively, because now candidates are unwilling to publicly support affirmative action. They like fairness and equality, but are mute on how to get there.

Look at Bush's infamous Willie Horton ad, designed to put racial fear of Blacks in the minds of white voters. Look, too, at Senator Jesse Helms (R-NC) commercial, used against his Black, U.S. Senatorial opponent, Harvey Gant. It depicted a white man (during a deep recession) receiving a rejection notice saying, in effect, that he would have gotten the job, except a (less qualified) Black had gotten the spot due to affirmative action.

David Duke represents the full-grown tree from the seeds sown by Ronald Reagan (welfare queen) and nurtured by Bush (Willie Horton). Let us remember this former Nazi and Ku Klux Klan zealot openly attacking Blacks in his platform, as he sought to be governor of Louisiana. Affirmative action bashing was his most trusted weapon. What is truly reflective of public perception is that he got over 40% of the vote and would probably have won, had it not been for the economic fears of the business and educational communities.

The 1992 Presidential election has already started with Pat Buchanan calling the Bush Administration a quotas ad ministration. Thus, the dilemma as to how anyone expecting to get Black support can avoid supporting affirmative action (anathema to whites) will continue. One of the shameful aspects of the Clarence Thomas Supreme Court nomination hearings was how he dodged the questions of Senator Arlen Spector (R-PA) regarding the use of hiring goals and timetables in the New York trade unions that had, for decades, denied Blacks construction jobs. Here was an educated African-American, seeking to become a Supreme Court Justice, who was a beneficiary of affirmative action in his Yale Law School admission, but who **could** not, **would** not, acknowledge that racially-based solutions should be used to solve racially-based problems.

Affirmative action generally refers to African-Americans, Hispanics, Asians and women. Why are only Blacks singled out in the ads and the other forms of retaliation against affirmative action? Where are the other groups voices and resources in this fight back that must take place?

If not affirmative action, what racially oriented solutions is any public official or critic offering? Educated, enlightened, socially conscious, and concerned citizens must demand answers from public officials, elected and appointed. They must be made to reopen to the contradictions including: the world of difference between the promise and the reality of empowerment for public housing residents, the way public officials glorify cutting budget deficits so as to have more available money to use for what--the politically-inspired rhetoric about the need to generate a thousand points of light in this country of over 22 million people?

On every conceivable front, at every opportunity we must initiate and encourage the non-confrontational education of white persons so as to help eliminate miseducation; reactivate older, Black groups focusing on strategies to continue affirmative action; and offer vocal support and engineer affirmative action programs--through contributions of time and/ or resources--ensuring the reinstitution of meaningful affirmative action in the public and private sector.

The great debate over the pros and cons of affirmative action and its effects on the prospect for Black Americans does not always take into account a key ingredient that is apparently in short supply in many quarters. That missing, or declining element is **hope**.

Waning and disappearing in Black neighborhoods around the country, hope is the eye of the needle through which the threads of affirmative action can be pushed and pulled to help ensure parity and progress for all Americans.

Affirmative action is an opportunity program that takes race into consideration, in the case of Blacks, due to past slavery and discrimination affecting generations of men, women and children of African heritage.

Contractor building something bigger

by John McCarron

NICE GUYS RARELY finish first, so it was good to hear that Paul Kings UBM Inc. has been named Chicago's top minority-owned construction firm by **Black Enterprise** magazine.

I've known Paul about seven years. He calls me from time to time to gab about the big projects around town: which companies are working on the Kennedy Expressway; who's lining up to bid on the downtown trolley, the new federal office building and the next expansion at O'Hare.

We've been talking ever since the Tribune ran a series of investigative stories on the bogus minority contractors that sprang up in the early days of government set-asides. Several reporters worked on the series. My contribution was an account of the debacle that was the McCormick Place expansion project.

On paper, 30 percent of the work was supposed to be done by firms owned by minorities or women. On the construction site, it was hard to find a black or Hispanic face.

Most of the large, white-owned construction firms on the $205 million project joint-ventured with minority-owned firms, or so their bid documents claimed. It turned out that several of the so-called MBEs (minority business enterprises) consisted of little more than a letterhead and a listing in the phone book. A white-owned firm would do the work and pay the MBE owner a fee for lending his or her name to the enterprise.

Among the most blatant was an outfit called Precision Contractors Inc., controlled by Noah Robinson, half-brother to Rev. Jesse Jackson. Precision was supposed to do 30 percent of the work on the enclosed pedestrian bridge that spans Lake Shore Drive. Subsequent inquiries revealed that company representatives rarely showed up.

Back then Precision scooped up huge amounts of set-aside work from the city, the state, the CTA and the sanitary district. Today Noah Robinson is serving a federal prison sentence for fraud and racketeering.

Nobody was more troubled by the MBE horror stories than Paul King, who has spent his life trying to open the construction business to legitimate African-American contractors. In the late 60s he helped negotiate the Chicago Plan for opening city construction jobs to blacks. Later he ran a training program for minority contractors sponsored by the United Builders Association of Chicago.

King founded UBM Inc. in 1975, and the company began to tackle successively bigger jobs, beginning with a piece of the University of Illinois Hospital, the James R. Thompson Center, the O'Hare expansion and an enlisted quarters at Great Lakes Naval Training Center.

All the while, he has defended the set-aside concept against those who see it as just another racial quota system, and one prone to fraud and abuse.

Owners always ask me: "Do you really do the work with your own forces?" They're surprised when we show up with skilled black tradesmen and laborers and get about our business like we know what were doing.

Today there are several large, black-owned construction firms in Chicago, companies such as C.F. Moore, for instance, that can compete with the best white-owned firms. But none has done more to advance affirmative action's cause than Paul King and UBM Inc. have.

Last week King played host to a luncheon to celebrate UBM's completion, as general contractor, of a $5 million, 150-bed drug and alcohol rehabilitation center on the West Side.

Michael Darcy, president of the Gateway Foundation, said he hired UBM on the recommendation of Wendell Campbell, one of Chicago's most respected black architects.

There's this fallacy out there that it's going to cost more if you use a minority contractor, Darcy said. I can tell you that Paul saved us money and that 70 percent of the work was done by minority or female hands, many hired from the neighborhood.

Darcy presented King with a check for $50,000, the agreed-to bonus if UBM completed the treatment center ahead of schedule.

King promptly announced the money would be donated to eight of his favorite schools and social-service organizations.

Paul King

Not everyone agrees that minority set-asides are a good idea. Last week, when the Cook County Board voted to make its 30 percent goal a legal requirement, suburban Republicans howled about mandatory quotas.

They have a point and I'm not convinced mandatory percentages are the way to go.

Maybe some day, when there are lots of Paul Kings out there, we won't need them anymore.

Originally published, November 1993. Copyrighted, Chicago **Tribune** Company. All rights reserved; used with permission.

N'DIGO Profiles™

FEBRUARY 1995

PAUL KING

Putting "Firm" In Affirmative Action

Putting "Firm" in Affirmative Action
by Rae Jones

Something has gone terribly wrong in affirmative action and minority set-aside programs.

Those who made the initial efforts and sacrificed the most for Black empowerment in this arena are not the direct beneficiaries of those efforts.

No one is more aware of this fact than Paul J. King, and his frustration is evident.

Chairman of UBM, Inc., a multi-disciplined construction management consulting agency, general contractor and engineering firm, King was a primary player 25 years ago in the local and national Black contractors movement.

Shutting It Down!

Representing a group of 80 Black building contractors and working with community organizations, King helped shut down three housing rehabilitation projects worth millions of dollars in 1969 on Chicago's West Side.

They wanted to force union leaders to the bargaining table where the issue of opening unions to Blacks could be resolved. At the time, the Unions were 97 percent White.

"We wanted our fair share of jobs, our piece of the pie, King said. Blacks would pass construction projects in their neighborhoods and see nothing hut White workers. It was a slap in the face, a daily insult."

"Our strategy was to initially try to get jobs on a site, then move on to being developers and owners of a site, then to gain control over business enterprises, jobs and all the commerce that interlaced with those enterprises," King explained.

Advancing Black Economic Empowerment

While the short-term strategy worked, the long-term plan didn't. King is frustrated that the early pioneers--Black contractors--no longer are benefiting from the hard work and energy they put into that movement.

"All the proponents, the core, in 1969, were Black, he said. We pivoted off of a Black presence, a Black commitment, and projects going on in Black communities. With all of that effort, if we look now at statistics in employment alone, without even considering development and owner ship, we are losing ground everyday.

Though the number of minority apprentices has grown, according to Department of Labor figures, King cautions that the numbers, when broken down by race and gender, do not bode well for Blacks.

"It is not that I am against any other ethnic group, King commented. It is that I believe that there should be a fair proportion going to the people who started all of this in the first place."

"At 10 percent of the Gross National Product, the construction industry represents one dime out of every dollar. One out of every seven jobs is in some way related to construction. It's a big, big business. So, in trying to advance the Black contractor, were talking about trying to stimulate an agent for the cause of Black economic development. It's not just trying to make an individual rich. It's a process toward Black economic empowerment."

Unfortunately, that has not happened. "We're at a crossroads," King says of today's situation. "We are experiencing a total erosion in what we initially meant for set-aside programs."

Pushing For Legislation

He knows what he is talking about. A prominent force behind the local and national push to institutionalize affirmative action set-asides through legislation, King's efforts began early.

As former vice president of the National Association of Minority Contractors, he traveled the country speaking and writing on the plight of minority contractors. He has also been instrumental in securing government funding for minority contractor assistance programs in Chicago and nationally.

Working with a Black brain trust facilitated through the Congressional Black Caucus, King wrote portions of the Public Works Act of 1976, calling for a 10 percent Minority Business Enterprise provision in construction of local public works projects.

"The situation now is a problem of conjunction," King stated. "We watched the original language in affirmative action legislation through various stages. It changed from 'Disadvantaged,' to 'Minority' to 'Minority Women,' then during the Reagan Administration to 'Minority and Women.' And, from where I sit, White women are the primary beneficiaries."

"The billions of dollars of construction set-asides that carried minority stipulation, with whole intent being to have greater development of minority firms so that they would be competitive and in a position to employ and train other people hasn't happened as proportionately for Black people as it has for other groups."

While his own company, UBM, which started in 1974, has done fairly well, not many other Black contractors have. Despite an agreement for the implementation of employment of minorities in the Chicago building and construction industry, not much ever really happened, mainly because of lack of commitment and insincerity on the part of the craft unions.

King attributes his company's relative success to several factors. His original partners, Sandra Giles and Sham Dabadghao, have provided commitment, dedication and continuity, he says.

And he explains, "I think you must be willing to sacrifice. A successful business takes a lot more time, and a lot more risk, than perhaps a job. You don't work for someone else, but you work harder. You can see and control the results of what you get. We have to associate our young people with a business zeal."

> **"We wanted our fair share of jobs, our piece of the pie,"
> King said. Blacks would pass construction projects in their
> neighborhoods and see nothing but White workers. It was a
> slap in the face, a daily insult."**

Assessing His Community

Fortunately for native Chicagoan Paul King, and others he has affected, his work ethic developed early. His father was an entrepreneur who owned a produce company and taught Paul at an early age the value of productivity.

"My father instilled in me a proper mode of conduct, of working long hours. My uncle taught me how to perform a task. I have had the best of it. "

"I was very inspired, but also very naive," he continued. "I thought that when we got through with the construction piece, back in the '60s and '70s, we could get that under control, then wed go after education. Then we'd go after the police. Then wed straighten out transportation. I had no idea that these struggles were life-long."

I never knew that we were operating without an agenda. There's no agenda about Black economic development, Black entrepreneurship, Black land ownership. I don't see anything about communication. But Black people have survived under the most terrible situations, so I'm not truly depressed. I have to rely in large measure on the proven survivability against the odds of Black people to improve our selves.

You can't tell me that we can't do it, but we need a collective will. We need some people to leap out here to be activists and advocates in areas of concern and action. And that's the funny thing shout Black people—every time you're ready to throw up your hands, ready to give up, somebody leaps our here with something that will give you some enthusiasm.

And that's also the thing about Paul King. Always ready to do something. He always has and he still is--doing something to help Black people.

Affirmative action:
The new racial sound-bite

by John McCarron.

We met for lunch at his favorite place in Greek Town and right away it was clear that Paul King, one of Chicago's biggest minority contractors, had something to get off his chest.

"With all the grief going on in the black community, with all the drugs, the crime, the unemployment, why do they want to go into the one corner where a little light is shining and snuff it out?"

He was talking, of course, about affirmative action.

More to the point, Paul King wanted to talk about the precarious state of government "set-aside" programs--the programs that have given companies like his UBM Inc. a toehold in the megabuck world of heavy construction.

I used to write about the big public works projects in town--the O'Hare Development Program, the McCormick Place expansion, the new Comiskey Park--and over the years King has become a valued source. Maybe even a friend. He's no angel, but in his business, angels get their wings clipped. King knows where the side doors are located in City Hall (He was one of the African-American businessmen who took heat for organizing a re-election fundraiser for Mayor Richard Daley) and he can cuss rings around any cement crew foreman.

Even so, his UBM Inc. has a reputation for showing up, for finishing on time and for staying within budget. UBM does not, like certain minority-owned contractors of yore, quietly subcontract their work to white-owned companies, while taking a cut off the top.

In the early days of set-asides such shams were the bane of King's existence, which is one reason he was such a good source.

"Not only did they steal jobs from blacks," he says of the shams "but they provided the anecdotes that are now fueling the fires against affirmative action."

Actually, the current attack on set-asides is much more fundamental than complaints about a few bad apples. The entire notion of officially favoring one race or gender is under political and legal attack. Resentful white males and the Republican majority they helped send to Congress are out to deep-six government-sponsored affirmative action programs, period. And earlier this month the U.S. Supreme Court, which has been known to peek at the election returns, threw out a Colorado set-aside program because there was no direct evidence that minority contractors there had been discriminated against.

That ruling doesn't affect Chicago's "25 and 5" program, which requires that 25 percent of city contracts go to minority-owned firms and another 5 percent to female-owned. Not long ago, the Daley administration redrew the city's program so as to acknowledge historic discrimination here in the building trades--a wrinkle that was missing from the Colorado program.

But the handwriting is on the wall. Congress is going after affirmative action, and Bill Clinton's political handlers are advising the president he'd be a fool to get in Congress' way.

All of which had Paul King waving his fork at me over his Greek salad.

"In 1969, when we started marching and shutting down construction sites, there were no blacks in the ironworkers union or the sheet metal workers. I mean zero. None. And there were no black contractors to speak of."

"Then Nixon came up with this idea of black capitalism. That, with a little help from government, you could start some black-owned companies that would have a ripple effect in the black community. And you know what? It worked. Look at UBM. Over the last five years we've paid $11 million in wages, $4.2 million in payroll taxes. And we haven't only helped blacks. About half our people are white, especially in the trades where it's still hard to find qualified minorities.

"At first we were getting a special break but pretty soon the industry found out we don't have horns, that we do the work, and so now we get calls from the big outfits who say, `Hey, that last job worked out OK. Why don't we get together again and bid on this bigger one.'"

"Now we're actually competing against the big boys on a low-bid basis. We're doing the concrete at the new University of Chicago diagnostic clinic not because we're minority, but because we had the best price."

Over coffee and baklava I tried to explain to King the thinking of the resentful white male. Like the contractors who under-bid minority firms but don't get the job. And the taxpayers who get stuck paying the difference. And most importantly, the white construction workers, none of whom ever owned slaves, who must wait at the hiring hall while blacks with less experience, get the call.

"But we're only asking for a tiny piece," Paul King shot back. "The biggest white-owned contractor in America does $25 billion a year. All the black contractors in America don't do $2.5 billion. You've got 5 million construction workers in this country and only 250,000 of them are black. There are more Hispanics in construction than there are blacks.

"Slavery has gone," he went on, "but not racism. The epithets are gone but the access is not there. You know the figures for black unemployment. You know the poverty and the despair that's out there. Affirmative action has been the one ray of hope. It hasn't worked in every field, but in mine it has been a big success. And now they say we don't need it anymore? Now they're going to take it away?

"If that happens," he said, "we'll be marching again. We did it in '69. Some of us remember how to shut down a job site."

The problem with that, I cautioned as we parted, is that white America might not respond the same way it did in '69.

He just shook his head. "Affirmative action has become the new racial sound-bite. It's a shame. It was working."

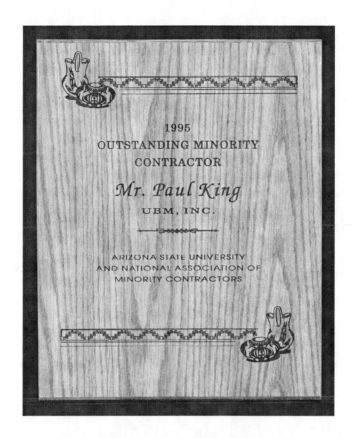

1995
OUTSTANDING MINORITY
CONTRACTOR

Mr. Paul King

UBM, INC.

ARIZONA STATE UNIVERSITY
AND NATIONAL ASSOCIATION OF
MINORITY CONTRACTORS

King Receives Minority Constructor Award

Paul King, chairman of UBM Inc., received **the 1996 Outstanding Minority Constructor Award** recently. The award, co-sponsored by the Arizona State University Del. E. Webb School of Construction and National Association of Minority Contractors (NAMC), was presented last week at the 8th Annual Construction Recognition banquet in Tempe, Ariz. King is a co-owner and founder of UBM Inc., which is the largest African American-owned and operated construction company in Illinois. For the past three years, *Black Enterprise* magazine has ranked UBM as the number one African American construction services company in Chicago. The company, which celebrated 20 years in business this year, provides program and construction management services, general contracting, specialty contracting and design/building services for a variety of private and public clients. King's contributions to education and to the advancement of minorities led to his selection as the award's third-ever recipient. He has spent more than 26 years fighting for the inclusion of minorities and women at every level of employment in the construction industry. A former NAMC vice president, King has traveled to 40 cities in 24 states to speak about the plight of minority contractors. He also helped to effect the first legislation that enacted affirmative action more than 25 years ago. Each year, King participates in the training of African American college students enrolled in UBM's summer intern program, which prepares students for professional construction careers. He also travels throughout the country to speak to young people about careers in construction.

King strives to introduce construction to kids

by Teresa Verbout

ASK PAUL KING, the 1996 Outstanding Minority Constructor, about the recent Supreme Court decision in *Adarand Constructors Inc. vs. Pena* and you can hear disappointment, not surprise, in his voice.

I think that it was unfortunate," King said. I think that the recent decision was somewhat anticipated, but it is not to be considered the death knell *for* affirmative action. It is somewhat unfortunate that all the major anti-affirmative action decisions by the Supreme Court have hovered around construction."

Opportunities that affirmative action has offered have helped King build his construction management and general contracting company, UBM, Inc., Chicago, into a successful firm, which has an annual revenue in excess of $15 million. His company's work and his own efforts to further contracting possibilities for minorities, in particular African-Americans, led to his being named the Outstanding Minority Constructor at the recent Construction Recognition Banquet for Arizona State University's Del E. Webb School of Construction. The award was sponsored by the Del E. Webb School of Construction and the Arizona Chapter of the National Assn. of Minority Contractors.

Sometimes King can't understand the attitude people have against affirmative action. "Affirmative action helped me create 350 jobs last year, over half of whom were white males who are supposed to be angry. Affirmative action helped me pay over $5 million in wages and $370,000 in taxes.

"A large portion of our subcontractors are white subcontractors who are against affirmative action. How could they be against affirmative action when we're creating the avenues for them to get action, for them to have work?" King wondered.

King's activism dates back to 1969 when he helped shut down a jobsite in protest of the lack of African-Americans on the job. "At that time I began looking at other avenues of helping black contractors get into other areas of work. We were pretty much at that time just relegated to the weld and the trowel trades."

King spends a lot of his time introducing African-American kids to the economic conditions that construction offers.

"When you don't get-the black person in the trades, you're not likely to get any evolution as a contractor. I am convinced that this is one of the things that I am definitely going to spend a good deal of my time on in the future. It also has to happen because we have to have, in companies like my own, more black professionals coming up. Because if the company is going to be really successful it has to be second, third generations of African-American people in my company, leading my company."

King spends time on two major projects. He has adopted a grammar school and created the Homework Club. Nearly 50 African-American sixth-graders go to the University of Chicago from 3-6 p.m. every Monday through Thursday to study. In return, King takes them to his office to see what he does for a living, to jobsites, to Chicago Bulls games or concerts.

His efforts have paid off. King recalls two sixth-grade boys he met through the program. One wanted to be a doctor and the other wanted to be a football player. Through the program, their math and reading skills increased, their self-confidence improved and their choice of vocations changed. Getting close to entering college, one boy is going to be an engineer, while the other will study architecture.

King's company also has an intern program for college students. Thirty interns have passed through the program, six of which have been hired full-time at UBM. King said even college students lack confidence and need two to three years of preparation time before they can handle a project on their own.

King is the former national vice president of the NAMC and one of the association's original board members. It's been more than 25 years since that pivotal shutdown in Chicago and King said sometimes race still becomes an issue.

"I think the biggest roadblock in effect—and it's still prevalent today—is no one wanted to entrust the responsibility of a major construction process or project to a black-owned firm. That's still pervasive today. Even with all the accomplishments we have made, there still is this blatant racial prejudice. And there's still this unbelievability that a black-owned firm really can be responsible for managing a $10 million, $15 million, and $20 million project. That was and still is the biggest problem."

During a special meeting held recently at City Hall, Mayor Richard M. Daley acknowledged the efforts of UBM, Inc., in sponsoring a summer Intern program for minority students interested in construction careers. Pictured are (from left) Monica Perry, Anil Singh, Larry Johnson, Paul King, Mayor Daley, Tapiwa Ziyenge, Sharlyn Brown, and project coordinators Geraldine Harris, James Watkins and Paul King Ill.

Minority intern program recognized

Chicago Mayor Richard M. Daley recently recognized UBM, Inc., during special ceremonies at City Hall for the firm's summer internship program. This is the third year that UBM has sponsored internships for minority college students in construction-related fields. The recipients were selected for the program based on their interest in engineering, architecture and construction management.

Each of the participating students was placed on an active construction site for the summer and worked with UBM field staff. The students also participated in workshops covering all aspects of the project cycle including estimating, project management, field control, job-site safety, and project close-out. The project coordinators kept track of the students' work, issuing reports on their progress while the students also made reports on their activities. The students received salaries for their work as project assistants.

Over the past three years the minority internship program has employed 15 college students,

This year, through the work of project coordinators Geraldine Harris, James Watkins and Paul King ill, a true mentor-protégé relationship was achieved with the students. In fact, Monica Perry, a senior at IIT and one of the participating students, continues to work part-time at one of UBM's field offices.

Daley said, "UBM does a great deal of business with the city of Chicago and gives a great deal back through programs such as this.

"These young people would never know the real side of construction without this opportunity provided by UBM."

He then encouraged the students to continue their work at school and pursue careers in engineering and construction-related fields.

Dodge Construction News®

"Serving the construction industry since 1946"

| Thursday, Oct. 20, 1994 | Vol. XLVIII-No. 202 | Copyright © 1994 McGraw-Hill, Inc. $5.00 per copy |

UBM, INC., recently completed its fourth summer intern program. The participants recently visited City Hall for a meeting with Mayor Richard M. Daley. Pictured are (from left)—Greg Wells, William Moppins, Maurice Thrower, Anil Singh, Callie Reed, Mayor Daley, UBM Chairman Paul King, Jesse Cooper, Rhona Moore, Patrice Harris, Project Coordinator Paul King III, and Christopher Ruthledge.

Minority students learn construction first-hand in summer intern program

Mayor Richard M. Daley recently hosted summer interns of UBM, Inc., at City Hall, extending his personal vote of approval to the firm's intern program.

During a half-hour meeting, the mayor praised the students' commitment to educational excellence and urged them to return to Chicago after graduation and put what they have learned at school and at UBM toward the good of the city.

The intern program curriculum consists of one-on-one instruction in marketing and sales, estimating, project management, scheduling, field control and safety.

The students worked alongside UBM project managers to improve skills already learned at school and to help bridge the gap from school to employment. Some students learned proposal preparation and development for the first time.

They were required to write a report each day about construction activity on the jobsite, including productivity of one or more subcontractors.

Rotation each week from project to project helped to provide a broader overview of construction management and general contracting techniques.

As a final exam, the students collectively designed, priced and scheduled a 2,800-sq.-ft. residential structure.

To date, UBM has employed 25 interns. Four have been hired full-time. ❑

Reprinted courtesy of Dodge Construction News, © The McGraw Hill Companies, Inc., 1994; All rights reserved.

125

Dodge Construction News CHICAGO®

"Voice of the construction industry since 1946"

Tuesday, October 3, 1995   Vol. XLIX, No. 189   Copyright © 1995 McGraw-Hill, Inc. $5.00 per copy

Interns receive 'hands-on' construction experience

Participants in UBM, Inc.'s, summer intern program learned the true meaning of "hands-on experience" this year. In short, they were up to their necks with project management work assignments such as scheduling and estimating, job meeting minutes and report writing.

Interns with good computer skills were essential in reducing the pressures on busy project managers often laden with heavy paperwork and computer-based work assignments. Students were helpful in completing routine tasks utilizing spread-sheet and word-processing multi-tasking software applications.

Construction assignments ran the gamut, from the preconstruction phase at Trinity United Church of Christ on the far South Side of Chicago to project close-out at Midway Airport for the Dept. of Aviation.

Perhaps, the most striking learning experience for interns was the restoration of the Reliance Building in the heart of downtown Chicago. Located at the busy intersection of State Street and Washington Boulevard, the 15-story restoration project poses a variety of constructability issues, such as deteriorating terra-cotta cladding securing scaffolding on the 100-year-old structure and pedestrian safety. From the ground up students witnessed a host of contractors scurrying in and out of the historic structure.

This year UBM expanded the program to include students interested in computers and marketing. These interns were assigned to UBM's corporate staff, where they were instrumental in stemming the tide of mounting office and marketing assignments.

The program ended in early August capped off by a gathering in the office of Mayor Richard M. Daley, who encouraged the students to take full advantage of UBM's intern program.

"Too often students are only exposed to routine summer jobs that are just desk jobs in the public sector work," said Daley. "This [UBM] program "gives full exposure and training in details of construction, which is what you need to pursue a career. Private sector efforts like this should be federally supported."

UBM celebrated its fifth summer intern program this year. The program is offered to college-age minority students, both men and women, pursuing professional careers in the construction industry. UBM has graduated 30 interns so far and five have been hired full-time. ◻

Reprinted courtesy of Dodge Construction News, © The McGraw Hill Companies, Inc., 1995; All rights reserved.

Bronzeville Credit

Don't let an African American firm's work go unnoticed.

Personal View by Paul King

The **Sun-Times** has been filled with articles and editorials about the historic Bronzeville restoration process.

UBM, Inc., an African-American construction company, was the builder of this project. McClier Corp. was the architect and UBM was the contractor. As chairman of UBM, I am concerned that virtually no reference has been given to the fact that that a black general contractor could provide the bonding, the financing, participate in the management of meetings, use a black superintendent to do the job and provide local residents with jobs.

At the Bee Building's opening ceremony, May 4, such leaders as Mayor Richard M. Daley and Rep Bobby Rush (D-I1L) praised UBM for a job well done.

Restoration of old, architecturally significant buildings is tough. For the Chicago Bee Building project, UBM overcame myriad challenges. We found a derelict, rat-infested structure that was being used as a crack house and chop shop.

We began by completely gutting and restoring the deteriorating structure, and constructed a new wing. This new structure blends seamlessly with the existing one and houses the children's library and an auditorium for community use.

The historic facade of the Bee Building was faithfully restored by replacing and refurbishing the terra cotta tiles and installing a new storefront identical to the original in appearance, but built with today's state-of-the-art energy efficiency standards.

New elevators, mechanical, electrical and computer systems were installed to meld a library for the 21st century into the gleaming, renovated jewel that today graces South State Street.

With the support of city and state funds, people working together to help African-American children improve reading and computer literacy skills, cooperation of this type can cure some of our social ills.

However, nothing can replace the pride that was seen in the black faces who knew a bona fide black firm worked to construct this structure.

And nothing will ever take the place of black children watching our superintendent, T.J. Alexander, an African American, direct this project. Not, only was T.J. a role model, but he was a real example for young black children to look up to. In too many cases, these young children are devoid of positive male examples in their everyday lives.

Paul King is chairman of UBM Inc.
Letter, courtesy of Chicago **Sun-Times;** *May 19, 1996.*

Commentary
Answering a child's cry

By Paul King

Commentary
Answering a child's cry

By Paul King

I am no social theoretician or practicing psychological professional. I am a Chicago-based, African-American businessman with a deep concern for black people.

With great interest, I noted a question posed in a Chicago **Tribune** headline pondering, "Can they be saved?" Both the query and the answer sought applied to two African-American youngsters of Chicago public housing. They claimed international headlines by literally throwing away the life of a 5-year-old neighbor. After dangling him from a high-rise window, they let him drop.

Anyone seriously pondering this question would do well to read **All God's Children**, by Fox Butterfield, which attempts to assess the life of Willie Bosket, a black prison inmate, originally incarcerated at age 9. The similarities in the lives of Chicago's neophyte killers, nicknamed Tony and Antoine, with those of New York's Willie are overwhelming. The basic indices of failure in the young men's lives are beyond mere coincidence.

These include:

- an insufficient presence of positive male examples;
- the paucity of affection, i.e., genuine caring;
- schools, courts and social service agencies that could not, or would not, do their jobs;
- and parents unable to respond to the emotional needs of the young men.

Reports from psychologists on the Chicago boys included statements such as: "feels unloved, disliked and mistreated by everyone," and "angry feelings towards his parents and parent figures, viewing his parents as unavailable to him." Bosket, whose father was in prison when he was growing up, and who had great difficulty relating to his mother, was questioned about his volatile anger. He responded, "Why am I so angry?" The reason is because Willie Bosket has been incarcerated since he was 9 years old and was raised by his surrogate mother, the criminal justice system. Bosket is only the monster created by the system he haunts.

What, then, must we do? First, we must reach some realistic conclusions about the capacity of those we wish could and would carry out their traditional functions (schools, social service agencies, and parents, for example).

Many urban public school systems are overwhelmed and often perform the Herculean tasks of disciplinarian, educator, and surrogate parents. In all too many instances, they are the most stable, predictable and safe place in some children's lives. According to The New York Times, at least 21 state agencies are under court supervision because they failed to take proper care of children who had been abused or neglected. There are more pressures being placed on these agencies than they can reasonably manage.

According to Butterfield, "the family is being pulled apart by centrifugal forces seemingly beyond our control . . . jobs are shrinking. We are less willing to spend tax dollars on public schools to teach students to sit still, obey the teacher and learn useful skills to compete in the global marketplace."

We are losing known and needed parenting skills as increased mobility and divorce sunder families, and as 15 year olds, who did not have proper childhoods of their own, have babies.

If we continue to probe the "Can they be saved?" query, we must conclude that schools, social service agencies and parents cannot perform the traditionally-expected tasks in far too many cases.

I propose the notion of prevention and intervention as the possible starts of a lifesaving process. Some effective examples of prevention and intervention I have personally experienced include an adopt-a-school program, a focused-mission school, a summer internship program and a special intervention project affected through my business hiring policies. My fraternity adopted a public school. The focus was on 6th and 7th grade

African-American boys. I teamed with another member to mentor two boys, both from single-parent homes.

I took this boy to lunch and dinner, brought him around my family so he could observe the interaction between husband, wife and children. I took him to Chicago Bulls games where he high fived Scottie Pippen. I put him in a homework club where Mondays through Thursdays, from 3:30 to 6:00 p.m., he studied. He visited my office where he could see a black man in a position of authority. I gave him books to read and discussed their ideas and values. Now, six years later, that young man is graduating from high school and plans to study engineering in college (no gangs, no drugs, no police record).

The firm I head, UBM Inc., has a summer intern program for college students interested in careers in construction.

What would happen if other Chicago-area businesses focused on African-American boys for three or four summers exposing them to approaches in problem-solving, learning how to work, and offering direction for a productive future? Again, maybe that's too simple.

After hiring an ex-offender who had learned drafting while incarcerated, UBM was featured on ABC-TV's "World News Report." We provided this black adult with a job and assigned him to two UBM employees to help him during his transition. He had two external counselors, as well. In his first year of work, he earned and paid taxes on an amount equal to what it cost to keep him in prison. On the first anniversary of his hiring, ABC's network news team returned to observe his development.

At the two-year mark, he was still not a statistic of recidivism. Surely, there were rough spots, but maybe the question ought not be "Can they be saved?" but rather, "Do we really want to save them?"

I believe that most at-risk youths can be saved if we intervene and prevent the mass emergence of more disfigured personalities who surface and fall through the cracks, only to be discovered, again, when a child is fatally dropped from a window several stories above street level. We all have a stake in the fates of Tony and Antoine, and their counterparts.

June 6, 1996

A MATTER OF PRIDE

Harvard law professor Randall Kennedy, in the May issue of The Atlantic Monthly, promotes for African-Americans something that Black psychologist Bobby E. Wright, in the 1970s dubbed mentacide--a cultural suicide of sorts, a psychological assassination. In his essay, My Race Problem-- And Ours, Kennedy argues that Black people should forsake racial pride in favor of individual achievements:

I eschew racial pride because of my conception of what should properly be the object of pride for an individual: something that he or she has accomplished. I can feel pride in a good deed I have done or a good effort 1 have made, he writes. I cannot feel pride in some state of affairs that is independent of my contribution to it.... I did not achieve my racial designation.

I, however, an African-American businessman born and reared in Chicago, reside ideologically in the same neighborhood as Pulitzer prize-winning playwright August Wilson. He states:

I believe that race matters--it is the largest, most identifiable and most important part of our personality. It is the largest category of identification because it is the one that most influences your perception of yourself, and it is the one to which others in the world of men most respond. Race is also an important part of the American landscape, as America is made up of an amalgamation of races from all parts of the globe. Race is also the product of a shared gene pool that allows for group identification and it is an organizing principle around which cultures are formed. When I say culture, I am speaking about the behavior patterns, arts, beliefs, institutions and all other products of human work and thought as expressed in a particular community of people.

By Paul King

I have pride in opera soprano Leontyne Price, who came from Laurel, Miss., at a time when Black people were lynched routinely. Yet she had the persistence, focus, discipline and talent to prevail in a Eurocentric medium in spite of hostile and subtle attempts to stop her.

I have pride in Glenn Harston, a young Black man who wanted to be an ironworker in Chicago in 1967. White union members threatened to push him from a high-rise girder to his death if he tried to integrate their union. Not only did Harston become a tradesman, but he went on to become a successful businessman who recently celebrated his son's college graduation.

I am proud of Harold Washington, who became Chicago's first African-American mayor. He prevailed despite the dismal predications of Whites that the city would collapse, bond ratings would plunge, city services would cease and the quality of city life would tumble if a Black man were elected chief executive.

I am proud of Nelson Mandela, who withstood decades of South Africa's apartheid, imprisonment and emotional torture. He had the strength of will and purpose to emerge victorious against his racist foes.

Nelson Mandela, Harold Washington, Glenn Harston and Leontyne Price succeeded in a climate of racial hostility and animosity that still persists today. Their courage, tenacity and refusal to surrender in spite of White resistance gives me racially motivated pride.

That pride extends to more ordinary accomplishments among African-Americans: to those Black mothers who struggle to obtain their associate degrees in community colleges and to their wayward sons who drop out of school but work hard to earn a general equivalency diploma (GED). To deny the joy of their winning against formidable odds would be the equivalent of me hating myself. That Black people succeed in a hostile environment gives me the moral basis to identify with and take pride in their achievements.

Kennedy rejects such racial kinship in favor of the unencumbered self. Quoting political theorist Michael Sandel Kennedy explains:

The unencumbered self is free and independent, unencumbered by aims and attachments it does not choose for itself:... Freed from the sanctions of custom and tradition and inherited status, unbound by moral ties antecedent to choice, the self is installed as sovereign, cast as the author of the only obligations that constrain.

Sandel Kennedy writes, that he believes the unencumbered self is an illusion. So do I. I embrace racial kinship because it is a necessity for Black survival. Unfortunately, being Black in America requires a double encumbrance: an extraordinary effort to achieve and a stubborn balance of mind to navigate the racist minefields that we African-Americans face daily. No one can expect to sail through life without the burdens and responsibilities that society demands.

How Kennedy can oppose racial kinship after having clerked for Supreme Court Justice Thurgood Marshall is beyond me. Marshall was obviously motivated by more than moral outrage in his legal championship of Black causes. Expressing his love and admiration for Southern Black people, he once said:

There isn't a threat known to men that they do not receive. They're never out from under pressure. I don't think I could take it for a week. The possibility of violent death for them and their families is something they've learned to live with like a man learns to sleep with a sore arm.

It is even more bewildering how Kennedy can invoke Frederick Douglass to support his outlandish ideas. Douglass, a former slave, felt enough kinship with slaves and later Black freed men to become a race champion and staunch abolitionist.

Kennedy may be ambivalent as to whom he owes for creating the environment in which he has achieved professional and material success. But he --like every other African-American--has his lineage tied to slavery and kinship with those Black people who over the centuries survived, thereby allowing us to carry on this debate today.

Still, for Kennedy, such pride, kin ship and loyalty are a burden, and he wonders whether Black people in positions of authority who choose to carry this racial loyalty will be dragged down by it. Black employers or personnel directors face the question of whether racial loyalties should shape their decisions, he writes.

Again, I must differ. My company, UBM, is the largest Black-owned construction business in Chicago. The construction industry has been one of the most racially exclusive industries in the United States, and the doors routinely have been closed to African-Americans at every level. In 1969, I led the first shutdown of Chicago construction sites. I confronted Whites-engaged in the worst kind of racial kinship--who said that if they allowed Black people into the union the buildings would fall down. Our shutdowns helped open up many of those closed doors.

Nearly 30 years later, African-Americans are still playing catch-up in this business. For some time, my company has been trying to hire Black project managers and other executives capable the prerequisite college diplomas or tradesman-level experience--credentials that impart the confidence, initiative and technical competence needed to qualify for project manager positions of overseeing $2 million or $3 million projects--a normal workload for such construction professionals. Guess what? There are none. The construction industry, with its decades of excluding Black people, has left us with a professional pool absent of African-Americans who have the prerequisite college diplomas or tradesman-level experience--credentials that impart the confidence, initiative and technical competence needed to qualify for project manager positions.

What would Kennedy have had me do? Wring my hands and give up?

Our company decided to take action and to develop our own candidates. My partners and I launched a college summer internship program. We hired a Black expert to help set up development programs. And now with an annual volume of $20 million, UBM has more African-Americans in decision-making professional positions--estimators, superintendents, computer engineers, civil engineers, marketing executives, accounting, safety, project managers--than many of Chicago's 10 largest White-owned construction companies, whose collective volume exceeds $9 billion nationwide.

Kennedy would leap to challenge us: How does this special effort to cultivate Black project managers affect other employees?

I have two partners. One is an African-American woman. The other is Asian Indian. Currently, our full-time staff, about 75 people, is a little more than one-third African-American. The others are White, Indian or Asian. The UBM family knows that corporate tenacity, the mutual respect I have within the Black community, as well as the depth of the relationships within the larger Chicago community, lend to the success that provides them with secure employment to sustain their own families and send their children to college. They know we are committed to giving them respect and a fair shake as we pursue these initiatives to help bring along the African-Americans who have been left behind.

Beyond profits, UBM seeks to give value to clients, to provide a means for employees to have a competitively paying and fulfilling career and to improve conditions in the African-American community. Our company, which will celebrate its 25th anniversary in the year 2000, is working on polishing our skills of management. We are perfecting our employee manual; there are merit awards, there are bonuses. There is a salary administration plan underway. There are written procedures and clearer paths for rewards and termination being developed. We are outlining for all staff the avenues for development and achievement. It's all a work in progress. But we are concerned about the well-being and betterment of everyone: Whites, women, Asians, everybody.

There is no conflict in the elimination of Black disparity and the running of a successful and fair business. A non-Black executive recently proudly reported to me that he assembled an all-Black workforce on one complex project that UBM won with the help of a local Black official. Our success proves there does not have to he a conflict if the owners and staff are committed to doing it.

I must say, however, that 1 do find one point of agreement with Kennedy: it is true that a Black person who adopts a racially disloyal position may he viewed by some Black people as threatening and deserving of harsh punishment.

At the end of his essay, Kennedy provides insight as to why he is so vexed by such solidarity:

My objection to the claim of racial pride and kinship stems also in large part from my fears of the stultifying effect on intraracial relations. Racial pride and kinship seem often to stunt intellectual independence. If racial loyalty is deemed essential and morally virtuous, then a Black persons adoption of positions that are deemed racially disloyal will be seen by racial loyalists as a supremely threatening sin, one warranting the harsh punishments that have historically been visited upon alleged traitors.

For most, the adoption of racially disloyal positions has a transitory effect. I hope that Kennedy's weird statements stimulate debate and that through such debate he will reconsider. Unfortunately, the reverse is more likely. Since White-owned media tend to seize on anti-Black views, Kennedy may end up with a throng of converts who do further damage to Black people.

Legal scholar Derrick Bell speaks to this curious phenomenon in his book, **Faces at the Bottom of the Well:**

Few blacks avoid diminishment of racial standing, most of their statements about racial conditions being diluted and their recommendations of other blacks taken with a grain of salt. The usual exception to this rule is the black person who publicly disparages or criticizes other blacks who are speaking or acting in ways that upset whites. Instantly, such statements are granted enhanced standing even when the speaker has no special expertise or experience in the subject he or she is criticizing.

But whatever the fallout of Kennedy's words, it pales by comparison with the ultimate disloyalty visited upon Black people by two men: Supreme Court Justice Clarence Thomas and Ward Connerly.

Connerly is steadfast in advocating a philosophy antithetical to Black advancement in the United States. He helped pass Proposition 209 with his posturing and pronouncements as a board member of the Regents of the University of California, Prop. 209 eliminated minority contracting, minority hiring and the minority university admission programs, since just last year he has helped reduce Black admission at the University of California at Berkeley's Law School from 75 to 14. Only one African-American student enrolled this fall. And in a spillover effect, at the University of Texas law school--formerly a major educator of Black lawyers--enrollment dropped from about 40 African-American students in previous years to only four this fall.

Thomas has Connerly beat though. Thomas is a primary beneficiary of affirmative action and racial pride--from his admittance to Yale's Law School, to his executive post at the Equal Employment Opportunity Commission. Even his appointment to the Supreme Court was a Negro thing--to fill Thurgood Marshall's seat.

Nonetheless, Thomas has taken an anti-black stance on congressional redistricting and a vehement position against affirmative action. He helped create the climate in which Prop. 209 was passed.

Let us hope that Kennedy eschews such a level of activism, and that his career never reaches the judicial bench where he could do more in irreparable harm to Black people. Let us hope that he remains in academia, where his ideas may he debated, then simply fade from the pubic arena.

Reprint of original, October 1997; courtesy of **Emerge: Black Americas News Magazine**

CAN YOU DIG IT?:
Affirmative Action and African Americans in the Construction Industry

by
Paul King

Paul King is chairman and an original founder of UBM, Inc., the largest African American-owned and operated construction service firm in the city of Chicago. This article was delivered as a speech to National Association for Minority Contractors 29th Annual Conference: Gateway to the 21st Century opening session, June 25, 1998.

On July 23, 1969, I was one of the leaders who shut down Chicago construction sites because of the absence of black workers and contractors in HUD-financed building projects. Hundreds of demonstrators were inspired by Presidential Executive Order 11246, which required contractors on federally assisted construction projects to not only cease discriminating against blacks, but take "affirmative action" to increase African American participation. Although employment, university admissions, and political districting rank high in the debate over affirmative action I would like to draw attention to the very distinct area in which I participated at the outset: Blacks in the Construction Industry. My argument will take the form of the question: "Can you dig it?," or, **DIG**, an acronym for Deception, Ignorance, and Greed.

Deception

There is no question that Blacks have been discriminated against by unions and trade schools with respect to construction careers. Thirty years ago, blacks were 0.6 percent of the electrical unions, 1.6 percent of carpentry, and 0.2 percent in the sheet metal trade. These closed doors, combined with the restrictive practices of banks and performance bond companies, enterprises. Affirmative action was intended to remedy racial exclusion and foster inclusion through the concept of correction and expanded opportunity, or (**CEO**).

Yet when the media, one of the chief agents of deception, discusses affirmative action, they substitute the word "quota" despite the fact that everyone knows that quotas are illegal unless imposed by court order. *Quotas close doors and set limits. While affirmative action opens doors by expanding opportunities.* Nevertheless, the print media continues to, purposefully I think, misapply the term.

Another deceptive device is the provocative use of the phrase "racial preferences," which suggests that one group (blacks) are unreasonably "promoted" over a more qualified group (whites) Affirmative action is not about preference, but the correction of past discrimination, such as increasing the 0.4 percent black elevator tradesmen in 1967 to a number visible on the radar screen!

Sociologist Michael Dyson states that the ingenuity of the conservatives and the far right is that they have deceitfully co-opted the rhetoric of the progressive and civil rights movements against the very principles of freedom, equality, and justice that the language originally stood for. Pollster Lou Harris essentially agreed, stating that "it is not only misleading, but deceitful to use 'affirmative action' and 'preferential treatment' interchangeably "

But the ultimate trick came with Proposition 209, audaciously known as, "the California Civil Rights Initiative," which banned the use of race or sex as a criterion for "either discrimination against or granting preferential treatment to" anyone doing business with the state. Prop 209 spokesperson, Ward Connerly, is as duplicitous as the language -- having once served as a paid lobbyist for the construction and roofing industry -- the same group that provided a vocal rear guard in recent Supreme Court affirmative action cases.

When the Harris Poll surveyed Californians, 81 percent supported the referendum. But when asked if they would still support the measure if it would "outlaw all affirmative action programs for women and minorities"-- that support fizzled to 29 percent, and opposition climbed from 11 percent to 58 percent. Simply put when the voters understand these mean-spirited ideas, they reject them. The citizens of Houston did not buy this verbal sleight of hand either, and refused to accept a similar initiative, when worded properly, even though they're Southerners, and like California, in a highly populated state.

Ignorance

What role does ignorance play in this equation? Most people do not understand the facts of black exclusion in construction. Generally, the avenue to becoming a skilled craftsman is to be sponsored by a contractor, complete a recognized training program, perform on-the job training, be admitted into a union as a journeyman, and then selected (highly subjective) to work by a contractor. Becoming a contractor requires knowledge of a trade, and/or architectural/engineering training, or college business preparation. *Prior to affirmative action, each of these doors had been slammed in the faces of blacks with the only open avenues being along the dead-end streets of unemployment and economic exclusion.* If blacks are not exposed through education and are ignored by employment trainers, then you don't develop skilled black construction workers, and by extension- no black contractors. In 1998, there is still a paucity of African Americans in civil engineering curricula at the top schools -- the University of Illinois at Urbana and IIT had only three graduates, and MIT, one.

Let's examine the consequences by looking at three of the Chicago areas largest construction firms:

1. The Walsh Group, founded in 1898 by a carpenter, with great-grandchildren still involved with the firm had a sales volume of almost $1 billion last year.
2. Pepper Construction, founded in 1927 by a carpenter, three generations old, $473 million.
3. Kenny Construction Co., founded in 1927 by a pipe-fitter, multigenerational, $469 million.
4. Power Contracting and Engineering, founded in 1926 by an engineer, $320 million.
5. Bulley and Andrews, founded in 1891 by an architect and mason, $65 million.

These major firms were founded in the 1890s and mid-1920s. Historians have called the former decade the worst on record in American race relations--from disfranchisement (taxation without representation), convict labor camps, to lynchings and segregation a la *Plessy v. Ferguson* (1896). Meanwhile, a generation later, in 1927, the new black migrants downtown department stores in the de facto segregated cities of the

North, like Chicago, where some local white contractors got their start. *Can there be any honest comparison of black contractors and these firms?* If each of these successful firms got their start through trade experience, architecture or engineering, and these fields have only been significantly open to blacks for less than 27 years, should not corrected and expanded opportunity (CEO = affirmative action) be extended until some form of parity is reached?

A huge advantage exists for a firm that is second generation, to say nothing of three generations or more -- the assembly of resources and business relationships (banks, sureties, clients) give companies enjoying these benefits an inherent and inherited advantage over newly emerging black contractors. The $7 billion volume of the top three construction firms in Chicago is more than double the total revenues ($2.65 billion) of all African American construction firms in the entire United States.

Greed

This leads me to the final component of the DIG paradigm -- GREED). *Why have the opponents been so relentless?* In 1970, the Associated General Contractors (AGC) and many unions said that buildings built by blacks would fall dawn. It is no accident that the biggest Supreme Court affirmative action cases, Webber, Fullilove, Croson, and Adarand, have centered around construction, and in each instance, the majority contractor organizations have opposed progress. But whereas the earlier cases, Weber (1979) and Fullilove (1980), upheld affirmative action programs in hiring and promotions and supported minority contractor set-asides in order to correct gross past discrimination and achieve equity in the workplace, (1983) and Adarand (1995)'s imposition of the "strict scrutiny' standard essentially ignored clear patterns of egregious discrimination and Inequity in the letting of public contracts.

But I will assume that these contractors are not all racists. The facts neither support the assertion that blacks have taken union jobs from white workers, nor that black contractors have deprived AGC members of a significant part of their business, which leads me to conclude that their continued assault is based on **GREED.**

Consider the volume of the top 25 contractors in Chicago, (none of whom are black), which for 1996, was $12.7 billion. All of the black contractors in the U.S. (UBM included) don't amount to one quarter (21 percent) of Chicago's top 25 construction companies. What do the affirmative action opponents want -- 100 percent of the work? The argument of reverse discrimination is patently false, whether advanced by unions or contractors.

Look at the case of the California electrical contractor who was upset because his firm lost a bid on a public contract because he did not meet minority business requirements. He wanted to perform all of the work himself. Let's examine the background to this situation. In 1970, there were practically no blacks in the electrical union (thus no black electrical firms in his specialty). So how does this guy expect the cycle of exclusion to be broken? If 28 years ago, there were virtually no blacks in the electrical unions, and today it's "immoral" to use a benign device like Affirmative Action to provide for some measure of inclusion, this guy seems to be saying that blacks should never be involved in electrical contracting. He doesn't want the cycle to be broken because he doesn't want to lose his power and privilege.

He goes on to argue that he never owned slaves and never discriminated against anyone, so why should he be burdened by minority business requirements? The answer lies in the simple fact that current generations pay for and benefit from actions/events that occurred during previous eras. All taxpayers are paying for the current budget deficit, though it isn't all of our own making. This guy doesn't complain about surety bonds; even though he may have never defaulted on paying or performing a job; or about expensive safety requirements, which are the result of accidents and fatalities caused by others; or union wages, which occurred as a result of worker abuse by others; or about ADA costs in building, even though he probably never caused anyone to become physically challenged or disabled.

Thus the greed is not all about money because blacks do not have a serious impact in the industry. It is not all about principle because concessions to public policy are a continued cost of doing business. This greed, though in part racially motivated, is about power. If a strong group of black contractors emerged across all trades with significant resource development extending across generations, there could be a change in who was elected to union local leadership; a change in the power equation when decisions about who will develop and own the land when public housing is demolished; who sits on public building commissions, Fair and Exposition authorities; who controls airport and transportation budgets – maybe even who sits in the Governor's mansion. It would change the complexion of those who make and interpret laws (the Clarence Thomases vigorously excepted).

Affirmative action might possibly lead to a power shift and I certainly do dig that.

In the wake of anti affirmative action spin-meisters and mistresses who continually engage in fictitious deceit, qua Abigail Thernstrom, and Linda Chavez, Ward Connerly and Clarence Thomas, we do have some sanity emerging. Faced with the clear evidence of the elimination of black students at major California campuses, a long time opponent of affirmative action has modified his position. Nathan Glazer, author of **Affirmative Discrimination**, stated in the March issue of **Commentary** that; "We do need black members of police departments if we are to police black areas effectively. ... Similarly, we...need black teachers and administrators in our schools." Regarding higher education, Glazer was even more emphatic:

> To my mind, there is good argument for maintaining this racial preference because the presence of blacks does change and on the whole benefit the education of all. But my principal reason is that our colleges and universities, and professional schools are the central gateways to positions of power, wealth, and influence, and applying strict autocratic principles would lead to a catastrophic drop in the number of black students ill those crucial institutions. That would send a terrible message to blacks, and would be bad for the country.

Ironically, even while the major contractor associations are fighting affirmative action, white contractors are privately saying they don't have enough workers; and developers are complaining because they don't have enough competition on their invited bid lists. They realize that it is unlikely that the future skilled labor supply will be sufficient without African American participation. To fight the remedy for this problem is either racist or stupid, or are they both the same?

About the author: *Paul King is one of the original founders of UBM, the largest African American-owned and operated construction services firms in the City of Chicago. For two years running, Black Enterprise Magazine ranked UBM the No. 1 African American construction services company in Chicago. Paul King is a leader in the business and construction high school. He is a much sought after lecturer and speaker and does so regularly for Chicago Public Schools, the De La Salle Institute, Roosevelt University, DePaul University, conventions, builder groups and various civic and community organizations Mr. King is the author of numerous articles that have been published in books, book reviews, trade newspapers and magazines. As recently as February 1994 Paul King was profiled led in a full-page editorial* *in N'Digo Magapaper. The feature-length article was titled "Putting 'Firm" in Affirmative Action."*

Paul King is a former vice president of the National Association of Minority Contractors (NAMC). He has also been a close advisor to Congressman Parren Mitchell (Democrat-MD). This is work led to the formation of a Black Business Braintrust responsible for the first legislation regarding mandatory percentage goals when utilizing minority contractors on federal contracts. He has been instrumental in securing government funding for minority contractor assistance programs in Chicago and nationally. He is the Chairman of the Chicago Business Council. Chairman and Founder of the O'Hare Development Group, (a Black development concern, presently developing a 41-acre site at O'Hare Airport.) Paul King is especially concerned about the well being of African American young people. Each year he gets involved in the training of college students enrolled in UBM's Summer Intern Program, created to help African American college students get started in professional construction careers.

Paul King attended the De La Salle Institute, the University of Chicago and Roosevelt University.

Originally published in **In Motion Magazine** February 6, 1999.

MEGATRENDS

THE SHAPE OF THINGS TO COME

CONSTRUCTION'S HECTIC DAILY pace—chasing proposals and bids, meeting project deadlines, getting out invoices, covering payroll—rarely gives its professionals pause to look too far into the future. But there is much to think about beyond the immediate challenges. To explore the changes and issues ahead for construction participants, ENR editors convened a first-ever panel of industry experts in New York City. The group of executives from contractors, engineering, architecture and technology companies, owners, labor unions, trade associations and management firms represented a cross section of construction. Questioned as hard by each other as by the editors, panelists offered hard-hitting and probing analysis of trends ahead in such critical areas as work force management, project delivery, technology and changes in the industry's own structure. This special report outlines that discussion and debate. It is the first of four special issues of **ENR** this year, marking the magazine's 125th anniversary. Together, they will offer an in-depth look at how far construction has come in that time and where it will be going.

ENR Megatrends: May 24 1999

WORK FORCE

Shortages of skilled, motivated and loyal employees, from craft labor to top execs, threaten construction's survival. Panelists suggest boosting pay, recruiting harder and cleaning up the industry's 'Diet Coke' image.

♦ 'As of last year, only 19% of architecture graduates eligible to take registration exams were showing up to do so."
LAURIN MCCRACKEN Global Design Alliance

♦ "Finding volunteers to preach the gospel of the construction industry is extremely important now, especially to girls and young women."
LES ROBERTSON Les Robertson Associates

♦ 'We need to snatch more knowledge workers, but the Holy Grail of becoming an overnight millionaire isn't in construction."
DEANE EVANS Architecture consultant

♦ "We have to think outside the box, and get a TV program that's really good and shows real images of engineering."
GENE FIGG, Figg Engineering Group

♦ Students show interest to guidance counselors to be craftsmen but mothers and counselors push two-year computer programs."
DAVID BACH ENSKI International Masonry Institute

♦ **"Students at black schools I've spoken at don't believe that a guy like me can be running a $40-million construction firm."**
PAUL KING UBM Inc.

♦ "What are we doing to expose students to the relevance of the construction industry if interest in subjects critical to it is wanting?"
FRANK LOMBARDI Port Authority N.Y. & N.J.

Nothing seems to frustrate construction industry executives more than the challenge of finding and keeping their workers. Megatrends panelists were no exception. As a people business, construction depends heavily on its human assets. With work booming in many sectors, shortages and turnover are already evident and competition for the best and brightest at all levels is fierce. Panel participants worry that Generation X is bypassing the industry for others with better benefits and more sex appeal and they say more must be done earlier to find and groom potential professionals and executives. Changing constructions traditional image as a dirty, low-tech, grunt-oriented career path is critical. But is a Wednesday night sitcom starring Joe Contractor the answer?

Unease in the ranks is growing, triggered by industry consolidation, a much improved job market, changing demographics and other factors. We used to bring young people on board, train them, and they became loyal to us and we to them. You don't see that today, says Leland Caldwell, vice president of MTA Bridges & Tunnels, a New York City agency.

Adds Donald Weisstuch, senior vice president of Sverdrup Civil Inc. in Purchase, N.Y.: "When I came to Sverdrup, the average tenure was 22 years. Now, its five years. People are leaving because they don't want to have to buy stock."

Others agree. "Last year, we had a sharp increase in our voluntary turnover, 9%, which to us, is panic level. Traditionally, its 4 to 5%," stated Richard D. Fox, executive vice president of engineer Camp, Dresser & McKee Inc., Cambridge, Mass. "Workers are leaving at two points in their career at 3 to 5 years and at 10 years. Younger staff are still in that dreamland where they say I'm gonna make it big and I can take the gamble. At 10 years, we lose people dissatisfied with the business because of mentoring or lack of training. We have a lot of flex time…[but] we were very concerned about losing women. They told us that as an organization, we weren't fixing things that were wrong soon enough."

Others point to more pressured work environments. "I don't think we as a profession take time to mentor our people," says Ron Wiss, chairman of engineering firm Edwards and Kelcey, Morristown, N.J. "We're all so busy we don't have a chance to do that."

COMING UP DRY

Sopping up new talent from traditional industry sources will be more difficult, panelists say. Engineering enrollment in [New York City's]

147

Manhattan College has dropped in half over the past 10 years, says Charles Thornton, president of Thornton-Tomasetti Engineers, also based there. There's a serious shortage now. Architecture is attracting more applicants, but they don't go into the business, says Laurin McCracken, CEO of the Global Design Alliance, Washington, D.C. As of a year ago, only 19% of graduates eligible to take registration exams were showing up to do so, he says.

According to McCracken, not one graduate of a recently started Masters level computer-aided design program for architecture students at Texas A&M University has gone into the profession. They've all gone to Hollywood or into the video game business, he says. Two students in the first class were hired away by Pixar [Studios] to work on Toy Story. How can any of our firms compete with that? Bruce C. Coles, chairman of Law Cos. Group Inc., Alpharetta, Ga., adds that more than half of all degreed engineers are not attached to construction.

REACHING OUT

Panelists say industry firms must be more aggressive in recruiting future talent reaching out to nontraditional groups and gearing outreach efforts to younger audiences. "We're not the best role models for our kids. We're not part of our communities, including schools," says Peter G. Vigue, president of Cianbro Corp., Pittsfield, Maine. "So what perception do we create for young people? If we can master the art of communicating that this is a great industry, if you commit yourself."

"Finding volunteers to preach the gospel of the construction industry, and, in particular, to encourage girls and young women to come in is extremely important," says Leslie Robertson, director of design & construction at Leslie E. Robertson Associates Inc., New York City.

Others agree. **"There has been no effort focused at minorities and women in inner cities to give them industry exposure,"** says Paul King, chairman of Chicago contractor UBM Inc. **"I have spoken at many black schools and they don't even believe that a guy like me could be running a $40-million-a-year company. It will take a special effort to correct what we've failed to do in the past, and we have to start now."** Panelists agree that taking the construction message to younger audiences is crucial so they can embrace critical math and science courses. "Educational standards, particularly in math and science, have been lowered over the past generation. If students do not learn to value these subjects in elementary and high school, the chances they will by college are slim," says Frank Lombardi, chief engineer of The Port Authority of New York and New Jersey. "What are we doing to expose students to the relevance of our industry, if interest in subjects crucial to it is wanting?"

Panelists lament the industry's perennial image as low-tech and dirty, and its inability to project the excitement and challenge that would attract the kinds of employees it sorely needs. "What is construction? Its not a worker in the media drinking Diet Coke," says James J. Moynihan, president and CEO of Heery International, Atlanta. "But where else do you combine math, personality, psychology, intelligence, common sense, and hard work of both your mind and your body. You get to see something and also take your children and grandchildren back to see something. That's what were not saying."

BEST AND WORST

Lombardi points out that the 1999 edition of Jobs Rated Almanac, which ranks 250 "best and worst jobs" based on factors such as salary, stress, security and physical demand, rates 14 construction trades nearly at the bottom. "Even a civil engineering job, 18th in a prior edition, has now dropped to 70th place," he says. "As the supply pool is diminishing, at the same time, the demand for these jobs is rising. This trend is disturbing for an industry that builds and maintains our nations infrastructure and helps support its economy."

HOLY GRAIL

Deane Evans, who heads his own architecture consulting firm in Falls Church, Va., and is a former American Institute of Architects executive, says construction will be hard-pressed to compete for talent with the medias high-tech darlings. "What you really want to do is snatch the knowledge worker and train him or her, but everything you see in Business Week is dot.com where overnight you become a millionaire," he contends. "And that type of Holy Grail really isn't out there in this industry."

Adds Irvin E. Richter, chairman & CEO of Hill International Inc., Willingboro, N.J.: "Our solutions to these problems are like the industry itself, long-term, hardworking, plodding and methodical. What can the industry do to create that kind of glamour and excitement about the projects we build?"

Several panelists called for some nontraditional approaches. "We have to think outside the box," says Eugene Figg, president and CEO of Figg Engineering Group, Tallahassee, Fla. "We have to get a TV program that talks about our industry and shows real pictures of engineering." McCracken suggests a movie with a "construction worker as the hero."

While the industry has yet to attract Hollywood's attention for next year's pilots, employers are taking small but effective steps to sell construction. Structural engineer Thornton notes success with his Architects, Constructors and Engineers mentor program. "We have 300 kids a year in high schools in New York City being mentored by representatives of 60 E&C companies, the cream of the crop, and they gave out $32,000 in scholarships," he says. "And were branching out to Stamford, Connecticut, and New Jersey. Thornton notes the city's overworked high school guidance counselors aren't steering students to construction careers. "There's one counselor for every 1,000 kids," he contends. "They can't make people interested."

Adds David Bachenski, area marketing director for the International Masonry Institute in Washington, which is affiliated with the bricklayers union: "Students show interest to guidance counselors to be craftsmen, but mothers and counselors push computers in two-year college programs. That often proves to be a dead end."

David Evans, CEO of David Evans and Associates Inc., Portland, Ore., has extended his firms outreach to a partnership with a local grammar school as well as sponsorship of local public televisions. "You get incredible exposure and we've been doing it for 10 years," he says. Its one of the best things that's helped us in recruiting because we're a recognizable entity."

TAKING BACK LEARNING

Just as important are new efforts construction employers are making to expand skill levels and promote education and career development among the current crop of employees. "I've long had a bias that the education of our industry is too important to be left to the educators," says Lou Marines, president of the Advanced Management Institute for Architects and Engineers in San Francisco. "We need to take back the schools to make sure that education that suits the end user is really happening."

But Marines also cautions that employees of the future must take their own career development in hand. "We need to support them in understanding that part of their educational development is their responsibility, not the mommy and daddy company's. Very few companies are setting up that expectation for young people."

Heery's Moynihan notes that the firms training program, which he dubs Heery University, offers a career incentive. "We're trying to make our company a clear choice in long term strategy versus short term benefit," he says. "We made a decision at our executive level that we would rather have people more concerned about a long term involvement."

NEW INCENTIVES

Construction employers are also taking steps to reeducate even the most hardened construction veterans to develop themselves and their staffs. **"I'm convinced that our managers don't have a clue to how to work with young people coming in today," says UBM's King. We've decreed that 40% of their compensation will be based on how they develop people. If they can't do it, our company won't be around.**

Jo Coke, president of the Dallas-based American Concrete Institute, notes success in fashioning a much-needed certification program for concrete finishers and related workers. "We went to Sylvan Learning Centers to offer our training," she says. "We're battling the lack of sex appeal in getting into the concrete business and we're combating the older contractor-finisher who doesn't want to change."

Upgrading the image of working in the construction trades through training is a key priority, Megatrends participants say. "Our industry is not known for flexibility or transition between different crafts. We must be serious about addressing the problem of training," says Nigel Parkinson, president of Parkinson Construction Co., Brentwood, Md. "We are trying to look at employment not as seasonal but as a long-term career choice from high school."

The training problem is compounded by worker shortages that force construction employers and unions to accept less well-educated applicants that need more preparation. "The level of education coming in now is very low," says Bob Durr, president of Durr Mechanical Construction Co., New York City. "So the union sector--labor and management together are developing recruitment programs to get that young child in grade school interested. That holds true for contractors too," he says. "An educated contractor is a good competitor," Durr points out.

Frank Williams III, president of Williams Industries Inc., Falls Church, Va., suggests extending benefits to younger workers. "If we can't do something with the wages, we have to be able to give the young a feeling of ownership in the business," he says. "There's a lot of bouncing around. As an enticement, offer ownership. The sooner you get that hook in there, the better off you'll be."

Thornton says the profession needs to fix its self-image. Architecture still has this perception that someone goes to school for 5 or 7 years and then is an intern for 2 to 3 years, and is still slave labor, he says. Law firms got smart in the 70s and got rid of that concept and pumped up starting salaries. Architects need a paradigm shift.

GREAT EXPECTATIONS

Others say the next generation will demand such change. "This is a very different generation growing up. Their expectations are different," says Robert Prieto, chairman of Parsons Brinckerhoff. "Someone coming out of college now may be more computer literate than my best designer with 20 years experience. Within 6 months, with some training or mentoring, they may be just as effective for 90 to 95% of our tasks. They recognize that and have expectations to spend 5 to 7 years in business to become a senior manager, not 20 to 25 years."

Prieto adds that "the challenge for us is to not resist that force, but to embrace and channel it. If we do that well, well be a successful industry. If we don't, we'll be sitting here in 25 years wondering why were the lowest paid industry in the country."

Marines call on employers to learn how to better use today's communication tools. "The better we get at using the Internet and speak the truth, and not industry babble, the more compelling we will be to young people," he says. We're doing that on our Web sites, but not enough. We have to convey the excitement of designing and building the infrastructure from which all of life happens." We need to snatch more knowledge workers, but the Holy Grail of becoming an overnight millionaire isn't in construction.

VIEWPOINT

AFFIRMATIVE
ACTION
PAUL KING

**AGC Blocks
Blacks' Progress**

Shame on contractors who fraternize with Ward Connerly, the arch enemy of affirmative action programs. Connerly, a black conservative on the University of California Board of Regents, led the successful 1996 campaign to end expanded opportunities for minori-

1969 Chicago whites opposed letting blacks into the trades.

ties and women in California. Now he wants to prohibit considerations of race and gender in government contracts, employment and college admissions in Florida.

At the invitation

of the Associated General Contractors of Greater Florida Inc., he visited the state in March to announce plans to put an anti-affirmative-action measure on Florida's ballot next year. Although rebuffed by Gov. Jeb Bush (R), legislative leaders and the state university chancellor, he received a warm reception from AGC.

No surprise. For at least 30 years, AGC has fought efforts to advance the cause of black contractors. I know from experience. In 1969, 1 was one of the leaders who shut down $60 million in work at Chicago construction sites to pro-

test the absence of black workers and contractors on federally financed building projects. AGC members opposed me and others.

White union adversaries blocked some of the entrances to the building in Chicago where Arthur A. Fletcher, then the assistant secretary for wage and labor standards, was convening hearings to investigate discrimination in the building trades. Fletcher, an African-American, entered the building another way. The hearings helped lead to the establishment of goals and timetables for the admission of blacks into the trades and helped create a framework for subsequent local ordinances and federal programs that benefit Hispanics and women, too.

Since that protest, the growth of black construction firms has been phenomenal nationally, no thanks to AGC. But today,

the total revenue of all black-owned construction firms across the entire U.S. still does not add up to even one-quarter of the revenue of the top 25 contractors in Chicago alone.

AGC has been relentless in opposing black contractors in legal, legislative and regulatory arenas across the nation. In *Fullilove v. Klutznick*, white contractor groups tried to block the 10% minority business enterprise provision of the Public Works Employment Act of 1977. In a 1980 ruling, the U.S. Supreme Court did not find the provision unconstitutional. But undeterred, various AGC groups filed a spate of anti-affirmative-action lawsuits: in Ohio in 1983, South Florida in 1984, and Michigan and San Francisco in 1987.

AGC's allies won big in 1989 in *City of Richmond v. J.A. Croson Co.* The city was requiring prime contractors to subcontract at

153

least 30% of each city contract to minority firms. The Supreme Court held that the plan was not narrowly tailored to remedy past discrimination. But testimony during the trial proceedings revealed that AGC did not have any black members in Richmond, Va., and that other contractor associations in the area had two blacks each at most.

AGC again made significant gains in its assault on affirmative action in 1995 when the Supreme Court ruled on *Adarand Constructors Inc. v. Peña.* Adarand, a white Colorado subcontractor supported by white contractor interest groups, had sued the federal government after losing a contract to a

disadvantaged business enterprise to install guardrails on a federal highway project. The case set a precedent because of the court's refusal to uphold a congressionally mandated affirmative action policy.

As the Clinton Administration has tried to comply with *Adarand* [and] "mend, not end" affirmative action, AGC has gone on the attack in the regulatory arena. AGC has fought to weaken the U.S. Small Business Administration's 8(a) program, which helps small disadvantaged businesses compete for federal contracts. Apparently, AGC has not been impressed that the program's graduates have emerged well-equipped with the experience and resources needed

to compete in the open market.

UNDEREXPOSED

The nation needs more black contractors and construction workers. But at a time of voracious demand for construction workers—especially in the building trades—few black youths are being exposed to the industry. In the Chicago area, for instance, AGC and union-sponsored apprenticeship training programs are located in the suburbs and away from most black residential areas.

How ironic. While major contractor associations are fighting affirmative action, white contractors across the U.S. are complaining that they cannot find enough workers

and developers are complaining that they cannot generate enough competition for construction bids. Without the increased participation of African-Americans, the future supply of skilled construction labor will remain insufficient.

The Washington, D.C.-based National Association of Minority Contractors will discuss the situation at its annual convention June 16-19 in Lake Buena Vista, Fla. Ward Connerly, do you dare join us?

Paul King, a former vice president of the National Association of Minority Contractors, is the chairman of Chicago-based UBM Inc., Illinois' largest black-owned construction company.

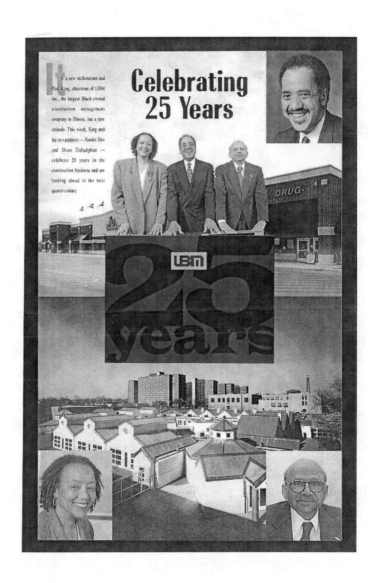

Celebrating 25 Years

Labor of love at Hales Franciscan

IN DEEP APPRECIATION OF HIS LONGTIME DEDICATION COMPASSIONATE SUPPORT, AND TIRELESS SERVICE

to

HALES FRANCISCAN HIGH SCHOOL

AND HIS EXTRAORDINARY LEADERSHIP IN THE RENOVATION OF ITS GYMNASIUM,

This Award is Presented To

Paul King

SUNDAY, JUNE 3, 2001

A great architect is not made by way of a brain
Nearly so much as he is made by way of a cultivated, enriched heart.

Frank Lloyd Wright

These are fat times for the construction industry. Especially downtown and along the suburban fringe, where Chicagoland seems a work-in-progress, dressed in scaffolds, dancing to the pop of rivet guns.

There are parts of the city and inner suburbs, though, that can only look on with envy. Other than a stray public works project or two, their new construction and rehab needs go largely unmet. It's a selective thing, this real estate boom.

It should not go unnoticed, therefore, when some of Chicago's biggest, busiest construction firms—companies that right now have more profitable things to do—dispatch highly-skilled crews to a have-not section of Chicago's South Side. Or when fierce competitors in a tough-guy industry not famous for philanthropy collaborate on, as they say in the trades, a little side job.

On Thursday morning, suits and hard-hats representing more than two dozen contractors will gather at Hales Franciscan High School at 49th Street and Cottage Grove Avenue to admire their collective handiwork. Together the firms contributed more than $700,000 worth of labor, materials and technical expertise, replacing the high school's windows and mechanical systems and rebuilding its worn-out gymnasium.

It's also the latest chapter in one of this city's most inspiring comeback stories. It began with the 1989 rescue of Hales Franciscan, which was about to be closed by the Catholic Archdiocese, and continues with Hales' flowering under a lay board composed mainly of middle-class, African-American elders. They are people who simply refuse to give up on the old neighborhood, or on a school that provides a Catholic, college-prep education to motivated young black men without regard to religion or ability to pay.

Credit Paul King, father of school president Tim King and head of his own UBM Construction, with putting a friendly arm on the likes of Bovis, Tishman, Turner, Pepper, Kenny, Power, MTH and a host of specialty sub-contractors. And credit-those companies with sharing the bounty of good economic times with a special client that otherwise could not have afforded their services.

As the boom roars on, so must such efforts.

WITH FRIENDS LIKE THIS, WHO NEEDS ENEMIES?

CONTROVERSY OVER "51% BLACK OWNED"

By Paul King, Special Correspondent

LYING BENEATH THE most recent affirmative action Supreme Court decisions has been an unrelenting assault on Black businesses, especially construction contractors.

The most recent reactionary anti-affirmative action Supreme Court decision (1993) and Adarand (1995 involve the construction industry. The twin demons of darkness on this path harming Black businesses are Supreme Court Justice Clarence Thomas and Ward Connerly.

Thomas' single vote could have defeated these attacks, but his psycho-political conservatism didn't allow it. Although primarily known for his orchestration and spokesmanship of California's Proposition 209, Connerly is a business operative whose ties to the Associated General Contractors and White construction interests are well known in the industry.

Following the havoc wrought by the judiciary branch, a well-intentioned Black Secretary of Transportation, operating in the mend, but don't end mode of the Clinton Administration, has come up with new rules requiring that owners of businesses designated as disadvantaged, must have a net worth of less than $750,000 and submit his/her personal tax returns, insurance policy information and all other private financial information to clerks at the city, state and multi-federal agencies, in order become certified.

Don't we already know that **Citizen** newspapers chain publisher, Bill Garth; **N'DIGO** publisher, Hermene Hartman; and **Essence** publisher,

Ed Lewis are disadvantaged, regardless of their individual net worth, in comparison to Steven Forbes and Rupert Murdoch? Each is light years away from these media mega-moneymen.

Why should they have to risk their privacy to prove it, particularly when the process of revelation could be used against them if they even inadvertently erred in reporting the information? Does this possibility seem far-fetched in an era when Black public officials are being investigated and hounded as never before? If these measures are enacted, the same thing could happen to other private citizens who do business with the government.

Then comes Florida's Gov. Jeb Bush with a new sleight-of-hand anti-affirmative action gimmick. He proposes elimination of all racial considerations in college admissions and MBE utilization programs in the state of Florida's contract awards.

His plan would admit the top 20 percent of all high school students into his states universities (regardless of their preparation or chances for success), while allowing MBE programs to continue in Miami and the Dade County area.

How can you call it wrong in Orlando and Ft Meyers, but acceptable in Miami? Could it have something to do with the Cuban-American political presence in South Florida? It seems inconsistent, but when you consider that the statement comes from a man whose father called Clarence Thomas the most qualified candidate for the Supreme Court, it is not surprising that this weird conclusion was reached.

Into this mischievous milieu enters the National Minority Supplier Development Council (NMSDC). This organization has long, been viewed as an ally to minority business. While leaving something to be desired in its advocacy/utilization of Black contractors, it has, nonetheless, been a proponent for expanded opportunity and utilization of Black-owned firms in the private sector.

Earlier this year, the Council expressed a position that a way should be found to infuse capital into minority firms that would reduce minority owners to below the 51 percent required for ownership and still allow the firm to be considered minority-owned and give credit to NMSDC corporations who utilize them.

On the face, of it, there is nothing wrong with minority firms seeking avenues of capital, strategic alliances, mergers, joint ventures and other arrangements in order to expand their growth and to allow them to more vigorously compete in the national and global market place. This is the ostensible rationale for the proposal.

However, I take the position that firms falling below 51 percent minority ownership and/or control should no longer be considered minority businesses--either for identification, utilization, or 100 percent credit toward minority business goals.

Why? Because ownership is critical. The majority shareholder(s) of an organization ultimately call the shots--right down to determining the management of the firm. They are exposed to both the risks and rewards of the company's decisions.

The whole purpose of affirmative action and minority business utilization was and is to assist business owners to become successful and thereby compete in the market place. It was not, and is not, set up to have profits gained, by MBE utilization go to non-minority investors. Simply put, this device was not intended, nor should it be used, to benefit White financial investors.

The big threat behind this move to dilute minority ownership and control is that it promotes the proliferation of fronts. Such a sweeping change, while benefiting a few, will open the door to abuse in other places. We are all too familiar with how White contractors in construction have used a minority firm to get a job, then pay them a fee and ask them to walk away, while allowing the White firm to control the project and the profits. In these cases, we create the twin deficits of deceit and a missed opportunity to develop a legitimate minority firm.

In the 1970s, here in Chicago, we had massive construction programs where White firms refused to work with legitimate Black contractors. Rather than develop a cadre of solid companies, the majority firms went the pass-through route, with questionable arrangements, which resulted in the failure of viable Black firms to emerge.

Control accompanies ownership, and conversely, ownership determines control. UBM is 100 percent minority-owned and controlled in a manner in which the policies, culture, practices and objectives of the owners are translated throughout the organization.

Non-minority individuals are authorized to make decisions on behalf of established policies, but safety violations, defaults, loans and surety bonds are borne by the owners, and the proverbial buck stops at his or her door.

But likewise, when UBM declares that we will be sensitive to the Black community, we can lead the charge to raise $700,000 for Hales Franciscan High School, while completing the $13 million Jewel facility on 95th & Stony Island, using 56 percent Black contractors (70 percent minority contractors) and creating 130 jobs for Black construction employees.

Given these critical distinctions regarding minority ownership and control, I could, nevertheless, support a well-crafted 18-24 month pilot demonstration program, wherein a minority firm could receive an infusion of outside capital (thus reducing control), and be given partial credit for involving an approved number of minority firms or subcontractors in a development plan.

For example, if General Motors had a minority parts supplier who received capital infusion and the supplier brought in a Black trucking firm, utilized a Black computer supplier/consultant, and another 100 percent minority firm provided a commercially useful function, this arrangement could be considered for a 40 percent credit. Simply put the partially owned/controlled minority firm would have to employ a long-term minority subcontracting plan, similar to that imposed on prime contractors by PL95-507.

As we see attacks on affirmative action in the public sector increase through both legal and legislative efforts, we must challenge the private sector represented by the NMSDC to do more, not less in the creation and development of minority businesses. Preparing an expanded minority business community for global competency is important, but the first step

and primary focus should be on how to get the private sector to quadruple their purchases from minority firms in construction, manufacturing, accounting, legal, media, advertising, computer purchases and consulting.

This is the critical issue for NMSDC in the face of the assault on affirmative action--to recognize minority and women business owners as a core consumer constituency, so that expanding their economic opportunities becomes a win/win situation for everyone.

Paul King is Chairman of UBM, Inc., "the man who put the 'firm' in affirmative action."

BUILDERS OF EQUALITY: ALPHA PHI ALPHA

by Brother Paul King

THE MODERN PERIOD of the Civil Rights Movement from 1954 to 1968, was historically bracketed by the brilliant and courageous leadership of two Alpha men. Brother Justice Thurgood Marshall and Brother Dr. Martin Luther King. Jr. The former, standing on an extensive body of case law that he had helped to establish as an NAACP attorney, successfully argued perhaps the single most important case in civil rights history: Brown v. the Board of Education in 1954. Though primarily concerned with school desegregation, the Brown decision overturned Plessy v. Ferguson (1896), and with it, the entire legal foundation for American apartheid. The following year, in 1955, sparked by the simple resistance of Mrs. Rosa Parks, Brother Marlin Luther King, Jr. met his cosmic destiny in Montgomery, Alabama, when he was chosen to lead that city's bus boycott. This event was the opening salvo in the non-violent battle against segregation and disenfranchisement that resulted in the desegregation of public accommodations (1964 Civil Rights Act), and voting rights (1965 Civil Rights Act). These legislative achievements were facilitated, to a large degree through another Alpha man, Brother Congressman Adam Clayton Powell. Brother Powell worked with President Lyndon Johnson to pass the most important Civil Rights legislation since Reconstructions constitutional amendments that abolished slavery and sought to establish the rudimentary rights of citizenship.

In previous articles in **The Sphinx**, and elsewhere, when the achievements of the 1960s are discussed, opportunity is generally equated with access. Whether that be the ballot, the right to sit anywhere on the bus, eat in any restaurant, sleep in any hotel, attend any school; or perhaps most significantly, the right to live without the continued brutality of the Ku Klux Klan's terroristic activity against African-American existence as human beings (although recent occurrences of church burning, lynchings [Jasper, Texas], and police brutality demonstrate the persistence of racist violence). But black Economic Development as an extension of the Civil Rights struggle is usually a critical missing link that must be understood, defended and protected. Brother Martin Luther King realized that access

163

must be accompanied by economic opportunity, but was stopped short in this quest by his assassination. Seldom examined, but inextricably connected to this era of progress is the entry into high paying job markets and the advancement of black business through Affirmative Action programs. This article will focus on the battle for Affirmative Action in the construction industry and how that struggle continues today as one of the linchpins for economic justice in the future. It is based on my own civil rights and business experience in that arena, along with the role and contributions of others Alphas.

Business opportunity is arguably the least documented and most neglected side of the economic civil rights movement, whose legal foundation is based largely on the Affirmative Action program advanced by11246, which required all government agencies and entities doing business with the federal government to end discrimination and take Affirmative Action to expand opportunities for blacks by developing programs to redress the historical legacy of racial discrimination and exclusion, with its consequent economic disparities. Demography was a primary barometer of change, in that the distribution of public sector jobs and contracts were required to positively reflect the population. This principle was also applied to the voter redistricting process. It should be noted that this Order was later amended to include women; consequently, white women have been the primary beneficiary of affirmative action in the workplace, as well as the business arena.

For many of us either not around or unfamiliar with the history of the last 30 years, it may be difficult to imagine what it was like to essentially have all political and economic authority vested in white elected and appointed officials, professional workers, civil servants, and private construction contractors, who built virtually every public building, shopping center, highway, airport and library; in large metropolitan areas, including inside the ghetto itself. But the current need for affirmative action is also clear: economic disparities abound and are easily documented. Today, the poverty level in the black community (35% and upward) exceeds the 25% unemployment rate for Americans generally during the Great Depression over seventy years ago. And this fact persists in the midst of what economists tell us is an economic boom period.

Still, Affirmative Action has helped to change the social and economic and cultural landscape of the country in ways that are too pervasive to recount. For example, the city of Atlanta today has produced numerous black million-dollar construction firms--all beneficiaries of Affirmative Action programs executed by Brother Maynard Jackson, the former Mayor of Atlanta. But in spite [or because] of the progress made under Affirmative Action, today, it is one of the most widely contested issues in the United States. Opponents of Affirmative Action use all types of misleading data to say enough has been done--that it results in illegal quotas and/or reverse discrimination. Their premise is that the attention given to race is unconstitutional, even though many blacks among them have benefited from such policies The most egregious case of the latter is Clarence Thomas (a George Bush appointee), who now occupies the Supreme Court seat vacated by Brother Justice Marshall (a Johnson appointee) and Ward Connerly, spokesperson for the campaign to abolish Affirmative Action in California, and an ally of organizations who have a similar mission in the construction industry. They are, in the words of one Black historian, "our modern day Judases."

Each application of Affirmative Action requires a different type of historical analysis and investigation. College and graduate school admission must be viewed through a different prism from that of the promotion of Black public service workers, such as firemen and policemen, for example. But one of the most significant, yet poorly understood areas of Affirmative Action as an engine for economic advancement and challenge remains the construction industry--traditionally one of the largest industries nationally constituting about 10% of the Gross National Product, and an area in which I have personally been active as a business man and advocate for over 30 years.

Affirmative Action in construction has its genesis in the construction project shutdowns that began in Chicago on July 23, 1969. During the summer of that year, the spirit of activism and black empowerment were like an infectious virus. The legacy of Brother Dr. Martin Luther King and the memory of his successful battles witnessed on television were fresh in our minds and gave us a "hopeful boldness" that inspired us to fight for whatever we believed to be right. Against this backdrop, 12 organizations, including the local black contractors association that I headed, came together under the leadership of the Dr. King lieutenant, Rev. C. T. Vivian, to form the Coalition for United Community Action, which closed down over $60 million dollars in construction in Chicago. The shutdown combined Dr. King's principles of non-violence with the traditional construction union protest practices of blocking access to worksites. Our approach was to focus on federally financed HUD-sponsored work, which could not be used to foster the inherent discrimination in the industry, based on the affirmative action guidelines of Executive Order 11246.

In 1969, construction nationally totaled $100 billion dollars, with 870,000 contractors, and 3.3 million construction workers. But only 16,000 of these contractors were black, with only 3,800 having paid employees, meaning that 75% were effectively self-employed operators with total receipts of $464 million less than half of 1% of overall construction volume. In Chicago, less than 2% of all construction workers were black and many of the trade unions like the Iron Workers, Sheet Metal and Elevator Operators had no African-American members. Without union membership, one could not work on public construction projects in Chicago. This situation was the same throughout the country in major cities, with some exceptions in southern and rural areas, where unions were not as powerful. Blacks were largely relegated to the Wet and Trowel Trades, i.e., painting, plastering and masonry. By virtue of this systematic exclusion, there were few black contractors in existence outside of the above-mentioned trades.

Although there was a long history of pioneering work by the National Business League, the NAACP and the National Urban League, the 1969 Chicago construction shutdown signaled the emergence of a new Black Business initiative on the national civil rights scene through non-violent direct action in a major industry. Thousands of persons were mobilized in. these actions over many months, which culminated in the signing of the Chicago Plan the following year, 1970. The Chicago Plan became the national model for the integration of the construction industry by establishing and enforcing goals and timetables for Blacks to enter all construction crafts. The principal signers of the agreement were Chicago Mayor Richard J. Daley; the Chicago and Cook County Building and Construction Trades Council; the Building Construction Employers Association; and myself, along with other Coalition leaders.

After successfully establishing the Chicago construction model of job shutdowns and the negotiation of an action plan, the effects of which still have impact, I became involved in organizing and/or applying the direct action model in other cities around the country, including Seattle, Pittsburgh, Memphis, and Denver. Meanwhile, several other developments propelled this issue into the national arena. The first was my participation in the founding of the National Association of Minority Contractors (NAMC) in 1969, organized by Brother Joseph Debro of Oakland, California, and upon his invitation becoming the Chicago representative. This ongoing organization represented the institutionalization of the national Black contractor movement.

The third national development phase stemmed from the publication of my essay on Black Elected Officials and the Black Construction Issue, in the early 1970s. After it came to the attention of Congressman Parren Mitchell (D-Maryland), he invited me to Washington D. C. to assist him in the creation and development of a Black Business Braintrust. This entity formulated the Black Business Agenda, which became part of the ongoing work of the Congressional Black Caucus. One of its primary purposes was to lead the effort to expand the economic participation of Black business, including construction firms, through federal legislation regulation and implementation. Parren Mitchell assembled an important cadre of industry leaders who worked to advance this new Black business agenda. My entry into this national arena was an offshoot of the '69 Chicago action. Thus we had combined Affirmative Action with administrative policies and our street enforcement capacity to get Black economic development on the national radar screen. This marked a turning point in the battle moving from the Local Street to City Hall, to the Congress, the Senate and the White House.

While some might say that their business success was never helped by Affirmative Action, there can be no doubt that the climate we created during this period caused government agencies and private corporations to seek out Black business in response to this public policy. The mandates required by congressional regulation, combined with a politicized and vocal Black community, aided established Black businesses that were able to immediately benefit from the process. There may have been publishers, bankers, insurance and accounting firms that had existed and performed well without Affirmative Action prior to its inception, but they were clearly enhanced by the external stimulus provided by the new attention on African-American business utilization.

As in all significant aspects of my life and work, Alpha men played pivotal roles in this struggle and were critical to this process as we moved forward. Brother John Wilks, director of the Office of Federal Contract Compliance (OFCC) in the Department of Labor during the Nixon administration's Black Capitalism initiative, converted our unbridled goals into a coherent, politically acceptable form, which, after his counseling, I could articulate. Under this policy, a number of economic development, technical assistance and business creation programs were funded by the U.S. Department of Commerce, the Small Business Administration, and various model city agencies that we effectively merged to promote the advancement of Black contractors. These programs and policies permitted our people to develop and work in all crafts and learn while they earned. Moreover, as construction contractors, we were the businessmen who had a natural interest in employing our people. That interest was viewed by majority contractors as a frontal attack on their traditional prerogatives that allowed them to control the entire industry.

We must understand that there is a huge difference between employment opportunities for Blacks and entrepreneurial empowerment, as conveyed through Affirmative Action business programs. After the initial resistance to integration by the construction unions in 1969 and the early 70s, there have been no Supreme Court cases against the mandated goals and timetables for Black construction workers (and later Hispanics and females). Yet, since 1969, there have been countless challenges all over the United States against Black contractor utilization goals--with the Croson (1983) and Adarand (1995) Supreme Court decisions that ignored egregious examples of discrimination in the letting of public contracts being the most damaging. The construction industry constitutes the primary challenge to Affirmative Action in the business world. Construction is a major Black economic engine that white corporations have rediscovered as an enemy to their total dominance of the Black consumer. Indeed, many of the civil rights that we acquired, such as access to public accommodations, are generally consumer in nature, and have further fattened the coffers of those who would keep us is a second-class economic status. Consequently, our job is to better understand and demand attention to Black business development.

Girded with a college education, and my experience as a contractor and advocate in the industry, I helped form UBM, Inc. in 1974. The firm has grown from two employees to being the largest black construction firm in the state of Illinois with over 100 employees, a multi-million dollar credit line, and $50 million dollar bonding capacity. We generate over 350 jobs annually and millions of dollars in contract awards to black subcontractors, UBM has gained tremendous opportunities by virtue of Affirmative Action; however, only good management and technical competence have allowed us to be financially successful.

We have examples of similar or greater Black success in the construction industry around the country, due in significant measure to the continued organizing efforts of the NAMC, and the emergence of black elected officials. But while these successes have been great, they are miniscule in comparison to the larger construction economy. The total of all Black contractors in the United States ($2.7 billion) is less than half the volume of the three top firms in Chicago alone. In fact, the number one Chicago construction firm's volume is more than one-third of all Black contractor sales nationally. This ever-widening gap is proof that the continuous attacks by the majority contractors organization, the Associated General Contractors (AGC), are having a serious negative impact on the quest for economic parity.

The role that Alpha Phi Alpha played in my personal and professional development that allowed me to contribute to this historic movement for economic justice is noteworthy. The glue that connected three Black men from Chicago (myself), Oakland (Debro) and Washington, D. C. (Wilks) was/is the principle of "First of all, servants of all, we shall transcend all," and the guiding principles in our collective effort were encouragement, education and guidance, along with a commitment and mutual cooperation with one another that we were taught and had per haps, unconsciously, incorporated into our thinking, worldview and actions. The desire to institute change and provide service to other Black people was a given. We didn't talk about it as a philosophy, nor did we have to convince one another as to why we should do this type of organizing. There was no strategic plan or development model needed to generate our enthusiasm.

But the social and cultural climate of the late 1960s is 180 degrees different from today. On the heels of the work of Brother King, the atmosphere in Black America was one of possibility and we valued the competition of how much we had read and could discuss about African History, politics and social theory among each other. From the time of my initiation into the Fraternity, I have been overwhelmed with good fortune-both, in terms of the men that were made with me and the national leaders who mentored me. The friendship that I currently hold with my fellow initiates and the mentoring I received from older brothers is worth examining. I can certainly credit my parents and family for their nurturing, values, example and financial support to go to school. But, where did the inspiration and challenge come from to excel in school or business? It came from being surrounded by other Black men of my Theta Chapter pledge line, all of whom graduated from college and are successful today. We are not only Ship Mates, but also friends who sponsor and host an annual dinner inviting other Alphas to meet and talk. One is a trusted CPA and another is a valued member of the UBM team. Brother Marv Wilson is a more recent addition to our company who serves as vice president for strategic planning, and continues the tradition of Alpha men playing key roles in my business development activities. This organizational genius is a key player in constructing a plan to make our firm multigenerational in the future. Do we foresee this type of closeness emerging among today's Black men and their families and lasting 40+ years?

The point is made best by citing a recent meeting where a representative of the Chicago Public Schools was trying to get two high school students involved in construction jobs, but could not find one or two with enough confidence to stand out by availing themselves of this opportunity. Compare this mindset to that of Theta Chapter in 1957. We were encouraged to be different. Nobody took me to a leadership class and said these are the strategies and tactics for being an effective leader or that this is what you do to behave as an upright Black man. My pledge group selected many careers, including chemistry, civil engineering, accounting, pre-med studies, aeronautical engineering, etc.--but we were all expected to succeed by graduating and using our experience to help others. This absence of great expectations, mutual support, encouragement and commitment to service is often absent from our current scene.

When I contemplated going into business, it was Brother Oscar Brown, Sr. who afforded me an opportunity by giving me my first painting contract while I was still in college. He schooled me in the ways of doing business through the many times we talked, as well as through his personal and professional example. He would loan me payroll money that I was always slow or late in paying back. But he never gave up and he would often counsel me by stating that I should continue to try and never give up on myself you have nothing to lose, but your own insecurity. What young man could not be successful with this kind of mentoring and positive intervention in his life?

If the attacks on Affirmative Action led by Clarence Thomas and Ward Connerly are not curbed, we will not only see a cessation of Black Business progress, but a decline in African-American youngsters development of the confidence, self-esteem and skills provided previously through university Affirmative Action admission and hiring policies. Therefore, I would urge the Brothers of Alpha Phi Alpha who read this article to become more knowledgeable about and protective of Affirmative Action, and recognize the fact that, like it or not, it has helped us all. Alpha Phi Alpha, as the first Black fraternity, with thousands of leaders in all fields of Endeavor, must take a lead in three key initiatives 1) Educating our young brothers about the facts of the Civil Rights era, including Affirmative Action. 2) Developing models for intervention and mentoring. 3) Helping to meet the challenge of engaging Black men in the Information Revolution--a task in which I have developed a strong personal interest, along with the others.

The Seven Jewels had a vision beyond our capacity to grasp, but it has sustained us for almost a century. Recently, we succeeded in developing [plans for] a Martin Luther King memorial in Washington, D C, and one only needs to read **The Sphinx** magazine to learn of historic achievements that Alpha men are making each day. Brother John Stroger, for example, the first Black President of Illinois Cook County Board, controls over 27,000 jobs and a budget of close to $3 billion dollars. Yet, these individual and chapter accomplishments will pale against the enormity of the problems challenging young Black men. It is my fervent hope that by sharing our experiences through the new energy of The Sphinx, we can institute a new sense of fraternal community, which is needed to offset the attacks on Black peoples quest for full equality.

The fact that I have benefited from fraternal life, particularly the guidance received from older Brothers, challenges me to see ways to help younger Black students. This spirit led my graduate chapter, Xi Lambda, to adopt the Adam Clayton Powell Elementary School in Chicago, where an Alpha Brother was principal. We must realize that there is a tremendous body of information requiring knowledge management, and we need a way to take the best ideas, concepts and practices that we have achieved and make them available to younger brothers. Perhaps the information revolution can yield devices for accomplishing this task.

Finally, we must recognize that the social constructs which allowed Brothers Adam Clayton Powell, Martin Luther. King, Ed Brooke, J. Herbert King, Judges Sidney Jones and Myles Paige, Clark Burrus, Brother Mayor Eugene Sawyer, Belford Lawson, and Charles Wesley to talk to me and embrace me as a protégé under their mentorship, no longer exist, particularly in urban areas. But just as Henry Arthur Callis had the vision to put an organization in place to successfully address the problems facing Black men during the early 1900s, it is our responsibility to make the Alpha Phi Alpha experience a relevant, exciting and necessary force in facing the challenges confronting Black men in this new century. My hope is to continue to participate in that struggle.

Reprinted courtesy of **The Sphinx** Magazine, Summer 2000.

Commentary
Going backward?: Deconstructing the construction business

by Paul King

Back in 1969 blacks made up less than 2 percent of America's trade unions and were excluded completely from certain trades such as elevator construction and sheet metal. Today, in the Chicago area, minority union membership has increased to more than 30 percent, with representation in all craft categories.

But now, all across America, we seem to be going backwards. In Florida, Gov. Jeb Bush has advanced a "One Florida" initiative--a scheme that goes as follows: eliminate race and gender considerations in college admissions and end all minority and female contractor utilization requirements on state contracts.

Apropos education, Bush proposes to guarantee the top 20 percent of each high school graduating class admission to Florida's state universities. This leaves it to Florida's racially segregated and underfunded public schools to prepare African-American and Hispanic students to swim rather than sink on campus. One critic noted that some Florida schools don't even have "enough chalk." Another likened Bush's "Talented 20" proposal to "vaporware," as in untried software using incomplete technology.

Yet, in an uncharacteristic rush to judgment, a **Tribune** editorial called the Florida plan "a smart play by the other Gov. Bush." Even more perplexing was columnist Clarence Page's take, that "for those who seek a sane, sensible way out of the nation's most vexing and volatile racial dilemma, the Bush plan offers welcome remedies."

Happily, many fair-minded people in Florida have accurately identified the enemy and are not content to be spectator-victims, as has been the case in other cities. They are supported by the National Coalition to Defend

Affirmative Action By Any Means Necessary and are organizing under the banner of "Stop the Attack on the Gains of the Civil Rights Movement." They have called for picketing of the Associated General Contractors of Florida, declaring that white- owned general contractors in league with Jeb Bush must be "called out by name."

As if this were not enough, we see the revival of the infamous Adarand case in which a white Colorado contractor convinced the U.S. Supreme Court in 1995 that he had been discriminated against by that state's minority set-aside program.

Still dissatisfied, Adarand has recently been "born again" and gotten certified as a DBE (Disadvantaged Business Enterprise). Now Randy Pech, the principal of Adarand Constructors Inc., is complaining his way through the courts, mutant identity and all. The Minority Business Enterprise Legal Defense and Education Fund compared the Adarand litigation to Dracula--"it refuses to die no matter how many stakes are driven into it."

Closer to home, John Duff's Windy City Maintenance sham has landed in the midst of this cluttered and confusing affirmative-action landscape. Reduced to its simplest form, we had an alleged white male- owned company posing as a female-owned business, and thereby getting contracts reserved for fledgling female-owned businesses.

The media immediately began to call this affair by another name. Instead of accurately describing the situation as gender-based abuse, one paper's headline read: "Janitorial firm loses minority edge," while The New York **Times** referred to the "minority program being misused." This interpolation of minority rather than female abuse is like calling affirmative action goals "quotas." That is inaccurate and seemingly designed to be divisive.

This plays right into the hands of the Builders Association of Chicago, which is proposing a suit against the city's set-aside program and will doubtless use the Duff case as evidence that the program doesn't work.

Mayor Richard Daley is one of the few mayors in the United States who has continued to promote and defend an economic opportunity program of the type we have in Chicago. His administration should be saluted, not sullied.

It's true, some abuse of minority set-asides has occurred. And yes, those abuses must be stopped. But don't throw the baby out with the bath water. Verification of authentic minority and female business activity can be achieved through improved monitoring mechanisms. Contractors are routinely required to prove up their insurance coverage, OSHA compliance, Chicago residency requirements and payment of "Davis-Bacon" wages on federally funded projects. Proving ownership and genuine contract performance shouldn't be a problem.

What fair-minded people need to know is that the enemies of black inclusion in Chicago's construction industry are the same forces out to end affirmative action in Florida, California and Colorado. The past 30 years have opened many doors for minorities in construction here, but there are those who would nail shut Chicago's effort to promote equity for minorities in building programs. They must not succeed.

Rather than curse the darkness of despair of blacks who loiter on urban streets, minority contractors are lighting candles. We are creating opportunities for them to learn a skill, support their families and ultimately, rebuild their own communities.

PAUL KING

Paul King was at the forefront of the struggle to push Blacks to enter the construction industry. He helped organize the National Association of Minority Contractors. He became a close advisor to Congressman Parren Mitchell, and he helped form the Black Business Braintrust that set in place important legislation that would benefit minorities working under federal contracts. King is the Chairman of the Board of UBM, Inc, the largest Black owned and operated Construction Services company in Chicago, IL. He is an author, lecturer, speaker and recipient of numerous awards. His passion is for today's youth, our leaders of tomorrow. He serves on several boards and committees within the academic community and sponsors his own Summer Intern Program at UBM. King is determined to pass on his great legacy of success by proving that hard work and commitment is definitely a winning formula.

the Gospel TRIBUNE

$2.00

Reaching Today's African American Congregations

April 200
Volume 8 No.

MASTER
CHURCH BUILDERS

Wendell Campbell   Paul King

Master Church Builders:
Wendell Campbell and Paul King
by Delmarie Cobb

FOR PAUL KING and Wendell Campbell, Trinity United Church of Christ represents more than a 20-year odyssey of the two companies working together. As chairman of UBM Inc. and the founder of, Campbell Tiu Campbell, respectively they have discovered the keys to success--both as individuals and as partners on multiple projects.

Teaming up to build Trinity United Church of Christ was the culmination of both men tirelessly working together and separately to break down racial barriers in their respective fields for years. An advocate for affirmative action, King traveled the country helping to formulate public policy and get legislation passed that would allow African Americans the opportunities to work on construction sites and head their own companies. Similarly, Campbell was working to form the National Organization of Minority Architects--of which he is a lifetime member and push the American Institute of Architects to accept more African American members.

"We came along at a time when affirmative action flourished and made all of these opportunities possible," recalls King. "That's why when I see the attacks on affirmative action, it causes me to be more adamant about wanting to make sure that this business goes into the future."

Helping King prepare for the future are his two partners--Sandra Jiles, an African American woman, and Sham Dabadghao, an Indian civil engineer. King calls their partnership the glue that has allowed UBM Inc. to last for 25 years.

"When I asked Sandra and Sham to join me in this quest, it gave me two people who had capacities different from me, but together we were greater than the sum of our parts," explains King. That's the single most important factor of this company's success. A factor that has helped UBM Inc. become the largest African American owned construction company in Illinois.

For both King and Campbell, their vocation is an extension of their avocation. Campbell's father and grandfather were contractors. He began working for his father at eight years old. By the time Campbell entered high school, he had become proficient in most of the construction trades. He was fortunate to study at the Illinois Institute of Technology when the college was developing its architectural department under famed architect Ludwig Mies van der Rohe. It was also a time when the catch phrase "urban renewal" was being used to describe wholesale changes proposed for black communities.

"I've always been involved with changing communities and the problems affecting those communities. Most of my life's work has been spent dealing with communities that were deteriorating and had to be redone," says the committed architect. So, I worked with people and helped them to organize themselves in a way where they could be involved in the redevelopment.

Today, the two men are actively taking part in rebuilding communities through church-sponsored projects. Both jointly and separately, their companies have built or are building dozens of structures for local churches ranging from places of worship, senior citizen housing, family housing and educational centers.

They believe the diversity of construction projects being developed is a natural extension of the church ministry in an effort to address the temporal and practical needs of their communities. As African Americans, they also believe their understanding of the historical significance of the church to the black community, gives them at an advantage when advising clients.

"When churches launch into development, they need to get legal and technical advice from a firm like ours that has a commitment to them so that they understand what kind of contracts they should get into and what kind of financing they should get," observes King. "I'm just amazed at the amount of money and potential that some of these churches have and do not use sufficient technical expertise that is available to them to insure they use people who want to see them win and not exploit them."

Helping churches to meet their spiritual and social objectives is also the corporate philosophy of Campbell Tiu Campbell. "We will go the extra effort to get the job done right. We found that a lot of our clients weren't familiar with developments and how to put projects together. Consequently, we would have to do their work for them, and they became a part of the building process," explains the firm's founder.

Campbell says that because of the growing number of church clients, there may come a time when the majority of his firm's projects will be church sponsored.

"My father says that churches are your best public relations tool. Whatever the size of the congregation, you have that number of people talking about you," acknowledges Susan Campbell, Vice President for Urban Planning and Business Development. Ms. Campbell is one of two daughters working for her father's architectural firm.

She says that in the black community, churches are the major developers. They are the ones who stayed in the community when other institutions left. Consequently, as a client group they are excited about their projects.

Like their church clients, both King and Campbell are striving to build institutions that will be multi-generational. "I believe too many black entrepreneurs made the mistake of thinking that if they can't continue the company with their own children, they won't put forth the effort. I believe that the new thinking about running and operating a business is going to be what distinguishes us in the future. That means that we are going to pay attention to ensuring that our employees not only make a living, but enjoy a life by working in a UBM environment." Therefore, as the company prepares to become multi-generational, UBM Inc. has put a management team in place that consists of a human resource manager, three vice-presidents and expanded its operational leadership to a six-person executive team.

In less than three decades, U8M Inc. and Campbell Tiu Campbell have grown from three employees to 50 and 30 respectively. Therefore, if past accomplishments are an indicator, these two companies will be around for a long time.

Remarks in Honor of Mayor Eugene Sawyer Birthday Benefit Celebration for the Wyatt Community and Family Life Center

by
Paul King, Chair, UBM, Inc.
Friday, September 21, 2001
Chicago, Illinois

To: Mayor Sawyer; Senator Braun; President Stroger; Reverends Wyatt; Alderman Ed Smith, who doesn't allow anything in his ward to happen without black people being involved; my mentor, Clark Burrus; "the legal eagle," Jim Montgomery; other elected officials and clergy; "the greatest gospel singer on earth," Albertina Walker; friends and fellow celebrants:

The Sunday before the New York attack, the hottest topic among black people was Reparations. Reparations was a call for those nations who aided and benefited from the slavery of black people to apologize and make some gestures to repair the damage done to a groups culture and sociopolitical future.

I believe that there should be reparations, atonement, and apologies given to Eugene Sawyer.

No black elected public servant endured the kind of attacks heaped on Eugene, a man who never sought revenge toward those who attacked him, as he became Chicago's second black mayor.

Chief among them was a black news writer working for the Sun-Times, who almost daily filled the minds of that paper's readers with malice and misstatements about Mayor Sawyer. He should apologize.

Black Aldermen, who after failing in a coup against the Mayor continued to disrespect him--they should apologize.

One very good friend of mine whom I respect, but with whom we had differences at this time, is now a chief judge of the Circuit Court, who achieved that post uncontested, according to Rev. Jesse Jackson, because another candidate withdrew in his favor. That's precisely what Eugene Sawyer and I offered him to support Gene. He should apologize.

A so-called political strategist from the Washington administration, now in radio and television, berated Mayor Sawyer. She should apologize.

I would hope that one day the book is written where those responsible for these unwarranted attacks are accurately identified, and an explanation provided as to why they sullied the reputation of this gracious black man. These peoples' attacks on him crucified and cut the Harold Washington coalition that laid the basis for the black community's political empowerment. In the meantime, since these people have not apologized, I want to apologize to Gene on their behalf, as well as to the black people of Chicago who lost a valuable political coalition because of the shortsightedness of a few.

I want to publicly state my gratitude for Mayor Sawyer being the catalyst for helping me develop the largest black-owned construction company in the State of Illinois.

Harold Washington invoked an executive order requiring minority business utilization in public contracts. Eugene Sawyer went on to make it work in ways that no one had ever imagined.

When the multi-million dollar international terminal at O'Hare was up for a construction manager, Eugene didn't require 25% MBE but 49.5%! This was the largest margin of minority participation in the city's history. From that my firm gained the airport experience to now be a partner in the one billion-dollar Terminal Six Project at O'Hare, one of the largest contracts ever awarded in Chicago.

Gene and I talked about raising the bar. We had achieved the required minority hiring and contractor objectives. Now it was time for black equity in real estate development. Gene awarded the development of the 40-acre site at Irving Park and Mannheim Road to the O'Hare Development Group, a black venture that teamed with a large white developer to complete the $50 million project.

This model provided valuable experience that enabled a black-owned venture to be awarded a second $40 million dollar development project on the military site at O'Hare.

With the overwhelming support of Ed Smith, that in turn, led to a $38 million development, the California Park, with blacks now having an equity position. Gene started the process and Ed Smith upped it and expanded it. Alpha men do not take backward steps. Now we see black equity requirements in the Burnham Hotel, the Madden Wells CHA Development, and elsewhere.

Although Alderman Ed Smith is a leader, he isn't alone. He's been joined by the majority of black aldermen on the Westside like Mike Chandler, Emma Mitts, and Ike Carothers. Championing the same values of expansion opportunities on the Southside are Alderman William Beavers, who stands out for the assistance he provided UBM in securing the Jewel-Osco Shopping Mall project on 95th and Stony Island; and other city council members like Freddrenna Lyle, who engaged in direct advocacy to enlist black contractors for the Chicago State University Library and Convocation Center; Arenda Troutman, who did the same with the 63rd Street YMCA expansion; Toni Preckwinkle, who brought black contractors into the Ancona School and Muntu Theatre Project; Leslie Hairston, who directly intervened on behalf of minority participation in the 79th Street Sears renovation; Tony Beale, who epitomizes black aldermanic initiative in insuring black participation in the far southside Y project in his ward; Madeline Haithcock, a low-profile warrior who supported the restoration of the historic Overton and Chicago Bee Buildings in a way that affirmed minority business opportunity and local community education at the same time; Dorothy Tillman, whose roots in the Civil Rights Movement under Dr. Kings leadership have made her a champion for black participation in construction in her ward, particularly in completing the first phase of the Lou Rawls Center; and finally, the late Lorraine Dixon, who epitomized the responsible public servant with a spiritual base, who facilitated UBM's involvement in the House of Kicks project at 95th and Cottage Grove.

These black aldermen, along with their counterparts: Carrie Austin, Walter Burnett, Shirley Coleman, Leonard DeVille, Todd Stroger, Latasha

Thomas, and Theodore Thomas--have made outstanding contributions in their wards with respect to minority business development. But it was Mayor Eugene Sawyer who paved the way with his visionary prescription for progress. We applaud the continuation of that legacy.

The beneficiaries of these actions by Mayor Sawyer have stepped up to say thank you.

- Robin Brooks whose husband, Frank (now deceased) sent in a $1,000 thank you.
- Tom Gilbane, from Providence, Rhode Island--$1,000.
- Joe Williams, $1,000.
- Odell Hicks, $1,000.
- Mitchell Watkins, $1,000.
- UBM, Paul King, $1,000.
- John Bolden and many others have made up over $8,000 to say, thank you.

We appreciate you.

If everyone Gene helped would support the Wyatt Center, we should raise over $1 million.

Gene Sawyer has been a man of principle and process, and not self-promotion, and that is why I am proud to call him my very good friend and brother.

Sir Clement launches Reading and Essay Competition

By Denise Major, *Guardian Staff Reporter*

Paul King presents cheque to Sir Clement Maynard to serve as an incentive for the Reading and Essay Competition. Photo by Patrick Hanna

Sir Clement Maynard, former Member of Parliament for the Yellow Elder constituency, yesterday launched the first Reading and Essay Competition to encourage reading and information concerning our heritage to the young Bahamians in the community of Yellow Elder.

The G.K. Symonette library, established in Yellow Elder in 1987, was the first community library established in the Bahamas and was named in honour of the late Georgianna K. Symonette, the mother of Sir Clement Maynard.

Paul King, leader in the construction industry in Chicago Illinois, the chairman and one of the original founders of UBM, the largest African-American owned and operated services firm in the city of Chicago, donated a series of Bahamian books to the library along with funds to serve as an incentive for the winner of the competition.

"I saw the potential for young fertile minds to be able to grasp information that have been kept from them by the absence of funds and interest, so I welcomed the opportunity to help them out," said King. King is a well-known philanthropist who is especially concerned for the well being of persons of African descent around the world. King introduced a series of books written by African-American authors, as well as Bahamian authors and poets to the library. In the latter part of last year Mr. King made similar presentations of adult books and children books, vowing to encourage versatility within the library by making this more recent presentation since a library should cater to all ages and races.

King, along with Maynard, and librarians from the various schools in the community launched the essay competition. There are three categories: ages 5-8, 9-12, and 13-16. The winner of each category will receive a monetary prize, and the first twenty participants who register will receive a T-shirt saying, "Knowledge is mine and I am getting it at G.K Symonette Library."

Some of the books that the children will be reading include--Young Martin Luther King Jr., I am Rosa Parks, Amistad, and Mandela.

Reprinted, Courtesy of Nassau **Guardian, 2002.**

Marilyn Cox, librarian at G. K. Symonette Library, displays the
T-shirt awarded to participants in the contest sponsored by King.

Essay Competition Winners Praised

by ANDREA M. MYERS

Three public school students, Dian Evans of Government High School and Rashad Rogers and Kristian Pratt of C. W. Sawyer Primary School are the winners of the first G. K. Symonette Library Essay Writing Competition.

The winners were announced on Wednesday at the library and received gift certificates to purchase books. All participants received T-shirts.

Dies, Rashad and Kristian were among eighteen students who participated in the first Black History Competition put on by the Library. They were asked to read books on Black history and write a report on their comprehension of the material.

Chicago businessman Paul King, who owns the largest black construction company in Illinois in the United States, donated the books to the library. His business employs over 200 people and does about $70 million in business annually.

Mr. King said that he started reading at age three and told the students, "I believe that reading is power and the gateway to understanding your life." He added that he realized that he could accomplish anything he wanted if he knew more and that the avenue to know more was to read more.

'Reading allows you to write, writing allows you to speak and between writing reading and speaking you can accomplish anything," he added.

The books include, "Dare to Dream" which addresses the life and reminiscences of Coretta Scott-King, the widowed wife of famed civil rights leader, Rev. Dr. Martin Luther King Jr.

Marilyn Cox, librarian at G. K. Symonette Library, said that the competition started in 2001. The competition, she said, was initiated by a need to encourage students to read the books.

Mrs. Cox said that modern society does not encourage reading. Calling Caribbean people 'oral people," Mrs. Cox said that we are more comfortable telling stories and talking to each other than reading. She said that the competition was great in that it encouraged students who would not normally take part in competitions to participate.

"What we often find is that children read, but sometimes lack the skill of comprehension," she said. She encouraged parents, grandmothers, and family members to read more to children as well as ask them to relate the story in their own words,

The G. K. Symonette Library, located in Yellow Elder, was built in memory of Mrs. Georgiana Kathleen Symonette, mother of the former Deputy Prime Minister of the Bahamas, Sir Clement Maynard. Also the representative for Yellow Elder under the Progressive Liberal Party government, Sir Clement said that he was encouraged to build the library and happy that children are making full use of it.

He thanked all the parents for supporting and helping their children.

Reprinted, Courtesy of *The Bahamian Journal*, March 21, 2002.

Cosmopolitan Chamber of Commerce

by Paul King
June 2002

Greetings,

I am honored to have been invited to speak before an organization with such a distinguished history as the **Cosmopolitan Chamber of Commerce**. Many of my old colleagues have been associated with this organization, such as Connie Miller from my CEDCO days, and JoAnn Siller, who was with us going all the way back to the **United Builders Association of Chicago** in the late 1960s. Through the years some other historic names have had leadership roles with this organization that I count as both friends and mentors, including the late Louis A.H. Caldwell and my great Alpha brother, Oscar Brown, Sr.

I want to applaud the work that Gloria Bell is doing with the Chamber, after doing such a great job for the State of Illinois CMS, We are grateful that someone of her caliber is responsible for carrying on this great tradition of advocacy for Black Economic Advancement.

I am equally aware of the Chambers role in mentoring other African American and minority business people through the years, and I doubt if there is another organization in the city of Chicago that can match its record of service. The Free School of Business Management (although I understand you finally started charging a few dollars for this service) is legendary for the guidance it provided to over 20,000 entrepreneurs since 1967. The Chambers leadership in fostering the Chicago Business Opportunity Fair in cooperation with the Chicago Business Development Council has been a pioneer event for today's huge Black Business Expos.

Many of these things came about because of the battles that we fought and the few we won during the civil rights movement. But before the birth of the modern civil rights movement, before the Chamber went from calling itself the Chicago Negro Chamber of Commerce in 1954, the year of Brown v. Board of Education, to its new interracial identity as the Cosmopolitan Chamber of Commerce, before there were any White House Conferences on Small Business, or cable TV shows on Chicago Business Issues, or weekly radio programs concerned with Business Building Business, the Chamber was fighting the good fight in both good times and bad.

In fact, the Chamber was not born with the helping hand of government, but was created by a courageous and visionary group of founders who decided to take a stand during the *worst of times*. The Chicago Negro Chamber of Commerce was founded during the Great Depression in 1933 by African American businesspeople who were fighting an uphill climb. They were unable to borrow money from banks; they were discriminated against by wholesalers who wouldn't give them the time of day, let alone a good price on quantity merchandise. They often had to service their customers by selling door to door, even though they were harassed by white salespeople. When most people were going out of business, they decided to start a business organization to promote their survival. And that organization not only survives, but is one of the oldest minority business groups in the country to remain in continuous existence.

Years ago, Chicago garnered the reputation of being the Black Business Mecca of the United States. Legendary businessmen like Anthony Overton and Jesse Binga were part of that heritage. One of the great leaders of the old Negro Chamber who shepherded the organization through 1947 deserves to be mentioned in that company, and that is S.B. Fuller. Most people don't know it but S.B. Fuller, was one of Chicago's first black millionaires.

So to the awardees, I convey my congratulations on being nominated by your peers and validated by this organization; but I also want to remind you that with awards comes the obligation to uphold a tradition by becoming and remaining an excellent business operation. I am sure you will meet that expectation with flying colors.

When the Chamber started out, some 75 years ago, it was clearly some of the worst of times, while today, as in Dickens' **Tale of Two Cities**, we are experiencing what may the best and the worst of times simultaneously. That certainly rings quite true for Black and other minority contractors.

1. The Good
- Under the leadership of Mayor Daley, Chicago is one of the only cities in the United States, which has a mandatory M/WBE utilization on all city contracts. Additionally it has a Target Market program that allows for competition restricted to minority firms.

- Recently we had the award of the **Terminal 6** Project at O'Hare. This $1 billion dollar project will provide over$250 million dollars in contracts to minority businesses.
- The CHA has a multi-billion dollar program, which includes not only the much needed demolition of the Black reservations along State Street, but also the construction of alternative housing for Public Housing residents elsewhere in the city. Under the leadership of Terry Peterson and CHA Chairman Sharon Gilliam, Black firms are offered a once in a lifetime opportunity to work to improve the quality of life for CHA residents.
- The Chicago Public Schools under the leadership of Michael Scott, a soldier of the struggle, is in a rebuilding mode that generates enhanced opportunities for black businesses to gain contracts.
- For the first time in history, we have an African-American head of Procurement concurrently with a Black Aviation Commissioner. David Malone in Purchasing monitors the award of all city contractors to ensure ethical procedures, including minority business utilization. And Tom Walker, head of the Department of Aviation, is charged with the mammoth responsibility of overseeing the city's airport expansion program.
- Beyond public projects, we also see a resurgence of private development in Chicago's Black neighborhoods like never before Walgreens, new cinemas, Jewel Food stores and LaSalle Bank, are just a few examples. IIT, the University of Chicago, Soldier Field, and McCormick Place are examples of other private/public mega-projects, while the 39-acre development on California Avenue represents the first warehouse development in the black community in 50 years. Viewing this landscape, we can only say that opportunities abound!
- President John Stroger at the helm of the County Board.

But there are some negatives raining on this bright horizon:

2. The Bad

- The evil of the BAGC lawsuit claiming that the city's MBE program is reverse discrimination. The suit has the audacity to say its 60 or 70 members are being denied because the 100-year monopoly on all Chicago construction was brought to an end by the City's MBE ordinances.

- The chaos in the insurance industry: In 2000 and 2001 the Stock Market took a big fall. Many insurance companies were heavily involved in the market where they made record profits during the Clinton Administration. These companies suffered big losses going into the 2nd quarter of 2001 when the September 11th destruction of the World Trade Center wiped out some of these companies. This was followed by Enron, which cost surety companies some $2 billion dollars in losses, and the K-Mart bankruptcy only added fuel to the fire. This combination of disasters has caused typical insurance workman's compensation, property damage and public liability rates to be sky-high, if available at all. Surety bonds for small and minority firms over a certain amount are becoming unavailable period. **The next 12 months will see contractors going out of business because they cannot get bonds!**
- A Supreme Court, which was once our friend, has now turned into a hostile opponent of our interests.
- One of the most devastating diseases infecting the body of the Chicago construction community is the proliferation of FRONTS. These are Black firms who lend their names to White owned firms in subcontract or so called joint venture arrangements which supposedly meet MBE rules, but in fact are very near FRAUDS. I have no quarrel with a joint venture that serves to develop a Black firm, and I would define development as a firm being able to perform independently after the job. We have Black fronts that do these shady joint ventures year end and year out, yet are somehow never able to estimate, staff, finance, insure and bond jobs for a fraction of the dollar value of their joint venture contracts.

FRONTS are wrong because:

1. They serve as an avenue to bring white contractors (with their cover) into Black neighborhoods and take job away from legitimate Black firms.
2. In some cases these fronts bring the very members of the BAGC (who are filling suit against City MBE programs) into our community to gain economic benefit to be used against us.
3. Fronts by their very nature do not use their joint venture expenses to develop their own companies. Thus, neither they, nor anyone

else, develop added Black construction strength and capacity.

4.   Firms from out of town are being encouraged to come into Chicago, set up shop and compete against local Chicago companies, but what we need is increased development of the Black firms that are resident to Chicago. This can be done by following UBM's example and mentoring local Black firms in the ways they need. How can a company from out of town help build capacity in local emerging Black firms when they don't know Homan Avenue from Stony Island, and are sending their profits back to another city? If we are serious about developing local capacity, let the Kennys, McHughs, Walshs and Powers set up open book mentoring programs in their bids and subject them to scrutiny to ensure no pass through Front activity is going on.

Over the past 3 decades, along with a few very dedicated and important people, I attempted to address some of the inequities facing Black contractors and by example demonstrate solutions to the "Bad Times."

I come out of a mindset of the 1960s where organizing with a single purpose was the most important thing we believed there was to do. We sacrificed money, personal comfort, sleep, and sometimes quality time with our families. Our central focus was to fight the ugly racism of the construction industry by any means necessary. It was through this dedicated organizing effort combined with the continued education of our people that we brought about change!!

At that time there were:

-   Less than 2 % Blacks in the trades. Not one iron or sheet metal worker, and no elevator operation contractors. **Now** minorities make up over 30% of all workers throughout the County.
-   **Then** Black contractors were excluded from work in our own neighborhoods and city procurement practices excluded our participation. **Now** we have city ordinances requiring our participation.
-   **Then** Black aldermen were afraid of "rocking the boat" and losing their seat. **Today** we have Black alderman shutting down jobs that don't have Black workers and who are willing to take a stand like Bill Beavers and Ed Smith.

Our role as trailblazers for economic justice in the construction industry has been marked by some important milestones:

- In 1969, I was one of the leaders that shut down construction sites to ensure that Blacks could go into the union.
- In the 70s, I authorized portions of the Public Works Employment Act of 1976 introduced into Congress by Parren Mitchell. This was the first law, which required mandatory integration for monitoring contractors.
- As a founder of UBM, I have the privilege of being the first Black general contractor to build a Jewel Food Store. The $13 million facility was the first time in Jewel's 100-year history that a new store was built by an African American firm.
- As Chairman of the O'Hare Development Group, we became the first Black development group to have an equity position in an airport facility.
- UBM has played an exemplary leadership role in employment and training programs, including our Summer Internships for college student, career counseling for high school students, the Project PRIDE employment track for CHA residents, and hiring previously incarcerated inmates.

This journey represents what I call the **Power Paradigm:**

1. Tradesman
2. Subcontractor
3. General Contractor
4. Developer

Each level of the paradigm is an advancement of additional power and responsibility. The tradesman gains experience and learns about productively. Also he/she shows young blacks that a career with HARD HATS and BOOTS IS OK!!!

The subcontractor has power over providing employment to tradespersons and has the discretion to purchase material from a number of different suppliers. The General contractor controls subcontractor selection, vendor purchase and installing policies of different types. The developer chooses the Architect, General Contractor, Bank, Insurance Company, Lawyers and numerous others.

With this power comes the responsibility to set an example along each step to use this extended influence to provide opportunities for other minority firms, in my case Black companies. What concerns me most today is that the people, programs and policies that enabled UBM to climb the power ladder will not be around to assist others.

So now, on what and where do we need to focus?

There is no structured management and technical assistance program set up in Chicago to service the needs of Black contractors. More than ever, emerging contractors need a place to receive estimating management, insurance, bonding, and administrative assistance. The time and effort it takes to review a set of plans and specifications often prevents contractors from responding to an invitation to bid. A Management and Technical Assistance Center (MTA) providing these services would help immensely. Cosmopolitan needs to develop a technical assistance center using state, federal, city, and private funding, which is fiscally managed by a CPA. Contractors need assistance in reviewing plans quickly enough to determine their feasibility and interest, followed by the preparation of sound bids.

UBM is mentoring smaller firms now, and we have teamed with Turner Construction to develop a specific number of minority firms between our two companies, as well as a training program for prison inmates. The other giant firms should be challenged to do the same thing. I don't mean using minority firms for hundreds of million of dollars in so-called joint ventures with the minority firm ending up with no independent capacity to do anything on its own. Such short-term front operations don't really develop the minority construction community.

Accordingly, a set of criteria for legitimate joint ventures should be established and monitored. Both the majority and minority firms who fail to meet these standards should be fined. These criteria should incorporate the following points:

A. That the Minority firms must perform the work.
B. They must do the estimates and budget a percentage of the trades?
C. They must put up money and be exposed to risk and loss.
D. Sign all checks.
E. Provide personnel from their company.

Other things we must do are:

1. Obtain a list of the members of the BAGC; circulate them among BCU, AACA, HACIA, the Chamber, FWC, and to the Alderman of the 20 Black wards. Advocate that no permits should be issued

to these companies until they resign from BAGC. This effort should be started to combat their assault on us.

2. Convene a series of monthly meetings on the chaos in the insurance industry starting in July for at least a one-year period. UBM hosted one in February 2002, and I am speaking at one that ENR is holding on June 18th here in Chicago, followed by one in Baltimore on June 21st.

3. Conduct a letter writing campaign to all Alderman, agency heads, and diversity officers at public and private institutions saying that before non-Chicago based firms are developed we want no out-of-town firms coming in to compete against local Chicago based firms capacity building.

All of this will require an organized effort by the people who have most to gain---the contractor and construction worker themselves.

Again, we need the Chamber to take up the charge of becoming spokesperson for these issues by teaming with IIT, the University of Chicago, Chicago State University, and Northwestern, (one or all) to obtain city, state, and federal funds to provide Management and Technical Assistance.

If Cosmopolitan takes up the challenge set forth by Oscar C. Brown, Louis Caldwell, and the other pioneers who set the Chamber in motion during the most hostile racist era, we will meet the current challenges head on, deflect them and lead scores of Black firms up the "Power Paradigm Path."

Acceptance Speech for JOHN McDERMOTT AWARD

Paul King, Chair, UBM, Inc.
June 2001

To Reverend/Clergy, Officers and members on the dais, honored guests, ladies and gentlemen:

I am deeply honored to be the recipient of the 2001 John McDermott Award from The Crossroad Center and Business Executives for Economic Justice.

It's a special privilege to have been recognized from such elite competition as reflected in the numerous recommendations that came to the selection committee. I know that my biggest champion in the nominating process was Bill Skalitsky, so I feel compelled to take a moment to share the story of how he and I became acquainted.

Five or six years ago, the Chicago **Tribune** published an article that I wrote about how businesses could intervene in the lives of young African American men. As is often the case, letters and calls (pro and con) came to my office in response. One call came in requesting a meeting with a group called "Lawyers for Social Justice." Now I must tell you that I was quite cynical about the young college graduates, the "generation xers" of that era. Many seemed to be self-centered, concerned only about their own upward mobility, and becoming Masters of the Universe. And I had particularly given up on most of the non-minority recent graduates because most of what I had read about them indicated that they were against Affirmative Action and exhibited very little interest in the kind of social change that would benefit Blacks.

Enter Bill Skalitsky and three of his cohorts: Bill was forming an organization of lawyers who wanted to provide scholarships for inner city boys, through a project called "The Enable Scholarship Program." And they were interested in making their first project a four-year scholarship for a young man at Hales Franciscan High School, where I was on the Board of Trustees, and my youngest son, Tim was President.

After I buried my surprise, shock and embarrassment at having lumped all young white lawyers into one big uncaring basket, I feebly asked why did they want to do this. Bill replied that each of them had been privileged enough to get a good Catholic upbringing and education and that he felt professionally and morally bound to do something to assist in the education of those who did not have access to such privileges.

Needless to say, Bill kept his word and the young man he co-sponsored graduated from Hales and went on to college. So I just want to acknowledge Bill as one of the reasons for me being here on this occasion.

On a very significant and personal note, I am especially honored to receive an award named after John McDermott. Like Attorney Earl Neal, who is in the audience today, and Clark Burrus and Cook County Commissioner John Stroger, John McDermott was a close friend and mentor. Thirty years ago, when we were protesting the fact that Blacks were not getting into the construction unions and/or receiving public contracts, and when they made up less than 2% of Union membership with no representation in certain trades, (in contrast to 30% nationwide today), John would quietly counsel me on the next move to make, and introduce me to people who could make things happen. John McDermott helped to propel our efforts far greater than I ever imagined. You should know for example, that John McDermott was responsible for facilitating the award of one of the first contracts that Illinois Bell ever made to a Black Contractor.

When John started the Chicago **Reporter,** he drafted me as his "unpaid construction consultant." In return, he spearheaded one of the most in-depth factual studies that had ever been done in Chicago on Blacks in the Construction Unions and on City awards to Black Contractors. This documented information gave me the ammunition to testify before Congress and push for more equitable laws and ordinances to be passed. In his later years, John was also active in supporting Hales Franciscan. Though he didn't do it directly, I am sure he was behind those who recruited me for the school's Board. So, it is this strong personal knowledge of the man behind this award, which makes it profoundly special.

At this juncture, I have to acknowledge that many of the efforts and contributions that have been associated with my receipt of this award, must be attributed to my company, UBM, where I proudly serve as a founder and chair. On behalf of the principals, executives and the entire organizational team, I would like to thank you for this honor.

UBM is the largest Black-owned Construction Company in the State of Illinois. Last month, we were selected to be a partner on a $1 billion dollar project at O'Hare Airport. This is the largest airport project in Chicago's history. Recently, we completed a $13 million dollar Jewel facility on 95th & Stony Island, which was the first time in Jewel's 100-year history that they had awarded a project of this size to a Black General Contractor. This would not have happened without the support and insistence of Alderman William Beavers and my fellow DeLaSalle Alumnus, Mayor Richard Daley. I also want to acknowledge Sam Jones, a Hales graduate, who ably served as the Project Manager on the Jewel Shopping Center Project.

Less than two miles from the Jewel project in my own parish, which is largely African American, another general contractor, who was not African American, was building a Senior Citizen's building. I let my disappointment with Catholic Charities be known to a few people. Shortly thereafter, through the efforts of Pastor John Breslin, and the Most Reverend Raymond Goedert. UBM received the largest contract ever awarded to an African-American construction company by Catholic Charities for the $1 million St. Ailbe's residential facility, which is currently being completed.

Our philosophy at UBM is that a Black Business must be internally well-managed in order to become financially successful. It should establish and transmit a corporate vision and mission that will lead the organization to become multi-generational, so that there is a continuity of wealth, knowledge and founding commitments. One of those primary commitments is to support institutions, individuals and initiatives that will create positive change within the Black community. This focus and purpose is clearly expressed in the Jewel Supermarket project, where we used 70% minority contractors and created 120 jobs for residents of that community.

Other projects reflect the same philosophy:

- ◆ CHA –We completed a million dollar project, which used 100% Black contractors, and created 60 new jobs for CHA residents, many of whom are still in the unions and working elsewhere.
- ◆ We fund a $1,000 annual scholarship for Black students at each of the 7 Chicago City Colleges.
- ◆ We employed a recently incarcerated man, who had learned drafting while in prison. Teamed with two-24 hour counselors and a UBM mentor, this African-American earned and paid taxes on $36,000 annually, which was about the cost of what it took to maintain him in prison. He worked for over 2 1/2 years with no recidivism.
- ◆ We sponsored and led the $700,000 rehabilitation of Hales Franciscan High School with a new gymnasium floor, windows, doors, etc.

♦ Established and funded Project Pride, an acronym for Personal Responsibility Individual Development and Empowerment. Provided $10,000 to Malcolm X College to train community residents to take and pass the union apprenticeship exam. This included the basics, such as Reading, as well as the communication and social skills necessary to enter and function successfully in the various construction unions. This program now involves St. Paul Church of God in Christ, Chicago Construction Unions, the Mayor's Office of Workforce Development, and others.

♦ Completed a project for the Gateway Foundation ahead of schedule and received a $50,000 bonus, all of which was donated to non-profit organizations for direct assistance to African American recipients. This included DeLaSalle High School, Chicago Public Schools and special Children's charities.

These are things that you can do when you are in authority and control the budget process. What we did provides an example to anyone that shares the same values.

How do these efforts connect to the principles of Business Executives for Economic Justice (BEEJ)? It can be debated as to whether they are motivated by the biblical intonations of "helping the least of these" or whether it is a sense of demonstrating that a mission-minded Black Business can create change in the lives of the community from which it draws its strength. But that is a debate where both sides win.

I am a Catholic, and it is that educational and value system that has helped to shape many of my decisions in public life. I practice the Catholicism taught at St. Anselm's by Sisters of the Blessed Sacrament, whose Founder, Katherine Drexel was recently proclaimed a Saint. It says that all people, regardless of their situation and stations are to be taught and respected, especially those affected by institutional racism. I practice the Catholicism taught by the Christian Brothers at DeLaSalle, which says that it is your responsibility to assist and help others in whatever way you can because the benefits you receive through education and access are to be used to bring others along--the Catholicism of Inclusion.

Being consistent with one's values while navigating the public arena is always a challenge. Now I don't expect someone like Antonin Scalia, in his capacity as an Associate Justice of the Supreme Court to practice Catholicism from the bench, but I do have to wonder how a man of my generation, raised with the same religious upbringing as mine can come to such different conclusions about public issues that I believe have moral underpinnings.

Antonin Scalia seems to hate Affirmative Action and has cast the vote to erase three decades of law written to expand Black and Hispanic participation in federal contracts. I must tell you that **UBM could not have done what we have done without Affirmative Action.** Scalia seems to practice a Catholicism of Exclusion that allows him to assert that you cannot take race into consideration when setting up voting districts, and permits him to rule that Black prisoners are not subject to "cruel & unusual punishment protections."

In conclusion, I would say that Scalia is probably hopeless and even I have a long way to go compared to others in this room on the issue of public life and our private faith. But I think we can all profit from the story of an Indian Guru, who prayed and meditated for hours each day, asking the Almighty:

1. Why do you allow poverty?
2. Why do you allow ignorance?
3. Why do you allow homelessness?
4. Why do you allow joblessness?

After 30 days of continued invocation to the Almighty, he got an answer in a Big Booming Voice, "why do **you** allow poverty, ignorance, homelessness and joblessness? In other words, what are **you** doing about this human misery?

This is the example that I have been guided by, and have tried to set for others, which is to use my education, experience, and business resources to advance others, and in the process, eliminate a portion of the human misery index within the Black community. But after looking at the committed examples from "Generation X," like Tim King who stepped out of his comfort zone to take in a parentless, homeless, young man and mentor him from a despondent high school student to a confident Georgetown University Junior; and that of Bill Skalitsky and his Project Enable Team, I am convinced that the best is yet to come.

Thank you.

Black Business: A View From the Bridge

by
Paul King,
Chair and CEO, UBM, Inc.

...The conviction is growing among them [leaders and businessmen] that the future of Negro finance and business is dismal....With the penetration of the chain stores and some of the better organized independents into Negro neighborhoods, racial protectionism collapsed."

From Abram Harris, **The Negro as Capitalist** (Rumford Press, 1936).

Black business development advocates, including myself, are facing both old and new challenges in attempting to ensure the continuity of these enterprises across generational lines. It is fine to celebrate Black expansion into the areas of information technology, financial management, and energy; but what if these businesses don't survive beyond the founder?

A case in point is that **there are no second-generation Black-owned general contractors (GC) based solely in Chicago who can bond and self-perform a contract (without a white partner) over $10 million!** One of the few, if not only Black construction firms with multi-generational credentials is Taylor Electric Company. Founded by pioneer Sam Taylor, the city's premier black electrical specialty firm rose to prominence under his son, Rufus Taylor's distinguished leadership, and is now being run by Rufus' daughter, Martha, after his untimely demise. This is the singular example in black construction of three generations successfully building upon the legacy of the founder. By contrast, Chicago's big three Black general contractors from a generation ago, Moore, Martin and Bush, known for their quality work and excellent performance, are no longer doing major jobs in today's market. Meanwhile, large White-owned construction firms, such as Walsh, Turner, and Kenny have a history spanning several generations. This disparity is exacerbated in today's environment where the bigoted, greedy attacks by the AGC on minority business programs, will assure fewer opportunities in the future.

Unfortunately, construction is not the only sector plagued by this lack of continuity. The Chicago **Defender** is a perfect example of a distinguished Black-owned business struggling to survive from one generation to the next. This historic newspaper was a veritable institution that provided information and encouragement for southern Blacks being brutalized, while denouncing the inequities of Black life in Chicago. It provided singular opportunities to Black journalists who later became featured columnists in major print, radio, and television media, and it gave Black people news about themselves that the white media didn't consider fit to print. Yet, the paper barely survived the founder's death, and was left with no viable plan to transfer this historic beacon into the next generation.

Independence Bank is yet another example. Once the parallel pioneer to Black-owned Seaway Bank, today it is owned by whites. Ironically, the very communities that Independence introduced to community banking are now being served by a proliferation of major downtown banks with neighborhood branches. What prevented the founders from looking forward to tap into this huge market now being seized by others?

Several reasons for this problem were identified in a **Black Scholar** (March-April 1972) article I wrote years ago: Firstly, many of these businesses were individual and the owners didn't take relatives or key employees into their confidence. Their children, in many cases, displayed extravagant rather than thrifty tendencies, or chose to go into other forms of livelihood. Finally, poor management combined with a lack of employee sacrifice, often reduced these enterprises to an individual effort, which compounded the problems noted above. Simply put, the founder/entrepreneurs did not transfer the determination they had in starting their businesses into insuring that the firms would survive their time of active involvement. This is the challenge today facing every forward-thinking successful Black business.

Looking at this question today, two major issues emerge: 1) Making the investment and commitment to create a business plan that will lead to the achievement of these goals; and 2) having the capacity to "change" the way business is done to be successful in today's environment. This requires a transformation from Entrepreneur to Executive leader in which, according to Patrick Lencioni, the following traps must be avoided:

1. Putting personal career and ego above that of the organization.
2. Seeking to be more popular than decisive; and attempting to ensure that all decisions are correct.

3. Failing to understand what accountability is and not applying it to employees.
4. Putting harmony over production/ideological conflict.
5. Failure to brag about people who work for you, and being vulnerable enough to trust people with your career, corporation and cash.

One of the biggest traps that black businesses today will have to beware of is large corporations going bankrupt. Vendors, suppliers, and professional services firms will land **far** behind privileged creditors when these firms go under. Few Black enterprises can afford to write off or discount hundreds of thousands (maybe millions) of dollars to United, Enron, Arthur Anderson, K-Mart, etc. Business plans must include a careful selection of clients to whom credit will be extended.

Successful planning for businesses today requires changing their culture and leadership thinking to adjust to consumers' shifting intent, the speed with which communication takes place, and the necessity to value people in the workforce. These changes constitute the foundation for continuity that must be fully embraced by company owners and leaders. The cost is great, but the payoff is huge. In the process, executives must change the way the company defines itself, operates, and treats its people. Whatever has worked in the past is not enough, and resistance to change can be unfathomable. Many of the best contributors to the company's earlier successes can become "player/haters" who will intentionally or subliminally fail to accept new ideas and practices. They may not be evil or mean-spirited, but people who fear the unknown; are too lazy to move out of a comfort zone; or are unwilling to reveal their lack of knowledge necessary for change.

Successful executives must develop teams that will balance the demands and expectations of clients, stockholders, owners (long term goals) *and* their employees. This will take a political effort and strong internal selling, and will require them to develop the necessary management skills themselves or acquire these skills through others. They must be in tune with employees and understand what motivates them. Business plans should require executives to be enrolled in management training programs, and if the results fall short, then supplemental support from other internal/external sources should be engaged. Persons who are committed to being with the company long term should be identified as "future leaders." Assess their potential on the key points of integrity, loyalty and passion for the firm's long-term goals, and require them to clearly articulate their personal career goals. Then determine what additional skills/experiences are required to reach these goals. Owners must then pledge to support this leadership development effort operationally and financially. Likewise, future leader candidates must have the honor and decency to remain and contribute to the company that has supported their leadership aspirations.

The challenge for the successful business in a dynamic environment will be to implement the transformation before the enterprise is rendered obsolete by competitors who have already mastered the art of change. An example can be seen in the contrast between United and Southwest Airlines—two companies in the same industry, both responding to post-9/11 economic downturns, but the former is bankrupt, and the latter, efficient and profitable. The answer lies is in the attitude, team spirit, and performance of the Southwest employees versus their competitors. This is the result of Southwest's leadership and commitment, as evidenced by their ability to envision, sell and implement their objectives.

Numerous articles in the **Harvard Business Review** advise executives to make **results** the most important measure of personal success. Your company's future is too important for customers, employees and stockholders to be held hostage to an individual's ego. Examine the commitment of key employees who must deliver if the company is to produce predictable results. Work for the respect of those who report to owners directly, and not their affection. Make clarity more important than accuracy. People will learn more if you take action than if you always wait for more information. It is the executive's job to risk being wrong. The only real cost in being wrong is loss of pride, whereas inaction means paralysis. Tolerate discord. Encourage people to air their ideological differences. Guard against personal attacks, but not to the point of sacrificing the exchange of ideas. Encourage people to challenge your ideas. Trust them with your reputation and ego, and they will reciprocate with respect and a willingness to be vulnerable among peers. In short: **Choose Trust over Invulnerability; Conflict over Harmony; Clarity over Certainty; Accountability over Popularity; and Results over Status.** UBM's mission statement seeks growth in the industry by satisfying clients through the effective contribution of all our people. This quest is led by the Executive Team and an energetic HR Manager, whose collective ideas and experience are awesome, and their kinetic and potential energy astounding!

As we celebrate successful Black Executives, we lament the demise of thousands of Black businesses that were once led by equally committed executives, but we recognize that the way of doing business in 2002 is dramatically different for all businesses today than for previous generations. We cited the historical reasons for Black business discontinuity and counseled vigilance in the face of the bigoted greed of MBE opponents who are shrinking future opportunities and causing an even greater need for multigenerational planning.

As owners, my partners and I have a single-mind commitment to reach our goal. The resources have been set forth and the policies outlined with clarity. As an executive, I know that I don't know everything, but as Leo Mullin said when asked: "How can you go from running a bank to heading an airline?" He indicated that he was not only determined to succeed; but was also willing to accept his "temporary lack of knowledge," by employing a Socratic approach of surrounding himself with knowledgeable people, through which ideas and solutions would emerge thus enabling him to reach his objectives.

UBM has turned the corner in the multigenerational quest. Although we suffered a few stumbles after coming out of the starting gate slowly, we're now in the homestretch with the finish line in view. I'll keep you posted on the final results.

Originally published as "The Nature of Executive Leadership: A View from the Bridge," March 2003. Reprinted courtesy of **N'Digo**, copyright The Hartman Group Publishing, Ltd., 2003. All rights reserved.

The Next Best Thing

Growth Areas for Entrepreneurs

by Barbrenda Loughlin-Wells

You've probably heard that when opportunity knocks, you should be ready to embrace it. The same holds true in business. If you know what to watch for in future entrepreneurial growth areas, you can prepare now for when opportunity comes a-knockin'.

The number of minority-owned businesses increased 16 times faster than other businesses between 1992 and 1997, according to "Keys to Minority Entrepreneurial Success: Capital, Education, and Technology," a report from the U.S. Department of Commerce. African Americans have strong showings in the service industries, particularly financial services and money management, as well as in technology, says Ramon H. Harvey, dean of Howard University's School of Business.

The growth areas for us continue to be technology, finance, manufacturing and construction. Barriers are starting to come down slowly and more and more African Americans are establishing themselves in these areas and serving as mentors to others, he says.

Harvey thinks entrepreneurs need to consider areas that will succeed economic downturns, or what he calls "bread and butter industries." "We're going more global," he says, "but we have to go back to basic manufacturing activities" that create jobs, such as textiles, manufacturing, plastics, steel fabrication and food processing. So, just where are the future entrepreneurial opportunities? Here are a few areas to consider.

Financial Services

Services is clearly a growth area," says Howard Anderson, founding partner of Boston Venture Capital firm YankeeTek and a professor at MIT's Sloan School of Management. "There are limits to what technology can do."

Anderson says financial services is definitely a growth area for entrepreneurs. The category includes money management, reporting on money and offering new kinds of wireless credit card services. Anderson said "family office" services, which cater to busy households by providing financial advice and help—from researching mortgage prices to selling stock shares on command—relieve people of time-consuming money management tasks. People are looking to buy these services from trusted third parties that can give them unbiased advice, either electronically or in person.

The cost of getting into this is not high, but the payoff is high for consumers," Anderson says.

Construction

Construction is 7 to 9 percent of the Gross National Product, says Paul King, chairman of Chicago-based UBM, Inc., the largest African-American construction company in Illinois. UBM is among the 8 percent of minority-owned construction firms in the United States, so there is plenty of room for those who want to enter into the scene.

Residential construction is up despite the weak economy because interest rates are low. King says. Rehab construction of existing residential properties is also thriving. "While everybody else is moaning and groaning, we are flourishing," he says.

Construction is essential to everyday living, King says. There will always be a need for health care facilities, especially in light of today's aging population. People also will need new schools and roads in the future. "Construction won't go away. It's like air."

While challenges exist for would-be construction entrepreneurs—difficulty in securing insurance and surety bonds for building projects and the ongoing war against affirmative action—King says construction is a rewarding field. "You can create change and make a difference in the community."

Paul King - Chairman UBM, Inc.

www.blackenterprisemagazine.com

22

The Next Best Thing
Growth Areas for Entrepreneurs
by Barbranda Lumpkins Walls

You've probably heard that when opportunity knocks, you should be ready to embrace it. The same holds true in business: If you know what to watch for in future entrepreneurial growth areas, you can prepare now for when opportunity comes a-knockin'.

The number of minority-owned businesses increased 10 times faster than other businesses between 1992 and 1997, according to "Keys to Minority Entrepreneurial Success: Capital, Education, and Technology," a report form the U.S. Department of Commerce. African Americans have strong showings in the service industries, particularly financial services and money management, as well as in technology, says Barron H. Harvey, dean of Howard University's School of Business.

"The growth areas for us continue to be technology, finance, manufacturing and construction. Barriers are starting to come down slowly and more and more African Americans are establishing themselves in these areas and serving as mentors to others," he says.

Harvey thinks entrepreneurs need to consider areas that will survive economic downturns, or what he calls "bread and butter industries." "We're going more global," he says, "but we have to go back to basic manufacturing activities" that create jobs, such as textiles, auto manufacturing, plastics, steel fabrications and food processing. So, just where are the future entrepreneurial opportunities? Here are a few areas to consider:

Financial Services

"Services is clearly a growth area," says Howard Anderson, founding partner of Boston venture capital firm YankeeTek and a professor at MIT's Sloan School of Management. "There are limits to what technology can do."

Anderson says financial services is definitely a growth area for entrepreneurs. The category includes money management, reporting on money and offering new kinds of wireless credit card services. Anderson said "family office" services, which cater to busy households by providing financial advice and help—from researching mortgage prices to selling stock shares on command—relieve people of time-consuming money management tasks. People are looking to buy these services from trusted third parties that can give them unbiased advice, either electronically or in person. "The cost of getting into this is not high, but the payoff is high for consumers," Anderson says.

Construction

Construction is 7 to 9 percent of the Gross National Product, says Paul King, chairman of Chicago-based UBM, Inc., the largest African-American construction company in Illinois. UBM is among the 8 percent of minority-owned construction firms in the United States, so there is plenty of room for those who want to enter into the sector.

Residential construction is up despite the weak economy because interest rates are low, King says. Rehab construction of existing residential properties is also thriving. "While everybody else is moaning and groaning, we are flourishing," he says.

Construction is essential to everyday living, King says. There will always be a need for health care facilities, especially in light of today's aging population. People also will need new schools and roads in the Paul King - Chairman UBM, Inc. future. "Construction won't go away. It's like air."

While challenges exist for would-be construction entrepreneurs—difficulty in securing insurance and surety bonds for building projects and the raging war against affirmative action—King says construction is a rewarding field. "You can create change and make a difference in the community."

Technology

"The United States has one of the most entrepreneurial societies in the world. We understand how to take technological breakthroughs and commercialize them."

> Dinah Adkins, President and CEO, National Business Incubator Association

Technology continues to be a growth area because businesses must be "technologically competitive even if they aren't a technology business," says Dinah Adkins, president and CEO of the National Business Incubator Association. Technology spans all sectors—from manufacturing to retail.

"The United States has one of the most entrepreneurial societies in the world," she adds. "We understand how to take technological breakthroughs and commercialize them."

New technology is the driving force behind state-of-the-art medical devices and pharmaceutical treatments, Adkins says. Entrepreneurs who have technological skills can use them in niche' markets such as medicine and health care.

"All emerging technology is propelled forward by people who turn the idea or product into a marketable commodity," says Corinne Kuypers-Denlinger, editor in chief of Trend Letter, a biweekly newsletter that tracks trends in business, technology and society. She adds that this is particularly true in biotechnology. Lucrative markets may exist for bioterrorism products such as anthrax exposure kits and pathogen detectors for home and office.

Energy

The energy and utilities industry is undergoing deregulation and restructuring, resulting in a more competitive market and opportunities for minority business growth, according to a 2001 Minority Business Development Agency report. There are $86 billion of sourcing opportunities available, the report points out.

Harvey says he sees a lot of activity in oil and oil refinement. No small wonder. The United States continues to seek to become less oil dependent while its oil demands increase. So, it makes sense that the energy sector offers many opportunities for entrepreneurs willing to take the plunge. Kuypers-Denlinger suggests focusing attention on alternative resources, small-scale generation and energy delivery as potential profitable fields.

Niche' markets

NBIA's Adkins says great growth has been noted in people developing businesses in specialized markets, such as home services (personal chefs, housekeeping) and arts and crafts. "People are used to a level of customization and sophistication," she says. "Look at cars. We can customize cars to fit ourselves. That's the way it is with everything now."

Smaller companies are more flexible and can move quicker than huge corporations to satisfy consumer needs and desires in specialty markets. "Manufacturing is difficult unless you're manufacturing in niche' markets," Adkins says. "There's a lot more interest and willingness to pay for artistic goods than in the past. This is a fabulous opportunity for businesses."

Resources For Entrepreneurs

Looking for help in starting your business? Log on to these Web sites:

- Entrepreneur.com (www.entrepreneur.com). Entrepreneur. com is an established online community where business owners access information, expert answers and comprehensive services to solve their business challenges.
- Entreworld (www.entreworld.com). The Kauffman Center for Entrepreneurial Leadership's comprehensive site provides a host of resources for entrepreneurs.
- Minority Business Development Agency (www.mbda.gov). MBDA, part of the U.S. Department of Commerce, provides leadership in fostering the growth and development of minority-owned businesses.
- National Association of Small Business Investment Companies (www.nasbic.org). NASBIC is the trade association for SBIC funds.
- National Venture Capital Association (www.nvca.org). NVCA represents America's venture capital community. This site contains excellent data on venture capital investments.
- Research Institute for Small & Emerging Business, Inc. (RISEbusiness) (www.riseb.org) An organization that provides information and substantive research on issues impacting the formation and growth of small and emerging businesses.
- State Science and Technology Institute (www.ssti.org). Provides complete information on state and community technology development initiatives.
- U.S. Small Business Administration (www.sba.gov). Contains resources for small businesses and useful data on its economic impacts.

Barbranda Lumpkins Walls is a freelance writer and editor in Alexandria, Va.

Summer 2003 Entrepreneur Issue
Reprinted courtesy of www.blackmbamagazine.com

CONSTRUCTION...
AS IT SHOULD BE
by Paul King

Fair-minded Chicagoans looking for a worthy New Year's resolution were pointed to a good one last week by Judge James B. Moran of the federal district court.

The judge warned that if Chicago wants to help minority-and female-owned companies get a fair share of city construction contracts, it had better come up with a different way of doing it. And he ruled that the changes had to be made within six months or the current program will be discontinued.

Those of us who have struggled for decades to gain a toehold in the construction business suddenly have a decision to make: We can get mad; or we can get better.

Not that there isn't reason for getting mad.

Shame on the Builders Association of Greater Chicago, an industry group dominated by prosperous, white-owned construction firms, for filing the 1996 lawsuit that created this predicament. Not satisfied with their near-monopoly on private-sector contracts, emboldened no doubt, by the popular backlash against affirmative action that now echoes from the federal bench, the association challenged the constitutionality of setting aside a minimum percentage of government work for minority-and female-owned contractors.

Do association members really think it is they who are being discriminated against? Do they really think that a city that is less than a third Anglo-white and more than half female shouldn't ask that 25 and 5 percent of tax-funded contracts go, respectively, to minorities and women?

Are they simply greedy? Or embarrassed at their historic failure to mentor and develop minority talent? Or at their furtive use of sham minority "fronts" to make it appear that they're doing their part? All to divert attention from Jim Crow tactics that have kept nonwhites out of apprenticeship programs, construction sites and bid competitions.

No wonder several of Chicago's most responsible contractors—big names such as Turner, Gilbane, Skender, Bovis and Power—leave shunned the Builders Association rather than be party to this disgrace. Good for them.

But enough of mad. The job now is to make Chicago's program better--or at least meet the criteria set by Judge Moran and recent case law.

In his thoughtful and compassionate 31-page opinion, the judge does provide some guidance. Instead of imposing a "rigid numerical quota," he suggests the city ride herd on winning bidders to make sure they give minority and woman-owned businesses a fair shot at subcontracts. There must, however, be measurement and accountability so if the winners don't make the effort, the city can impose fines or liquidated damages.

Strangely, Judge Moran accurately traces the historic impact of racism on minority hiring and the awarding of public contracts. Then he repeats the neo-conservative mantra that racial considerations ought not play a part in setting things right--hmmm.

Stranger yet is his suggestion that minority firms be "graduated" from the program once their annual revenues reach just $17 million, as opposed to the city's more generous $27.5 million.

Experience tells me the city's graduation level is, if anything, too low. Size matters in construction. A $27.5 million company is barely able to maintain the back-office capability--estimating, accounting, purchasing, scheduling--necessary to bid on, say a district police station or branch library. How are they supposed to compete with a $1.8 billion giant such as Walsh Construction on, say, a college dormitory or—dare I suggest—an airport terminal?

Or is it our "place" to stay small? To be grateful for any leftovers once the majors have their fill?

Yet it is the small firms, not the $27 million mediums, that now face extinction. Recent experience shows what's in store. Even Judge Moran acknowledged that minority contracting fell by half after the elimination of set-asides at Cook County and at the Metropolitan Water Reclamation District.

Paul King

I am not convinced set-asides can be replaced. But if they are, do know that only a widespread effort at voluntary affirmative action could begin to fill the void.

By that I mean a full-court press by Richard Daley, Gov. Rod Blagojevich and our region's top business and civic leaders. By that I mean that no government, hospital, university, financial institution, major downtown landlord or responsible corporate enterprise would begin a rehab or construction project without a significant minority presence on its construction team.

A reasonable expectation? I don't see why not. Daley has been a strong backer of economic opportunity for minorities and women. Civic groups such as Metropolis 2020 have argued that our region will not thrive as a house divided between majority haves and minority have-nots.

And that, ultimately, is what's at stake. Not the survival of a few hundred small construction companies, but of hope itself.

Construction is one of the last industries where a nonprofessional can earn a decent wage. It is a last hope for thousands of unemployed black youths in this region; not to mention thousands more now behind bars, who will soon walk our streets, looking for honest work.

Chicago's minority contracting program must be saved and improved, not condemned and enjoined. This is a New Year's resolution worthy of all fair-minded Chicagoans. We have six months to make it happen.

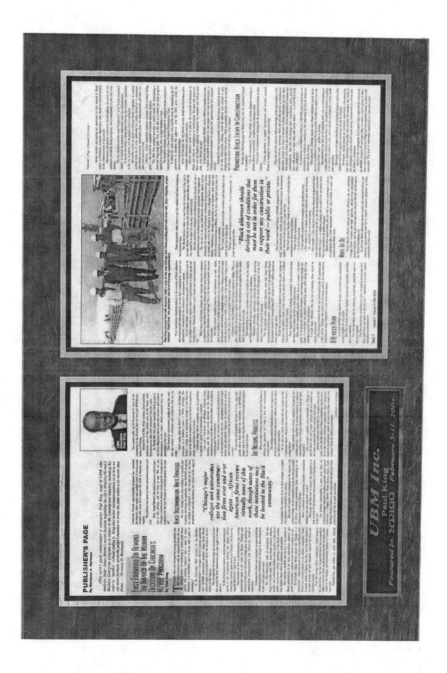

Fast Forward or Rewind:

The Impact of the Moran Decision on Chicago's M/WBE Program

by
Paul King,
Chair, UBM, Inc.
January 2004

We can clearly see that Mayor Daley and the City of Chicago have demonstrated a strong commitment to the goal of economic opportunity for minority and women businesses. This article will analyze Judge Moran's recent decision regarding the city's M/WBE program, including his order to "mend it" without ending it, and will make recommendations as to how we can move forward, given his mandate to revise the plan within a six month timeframe. This final plan should be reviewed before submission in order to gain the support of the three major stakeholders: unions, minority contractors, and worker advocates. A 2,4,5, and 6-month schedule must be established and published for the stakeholders' taskforce. These deliverables must include the input and support of the city's Procurement and Legal departments, and the Mayor's office. This article takes into account the strong possibility that the current program may be enjoined before the six-month deadline for modifying it, which could throw current and pending contracts into a state of chaos. Therefore, it is incumbent upon us to act with a sense of immediacy!

Judge Moran's comments on Race: Cause and Remedy

In his December, 2003 decision on the BAGC's lawsuit against the City of Chicago's M/WBE construction program, Judge Moran acknowledges, in considerable detail, the historical discrimination in the industry. This recognition obviously begs the question as to how this racism has been manifested and what ought to be done about it. In the construction industry, this pattern of racism has functioned primarily in the exclusionary policies that denied African Americans training opportunities at Chicago's de *facto* segregated Washburne Trade School, thus blocking the door to apprenticeships and eventual journeyman status in the trades. Without these avenues of entry into the industry being open, the pathway to construction entrepreneurship was effectively closed to minorities. Consequently, there was essentially no pool of African American general contractors in Chicago to draw from prior to the civil rights movement. The well-constructed walls of segregation did not begin to crumble until 1969, when black workers, businesspersons, and community leaders came together to shut down public sector construction activity operating in the black community without black labor or contractor participation.

This watershed moment provides not only the key to the genesis of black participation in the local construction industry, but points us towards a solution to the current situation as well. For example, Judge Moran states that Chicago is a union town—what does that mean? As we saw above, what it meant in the past is that blacks were locked out of participation in the industry altogether. What it means today is that unions recognize that they must be more inclusive in order to meet the labor demands required by local construction activity. With the average white construction worker being in their mid-forties, the pool of qualified labor had to expand in order to survive. Even so, discrimination has not been eliminated in the training and certification process of construction work. Nonetheless, our efforts to push more African Americans through apprenticeship programs has both expanded the minority labor supply and created a pool of construction workers who went on to acquire the skills to become contractors. *This process has taken an entire generation to bear real fruit.* Thus, Judge Moran's decision comes at a critical juncture in this process, and we have to ask: Will we see Chicago's construction industry build upon the foundation of progress over the last thirty years, or are we facing a new century in which this progress will be eroded?

We have already seen clear evidence of minority participation declining precipitously when minority/women business enterprise programs are cutback or eliminated—that should tell us that these programs are not only necessary, but critical, at this stage of development for minority firms in their struggle to acquire and maintain a foothold in the industry. We all know that in any development program, if the instruments of growth are removed too early, it can result in permanent injury. *Why then, should an effective program be dismantled too soon?*

Judge Moran advised that the city's program use a laser beam rather than a baseball bat to remedy the historical racism in the industry. But meanwhile unions have a variety of tools at their disposal to enforce their rights--from legal redress in the courts, to picketing sites and shutting down projects that do not adhere to standard labor practices or violate their prerogatives. Clearly, these remedies are more like baseball bats than laser beams. If it's appropriate for the unions, then why not for those who seek economic justice in the face of a legacy of past discrimination? To be more specific, why shouldn't M/WBE advocates exercise the same prerogatives?

We have pointed out that because of the rampant discrimination in the industry and the society at large, we are essentially seeing the first generation of African American construction firms operating in the commercial sector in Chicago. What is involved in developing a healthy construction company and how long does it take? Obviously, the best way to answer that question is to look at some of the common characteristics of the top firms in the city. One primary commonality is quite clear: they are multigenerational, and their founders generally started out as tradesmen. Pepper, Turner, Walsh, Kenny, Bovis, Clark, McHugh, Bulley Andrews, and others like Bechtel have been a business for two or more generations. You cannot make up for hundreds of years of discrimination in the 20 years that we have had M/WBE programs in Chicago.

Before the Civil War, black workers, slave and free, performed most of the skilled work in the South. After Reconstruction, they were eliminated from the crafts. By World War One, those who came North as part of the Great Migration had to face the pervasive and virulent discrimination in the trades, which continued from one generation to the next. This historical environment produced both the tradition and culture of exclusion and exclusivity that we see today. That's really what the BAGC lawsuit is all about: the protection of a northern culture of white privilege. The BAGC's actions are a reactionary attempt to turn back the clock on the effort to construct a society based on equal economic opportunities for everyone.

Although Judge Moran recognizes race as a problem, he appears to ignore it in formulating a solution. Last year's University of Michigan Supreme Court Decision and the most recent decision on the Adarand construction case both allow race to be taken into account in remedying past discrimination. Obviously, the elements involved in the problem have to be incorporated into the cure, and prudent counsel would advise that preventive measures be considered as well in order to not only eliminate the problem, but prevent its reoccurrence. If minority participation declines to levels only marginally above those before the institution of M/WBE programs, then it is obvious that preventive mechanisms need to be developed further. What are some of these preventive devices?

In order to address this question, let's look at how the construction process works. The bidding process breaks down into two major areas of activity: *Public and Private Sector* contracts, each of which has different procedures. In the Private Sector, Contractors are **invited** to bid. Credentials matter, and previous experience with the client is a huge factor. In fact, Private sector clients routinely circumvent the bidding process altogether by giving contracts to majority construction firms through negotiation rather than an open bid process. For example, a pattern seen repeatedly in Chicago, is one in which the city's major colleges and universities use the same construction firms over and over again. African American firms receive virtually none of this work, even though many of these institutions may be located in the African American community, have substantial minority enrollments, and/or are receiving major grants and contracts from the federal government. These institutions should be subject to the scrutiny of black aldermen and Congressmen so that their constituencies' interests are appropriately factored into the institution's development agenda.

Contractors seeking public sector projects must be *pre-qualified* in order to submit a bid. Pre-qualification is based on the following criteria: financial, insurance, surety bonds, and experienced personnel. With respect to the latter category, one must ask where the experience is supposed to come from if African Americans have been denied access to the requisite education and training? This is the first major hurdle that must be overcome. The other criteria require resources and experience as well: banks don't loan millions of dollars to owners who are not personally solvent, nor do insurance and bonding companies support firms without a proven track record and a sizable net worth—it's a case of the proverbial vicious cycle—and in this, case that cycle begins with racial exclusion.

Contracts are then awarded to the lowest responsive bidder. This is a place where the bid process can be intersected in order to promote equity: General Contractors get prices from subcontractors and suppliers that enable them to submit the lowest bid. Subcontractors are also a primary source of labor for the job, usually providing between 60 to 80% of the workforce; therefore, economic opportunity should be provided by identifying subcontractors and workers who reflect the ethnic demography of the community where the project is located.

The Bid Process raises another important issue that the Judge incorporated in his decision, i.e., he believes the size of the minority firm in the program should be lowered from $27 million to $17 million (based on 3 year average sales). To put this in perspective, it should be noted that *the sales volume of Chicago's top majority firms is four times the annual volume of all black contractors in the entire country.* These firms have banking relationships with preferred rates that have been in place for two or three generations. How can we reasonably expect smaller firms to compete with these giants in securing the financial, insurance, and bonding requirements necessary to even enter the general contracting arena when facing this longstanding majority firm advantage? I would argue, therefore, that the size of minority firms should be raised, not lowered. The average revenues for the top contractors in the Chicagoland area is $86 million. Perhaps that should be the target goal to develop minority firms that are truly competitive in the local marketplace.

A revised M/WBE plan should include a two-tiered size certification process eligible for city credit:

1. Tier One are those that are minority owned and controlled and under the size standard.
2. Tier Two are those who are minority owned and controlled and over the size standard. Tier Two contractors would have to agree to mentor at least one certified small firm, and agree to directly hire a minimum of six new workers through its subcontractors.

These arguments make sense to any fair-minded individual examining the historical facts. The Moran Decision takes its cues from the notion that if the city in the past did not directly or indirectly discriminate against blacks, then the city cannot be an agent to a *racially oriented* remedy. But this conclusion contradicts the historical facts—because the city's participation in past discriminatory practices is precisely what happened.

Consider these facts to illustrate the point:

You plant a seed; nurture the soil, a plant grows.
You abuse a child; miseducate him, and a socially dysfunctional man emerges.

> You provide a person with an example of the opportunities in the construction industry: encourage them and provide access to construction education; arrange for them to become a union craftsman; provide them with enough work hours and promotions (from chargeman, to foreman, and superintendent); then after developing their construction skills, provide them with access to bank loans, and surety bonds, and **A CONTRACTOR WILL EMERGE!**

In each of the above areas, the city has in the past, both directly and indirectly, denied African Americans the opportunity to become contractors. From permitting unions to dictate who would be allowed to attend a Chicago Board of Education facility (Washburne), through continuing to do business with banks that refused commercial loans to Blacks, the City has a legal and moral basis for participation in the remedy.

The Courts, however, seem to be like ostriches with their heads in the sand in the face of these facts. The key case to be looked at here is BAGC v. Cook County in the U.S. Court of Appeals, Seventh Circuit in 2001. The Court found Cook County's M/WBE program to be "overinclusive," and should only include groups that have been clearly discriminated against. Africans Americans clearly pass this test.

The Court decreed that there needs to be a narrowly tailored plan that incorporates the following elements:

- Proof of prior discrimination;
- A fixed time period;
- A non-specific proportion of contracts that shrinks over time;
- The owners of the business must be relatively poor, and unsuccessful, which flies in the face of reality. For example, a firm must have sufficient resources to guarantee bank loans and meet payroll for the 90 to 120 day period that public entities routinely take to pay, in addition to being able to qualify for the surety bonds that are required on all public projects. Given these requirements, the city will be sorely challenged to develop a program which is both meaningful, useful, and available to small and medium sized black firms.

What to do:

1. Black elected officials must go on the offensive.
2. The City, including CPS and other agencies should establish a revision of procurement process policies.
3. The Governor and state elected officials should amend the Illinois Purchasing Act.

Black Aldermen should consider all construction firms and contractor organizations that fail to support inclusive programs as being unwelcome in their wards. BAGC members have been previously published in **N'Digo**. Before permits and zoning are approved, or fees waived in black wards, a community economic opportunity Plan should be presented prior to the commencement of the project. Developers and General Contractors should address the issues of subcontractor utilization, hiring programs, and commitments to jobs after completion.

The City should revise the word "responsive" as in "lowest responsive bidder," to include an economic opportunity plan for subcontractors; and a hiring plan reflecting the resident's population in the city in general, and the project ward in particular. Just as Bid Credits are given to Chicago-based companies, in contrast to those from out of town, additional Bid Credits should go to contractors who submit economic opportunity plans for Subcontractors and joint ventures with

minority firms. Likewise, certain municipal contracts mandate local resident hiring goals; this should be expanded to include minority workers.

The SBA 8(a) program provides a useful model for formulating a short and long-range plan. First of all, this is a federal set-aside program approved by Congress, thus it's legal standing is clear. The program promotes development by helping to create competitive businesses through a Fixed Program Participation Time (FPPT). It allows for joint ventures with non-8a firms by submitting the JV agreement in advance for approval. And the SBA gives credit for Mentor/Protégé partnerships. **In the revised plan, the city should use this model for developing mentor/protégé relationships and joint ventures.**

Specific attention needs to be paid to the hundreds of thousands of black men who are unemployed or incarcerated. We must ask ourselves: How can non-English speaking immigrants be coached into $20 an hour jobs when blacks are not? Programs such as Project PRIDE, which UBM co-founded and totally funded, should be established for individuals who want to participate in training programs to prepare for and pass the apprenticeship tests and applications. Funding for those incarcerated, such as Pell Grants, should be provided, so that construction training could be offered and utilized to gain employment after their release. UBM successfully did this with an individual who was hired within 90 days of his release. In sum, the following Steps for Black Entry into the workforce should be considered:

A. For the unemployed, Project Pride, or similar program training to prepare them to successfully complete union entrance tests.
B. 2 years of construction training for those incarcerated prior to release
C. Union agreement to support unemployed and recently released blacks in training for immediate apprenticeship.

In conclusion, it is clear that if the city's plan is suspended or eliminated, the leadership of African American Aldermen will be critical. Although every alderman should care, Black aldermen should develop a set of conditions that must be met in order for them to support ANY construction in their ward—public or private. Any committee that they sit on requiring their vote, on such matters as zoning approvals, waiver of permit fees, etc. should be evaluated according to the criteria of contracts, jobs, and economic development. Developers should team with black development partners, black general contractors, and/or joint ventures with black general contractors should be utilized. The developer should present an economic opportunity subcontracting plan and a community hiring plan that includes the number and kinds of jobs community residents should expect during construction, as well as after the project's completion. Just as it was a courageous City Council that supported the creation of the M/WBE Program twenty years ago, today we need a CREATIVE group of Aldermen to develop a revised set of legal and time-honored means to achieve the same goals. This level of Aldermanic Leadership is a **trust and a must.**

"Black Chicagoans Need Access to the Taping Monopoly,"

N'Digo Magapaper; February 16, 2005

by Paul King

In his Sunday, September 26, front-page article, "Taperos' break down union walls," reporter Geoff Dougherty seems to celebrate the literal takeover of the drywall-taping trade in Chicago by Mexicans from 600 miles south of the U.S. border. The article cites estimates that **95 percent of tapers** [a virtual monopoly], represented by the Chicago Painters Union are from Mexico, most from a single region around the town of El Fresnito.

Taping is a relatively simple part of the drywall installation process that can be easily taught, and provides fully employed tapers with an income of $60,000-a-year or more. Many of the immigrant "*taperos*" are able to send part of their earnings back to their families in Mexico, Dougherty reports, where new U.S. pickup trucks and recently constructed homes line the dirt streets of their little towns, alongside the "gaunt cattle" that symbolize the absence of local economic development. It is reported that half of some these Mexican villages were built by money earned by tapers in Chicago

The *tapero* monopoly highlights the growing Hispanic membership in the Chicago's building trades [the Bricklayers and Carpenters' unions are notable examples] that have traditionally been dominated by white ethnic groups who often practiced exclusionary policies towards African Americans. The increased number of Hispanics at construction sites, the **Tribune** writes, has resulted in the unions being "forced" to print magazines and membership materials in Spanish, while others have gone so far as "to promote Hispanics into management positions."

The *tapero* phenomenon was actually started by one man who migrated to the U.S. as a "guest worker" during the World War II labor shortages. His ambition soon bore fruit when he found himself being paid by the day for a job that he could finish by noon. After searching for a way to capitalize on his extra time, he came across the trade of taping drywall joints, and soon became one of the first Hispanics to join the local Painters Union. When a friend started a construction company, he became the drywall foreman, and in this capacity, he found over 100 jobs for Mexican immigrants and friends through the years. Now retired, this enterprising journeyman from a little town in Mexico now has a home in Chicago's south suburbs.

"Good for them!" Some may say that our high wages and liberal immigration policies are stimulating the economies of Central America. I say wait a minute! Back here in Chicago, don't we have an unemployment rate of about 40 percent among African-American men aged 17 to 38? How and why have we somehow passed over them, and ceded this easily learned, but lucrative trade to foreigners. If immigrants can be taught the trade in *six months*, then why can't we train inmates how to perform this work during several *years* of incarceration?

I ask this out of frustration, rather than any hostility to Hispanics: **How do non-English-speakers from outside the country win quick acceptance in the building trades while so many American-born Blacks remain jobless and effectively blocked from the key construction unions?** Why is it that a training coordinator for the painter's union can state straightforwardly that "We are a labor organization and we represent workers in the construction industry," and if they [Mexican immigrants] want to work in our industry, then we want to be there for them."

Are Hispanics more acceptable because they work harder, are always on time, and are more respectful? Or are they more docile, as Dougherty suggests, because the "fear of deportation prevents them from complaining about shoddy treatment from contractors and safety conditions?" On the other hand, do contractors find African American workers to be more contentious, less disciplined and disrespectful? Obviously, we do not want to paint a picture with too broad a brush, but we must honestly address the real issues or *perceptions* that guide the decisions of people in the industry, if we want to move forward.

Thirty-five years ago, Black people shut down over $60 million in construction because there were neither Black subcontractors, nor Black involvement in union apprenticeship and training programs. Nelson Carlo and the late Paul Moreno were among the three or four Hispanics who joined us. Today we have construction sites requiring taping and painting throughout the African American community, such as the replacement of some CHA buildings; new Fire and Police stations, along with private sector contracts being reviewed by Aldermen on the South and West Sides.

Why can't young African American men and women get jobs in their own communities and be given the opportunity to develop themselves, as well as the local economy?

My Black-owned firm, UBM Inc., is a 30-year-old company that was born in a struggle, which continues to this day. For the past decade, we have been the largest Black-owned builder in Illinois, working on the mixed-income developments that are replacing public housing, on fire and police stations and other public works contracts. *All of these projects need drywall tapers and other skilled trades, yet it is difficult to find unionized African-Americans in all but the least-skilled "laborer" category.*

Several things need to be done *post haste* to address this issue:

1. Educate our young people, starting at age 10, about employment opportunities in construction.
2. ACE, the Coalition for Commitment Action, and the Chicago Urban League should establish the goal that within five years, 50% of all tapers and painters should be African Americans.
3. Third, Black members of the City Council should summon union leaders to explain how and why recent immigrants have rocketed to the front of the hiring lines. Aldermen should explore the issue of fairness with respect to the city's employment of immigrant workers who can send funds back home to another country when our own neighborhoods lack sufficient economic development.
4. Finally, a task force should be set up by Gov. Blagojevich; Cook County President John Stroger, to explore how non-violent offenders in our prisons can be taught construction trades and, more importantly, the social behavior and discipline necessary to keep jobs in this field.

I understand that not every unemployed Black person can be reached. But the vast majority can, and as Americans, our failure to reach out to them impoverishes our lives no less than theirs. Although I have often disagreed with sociologist Glenn Loury when he took anti-affirmative action positions, I concur with his assessment that the "vast disparity over representation of African-Americans in prisons and jobs" is our "deepest problem."

Such a problem, Loury stated, in a presentation entitled: "The Blame Game: Personal vs. Social Responsibility in the Race and Poverty Debate," marks "the failure of a civilization, not the success of it." Job training for willing prisoners would be a good start in correcting this imbalance and reversing this process! This time I agree with Loury 100%.

"Passing on Lessons Learned through the School of Public Policy"

Submitted by Paul King, Chair, UBM, Inc.

This proposal has been developed in response to my presentation at the National Black Political Convention at Chicago State University in July 2004.

Background: We can observe from the vantage point of July 2004 that Chicago has many Black people who have achieved great milestones in the areas of Business and Economics, Education, Politics, Governance, and Medicine. These people are advancing in age with a tremendous collective body of knowledge, but many are virtually unknown to the public at large, and certainly to younger generations. Their names may be rarely mentioned in public discourse; they are seldom the subjects of interviews in the broadcast and print media; and they sometimes even escape the net cast by those engaged in academic research. In the field of Politics and Governance – we have such luminaries as Mayor Eugene Sawyer; County President John Stroger; Budget Director, Sharon Gist–Gilliam; Corporate Counsel, James Montgomery; State Senator, Emil Jones; the first Black female Senator, Carol Moseley Braun; Congressman Bobby Rush; Consumer Affairs/Commissioner Brennetta Howell Barrett; Budget Director, Clark Burrus; State Controller, Roland Burris; and Earl Neal, legal counsel to four generations of Mayors. In the Business arena, we have groundbreaking entrepreneurs like Tom Burrell, John Johnson, Dempsey Travis, Ed Gardner, and myself, Paul King.

The lives of these people have been documented or referred to in books like Dempsey Travis' **Autobiography of Black Chicago**; Timuel Black's study of several generations of leaders in Chicago's Black community; and the video documentation program conducted by the HistoryMakers project, as well as other media efforts.

Objective: The objective of the School of Public Policy would be to engage these historic figures to participate (on at least one occasion) in a

Distinguished Guest Lecture Series, in which they would expound on the following points:

1. A general description of what they do or did.
2. A discussion of the level of responsibility they carried.
3. The number of people employed, supervised, and/or in their constituency.
4. The size of the budget for which they are responsible.
5. Identify what they regard as their key achievements.
6. How did they acquire their position?
7. Discuss the amount of time and effort it took to achieve their position.
8. Discuss the reasoning behind their career choice.
9. What advice would they offer others seeking public service.

The **Lecturer** would be asked to give a 40-minute presentation, followed by at least one hour of questioning. Each **Lecturer** would be asked to speak without a fee, although the CSU Foundation may want to explore compensation based on a named opportunity.

The audience would be invited (developed) to include:

1. Students enrolled at Chicago State University (for possible credit)
2. Students from the City Colleges of Chicago
3. Community residents seeking to understand the purposes and processes associated with the careers of these Distinguished Lecturers.
4. Aspirants to public service and leadership roles, or young people who constitute an emerging leadership group, but do not yet hold an office.

Schedule: If we choose eight lecturers across six disciplines – that would lead to 48 lectures per year, four per month, or approximately one per week, with an allowance for several holiday recesses.

Points to consider:

1. Our young people do not read as much as they should, thus verbal exchange might be a more stimulating means of educating them about the rewards of public service and the legacy that they inherit as they prepare for leadership roles in the future.
2. This could start off as a pilot project in Public History, and

constitute a class on Public Policy, which could be offered as a four-credit course at Chicago State University and the City Colleges of Chicago that could be audited by both registered and non-registered attendees.

3. Public Policy in this context is basically defined as the key impact areas affecting African Americans in Chicago.
   A. Jobs
   B. Housing
   C. Education
   D. Politics/Governance
   E. Business

The Lecture Series will explore how these impact areas are funded, administered, and **CHANGED**. Two examples will be offered to illustrate this point:

- The construction unions, in league with a racist Washburne Public School, had less than 2% African American participation in 1969. Today, that number has grown to a factor of 10. What was done? How was this accomplished? Why?
- James Montgomery was the first Black Corporate Counsel to Chicago's first Black Mayor. What is a corporate counsel? What does he do? What challenges did he face, etc.?

Cost:

1. Staff person/instructor to coordinate the Lecturers and follow up with students.
2. One administrative person to provide non-instructional support.
3. Telephone, computer, copy machines, and consumable supplies.
4. Audio-visual equipment
5. Syllabus
6. Possible honorarium to stimulate and/or support written presentations.

Sources of funding:

1. Chicago State University would provide space.
2. City Colleges and Chicago State University budgets.
3. State grants
4. Business and Individual donations
5. A budget must be developed to cover project costs, including in-kind contributions, such as class space rental.

Challenges:

1. To secure Lecturer participation.
2. To develop a generationally diverse audience and sufficient attendance
3. To ensure that the effort is non-partisan
4. To develop a plan to implement the objectives.

In sum, the objectives are to inaugurate a "Conversation and Question" **Distinguished Lecture Series** with current and former public policy figures in order to provide a forum through which their collective Body of Knowledge can be verbally communicated, videotaped, and possibly processed as the basis for a syllabus, or curriculum for future use.

Originally published as "Passing on Lessons Learned through the School of Public Policy." Reprinted courtesy of **N'Digo**, copyright The Hartman Group Publishing, Ltd., 2005. All rights reserved.

Comments on Business and Economic Development in The Covenant by Tavis Smiley

Forum at the Metropolitan Community Church

April 7, 2006

Like the late August Wilson – I am a "race man." **Stated simply, I believe that race matters.** That is the largest, most identifiable and important part of our personality. It is the largest category of identification because it is one that influences your perception of yourself and it is the one to which others in the world of men most respond.

Race is also an important part of the American landscape, as America is made up of an amalgamation of races from all parts of the globe. Race is also the product of a shared gene pool that allows for group identification and it is an organizing principal around which cultures are formed. When I say culture, I am speaking about behavior patterns, the arts, beliefs, institution and all other products of human work and thought as expressed by a particular community of people.

Quoting Wilson further...."we do not need our Blackness couched in abstract phases like "Artist of Color." [People of Color used throughout "Covenant"] Who are you talking about? A Japanese artist; an Eskimo, a Filipino, a Mexican, a Cambodian? Are we to suppose that one white person balances out the rest of humanity lumped together as non-descript "People of Color" and reject that we are unique and specific?

The fact that **The Covenant** exists as a book is testimony to the admonition of Carmichael and Hamilton that before a group can confront an open society, it must first close its ranks. The fact that my long time, good friend Haki Madhubuti would collaborate with Tavis Smiley to publish this book represents committed Black men closing ranks and marshalling resources. Clearly Tavis Smiley's presence and respect in the media make this book gain the attention of the larger, white society.

Covenant 5 – Ensuring Broad Access to Affordable Neighborhoods

Angela Blackwell's essay is reflective of what many of us experience.

However, this section, by necessity must assure that Black people have jobs of at least $15.37 an hour (a national average).

Where are these jobs to be found? Where are the jobs to navigate the transportation between residents and places of employment? The jobs are in the building, remodeling, developing and maintenance of existing houses and new developments. The jobs exist on the highways, roads, and bridges which this covenant describes.

This means that jobs in construction must be provided for Black workers during construction, as well as maintenance jobs when the buildings are up and running.

The average age of a union construction worker is over 44 years old. There are 150,000 constructions jobs that go unmanned each year.

This covenant is silent on the use of black contractors and black workers in realizing its goal. I agree with the fact that we should demand that elected and appointed officials be responsive or ousted. Some are so fearful of losing their jobs that they won't do anything that could be controversial, such as assisting Blacks. Some of these agencies, led by Blacks, put black vendors out of business because of their failure to make timely payments.

What is Needed?

1. Where there is residential development going in our communities, we should have black developers as part of the development team
2. Those developers must be forced to use black general contractors where the capacity exists – joint ventures when necessary.
3. Black professionals – lawyers, accountants, engineers, architects, tax incremental financing specialists and black banks should be involved
4. Black subcontractors must be used alone or in joint ventures.

However, most attention must be given to providing the jobs to local residents. Clearly one house or one development cannot employ all who seek it. Yet an opportunity conference about a development can be held with community residents, job applications can be taken, a schedule of when projects will start can be provided to job applicants.

In one trade alone in the Chicago area, 95% of the union members are Hispanic. They come from Mexican towns over 1200 miles from Chicago.

Why are Black people going unemployed while these $20+ per/hour jobs are going to other groups?

As we contemplate this covenant, we must confront this contentious subject.

What has worked?

1. My firm, a general construction firm, hired two black men recently released from prison. Peter Jennings featured the interview and hiring on "World News Tonight".

   - These two men had received drafting training and construction training while in prison.
   - This training while incarcerated was maliciously cut back and should be reintroduced on a list of demands we seek.
   - These men, however, had a counselor available to them 24-7 for purposes of adjustment assistance. Our company provided them with a mentor and they worked for three years with no problem or recidivism (while earning and paying taxes or just about what it cost to keep them in prison).

2. **Project Pride** – this is a program started by my company in association with St. Paul Church of God in Christ. We provided $10,000 to pay City College of Chicago faculty to prepare job seekers to enter the world of work.

   This includes but is not limited to:

   1. How to take the union apprentice exam
   2. The behavior expected on a construction job
   3. The safety requirements
   4. How to ask a question without feeling "stupid"
   5. How to take instructions without feeling "dissed"

These black people went through the course, passed the test, joined the union and some are still gainfully employed.

Covenant 5 makes a glaring omission in failing to include business and construction job opportunities that will occur as it pursues that vision.

The mentoring and assistance to Black job seekers must be addressed simultaneously.

Walter Mosley persists in his urging that we include the young people we seek to employ in the policies we form for doing so. [**Life out of Context**]

6A – What Works

-In Chicago, we have a charter high school called ACE (Architecture, Construction and Engineering). This high school exposes youngsters to core curriculum in addition to early exposure and training in construction-related subjects.

-Another ACE program sponsored by the large majority group firms takes youngsters from the Chicago Public Schools and gives them intern positions. This program also provides summer jobs, mentor-protégé relationships and possible college tuition assistance for construction careers.

-Chicago also has the Coalition for United Community Action which trains people to enter the construction field; it trains for advancement in the field from a Tradesperson to Foreman and Foreman to Superintendent.

-The preponderance of these students is black men and women.

-These programs should be replicated throughout the country and funded to the level required to expand the respective student population.

Covenant 8

Marc Morial's father was a fraternity mentor to me. Though I have talked with him on occasion, I am surprised at the failure of this covenant to address Black Economic Development, particularly as it relates to Black Contractor Utilization.

As a former President of the U.S. Conference of Mayors, he must have been aware of the example set by the late Mayor Maynard Jackson of Atlanta.

Jackson was adamant that the construction, concessions, design and maintenance contracts of the Atlanta airport included a substantial share of the business opportunities went to black firms.

What Worked

30 years ago, we shut down construction sites where there were no black subcontractors and no black workers. That demonstration led to a plan eventually put to executive order by the late Mayor Harold Washington and signed into law by Mayor Richard M. Daley.

The Black contractor movement grew out of this with the formation of the National Association of Minority Contractors. This organization, with directors from all over the country, was formed in San Francisco – by Ray Dones and Joe Debro in 1969.

As a Chicago director, I became a member of Congressman Parren Mitchell's (d-MD) Black Business BrainTrust which provided him with input on laws and governmental agencies affecting manufacturers, media publications, construction, architects, engineers and other businesses.

The NAMC still exists and, even in the face of the anti-affirmative action agenda of the **AGC,** Chicago continues to have a 25% minority business requirement on public contracts.

Why do other ethnic groups provide services in our community and we don't?

  -Chinese Restaurants
  -Jews
  -Koreans
  -Arabs

-Do we know why the subsequent covenant discussion should research this and determine if they work harder, spend less--are more disciplined or what?

-We now have major chains re-entering Black neighborhoods – what demands will be put on them to force support of our community?

-We need business technical assistance centers set-up in black communities where (a) procurement assistance, (b) management assistance and (c) financial assistance can be taught and provided for start-ups.

De LaSalle High School 50th Anniversary Remarks

by Paul King
September 21, 2006

It is a special honor for me to receive this award on the occasion of the 50th Anniversary of the De LaSalle class of 1956. This school is a much different place than it was in 1952. No one here is very interested in the past, but I cannot accept the honor without reflecting on the beginning years and the impact it had on the success of my life.

1. **Tolerance** and **understanding** of other ethnic groups. I had never had any sustained contact with any group other than African-American when I was admitted here. The only exceptions were the priests and nuns at St. Anselm and the teams from St. Raphael and visitors we played basketball against during the St. Sabina tournament. Therefore, my first exposure to Irish, Italian and Polish people came during my four years at De LaSalle. This was a huge culture shock because I came to understand their tradition, biases and ideas about success. It is noteworthy that I never experienced a hostile racial incident during my time here.

2. **Quality of Education:** Today 50% of all students entering 4-year colleges must take remedial work in order to be admitted into the standard curriculum. De LaSalle prepared me to place out of or "skip" first semesters English and math when I entered the University of Chicago because what they asked on the tests, I had already learned. The foundation in English, gained at De LaSalle, put me in a position to read, write, speak in public and publish hundreds of articles, papers and books--in addition, to Business proposals and negotiations.

3. **Values:** While having a two-parent family and scores of uncles, cousins and relatives living with me, I entered high school with a set of ideals that I was steered to embrace. But it was here that those ideals crystallized into **values**. I was placed in a college bound class where I was expected to succeed. Others around me showed me

239

that marriage after college, or work, taking responsibility for your children, guaranteeing their education was not a random choice, but an expected behavior you had to do. Many of my classmates brought these values from their various backgrounds and I also learned from them.

4. **Friendships**: The measure of a high school experience are the relationships you establish and maintain throughout your life. Some of my best friends are from the class of 1956. Our children have gone to the same high schools and colleges. As our careers advanced, there was never a time that we asked a favor of one another that was not done. Friends tell you when you are acting out of line or are just plain wrong. These friends have done that for me and likewise have taken it from me over the years. We go to dinners periodically every week; we visit one another in the hospitals; we attend the wakes and funerals of family members, in addition to anniversaries, baptisms and weddings. But most of all I witnessed the equal treatment of those who did not have as much as some had and learned the value of treating people with respect regardless of how much money they did or didn't have; or how much influence they may have had, and that just because they were honorable, they were due respectful treatment.

I could not take this honor without acknowledging my wife of 45 years, Loann, as well as Tom Ward, Kevin Forde, Jack Moody, Bob Cull, and John Lindsay.

Our class will make a gift for future classes that you will hear about later. But today, to the classes that follow, I will borrow from another man named Paul who said, "We have fought a good fight, we have finished the race, and we have kept the faith"

That is the tradition of the class of 1956 and I am proud to be a part of it. Thank you.

GOVERNORS
S T A T E   U N I V E R S I T Y

PRESENTS A PUBLIC FORUM

LESSONS FROM OUR LEADERS:
A Conversation Towards a School of Public Policy

SATURDAY, FEBRUARY 3, 2007
10 AM - 12 PM

GOVERNORS STATE UNIVERSITY
SHERMAN MUSIC RECITAL HALL
MAIN BLDG., F WING (OFF OF PARKING LOT C)

SPEAKERS:
Paul King
Jim Montgomery

MODERATOR:
Dr. Gwen Robinson

SPONSORS:
Alpha Phi Alpha Fraternity, Inc.
GSU Black Student Union
GSU Student Senate
Illinois Torch

"Lessons from Our Leaders: Towards A School of Public Policy"

Remarks, Governor's State University; February 3, 2007

I. The change created in the construction industry; and using affirmative action for the first time in the nation.

How it was done:

I stand here today as a living expression of the story of African American participation in the construction industry as a consequence of the civil rights movement. We know about civil rights as it affected segregation in public accommodations, the extension of voting rights, and integration in the public schools. But before Brother Martin Luther King was assassinated in 1968, he had turned a corner and had mapped out a program for economic parity that involved jobs and black business development. He said what good did it do to be able to drink a cup of coffee at a downtown lunch counter if you didn't have the money to pay for it? And that was before we were paying the cost of double lattes at Starbucks.

Although employment and university admissions are the most talked about subjects in the debate over affirmative action, I want to highlight another very distinct area in which I participated from the outset, i.e., Blacks in the Construction Industry business. The focus of some of the most important Affirmative Action cases to reach the Supreme Court, like Webber (1979), Fullilove (1980), Croson (1983), and Adarand (1995), have centered around construction. Interestingly, while the earlier cases, i.e. Weber and Fullilove, upheld affirmative action programs in hiring and promotions and supported minority contractor set-asides in order to correct gross past discrimination and achieve equity in the workplace, the latter cases--Croson and Adarand imposed a "strict scrutiny" standard that essentially ignored clear patterns of egregious discrimination and inequity in the letting of public contracts. If this sounds like retrogression to you— that would be a correct assessment.

The story of discrimination in construction started well before my lifetime. Before the Civil War, black workers, slave and free, performed most of the skilled work in the South. After Reconstruction, they were eliminated from the crafts. By World War One, those who came north as part of the Great Migration had to face the pervasive and virulent discrimination in the trades, which continued from one generation to the next. This historical environment produced both the tradition and culture of exclusion and exclusivity that we see today, and that organizations like the white Builders Association of Greater Chicago [BAGC] are still trying to protect and maintain.

In the local construction industry, this pattern of racism has functioned primarily in the exclusionary policies that denied African Americans training opportunities at Chicago's *de facto* segregated Washburne Trade School, thus blocking the door to apprenticeships and eventual journeyman status in the trades. Without these avenues of entry into the industry being open, the pathway to construction entrepreneurship was effectively closed to minorities. Consequently, there was essentially no pool of African American general contractors in Chicago to draw from prior to the civil rights movement.

To put the consequences of this discrimination into context, ten years ago, the volume of the top three construction firms in Chicago was $7 billion. **This figure was more than double the total revenues of $2.65 billion of all African American construction firms in the entire United States.** At the same time, the dollar volume of the top 25 contractors in Chicago ten years ago, (none of whom were black), was $12.7 billion, which meant that the revenues of all of the black contractors in the United States did not amount to one quarter (21 percent) of Chicago's top 25 construction companies. Aside from being white, what do almost all of these major firms have in common? The answer is that they are multigenerational establishments and their founders started out as tradesmen. Most of the major Chicago construction firms were founded between the 1890s and mid-1920s, the same era that launched segregation, namely the "separate but equal" Supreme Court Plessy Decision in 1896, and disfranchisement, which also meant taxation without representation, that was not remedied until the 1965 Voting Rights Act. It also included convict labor camps [today the U.S. incarcerates more of its citizens than any country in the world and we know who is disproportionately represented); and lynchings— unfortunately the contemporary list is too long to recite, especially if we include the atrocious examples of black victims of police brutality and killings in urban areas like Rudy Giuliani's New York City. Meanwhile, a generation later in 1927, the same year of the great Mississippi Flood that was comparable to Katrina in so many ways, some of these local white contractors were getting their start with projects in major downtown department stores. This was at a time when **the new black migrants of the Great Migration, could not even enter, let alone work in these same stores in de facto segregated northern cities, like Chicago,**

These well-constructed walls of segregation did not begin to crumble until 1969, when black workers, businesspersons, and community leaders came together to close down public sector construction activity operating in the black community without black labor or contractor participation. On July 23rd of that year, I was one of the leaders who shut down Chicago construction sites because of the absence of black workers and contractors in HUD-financed building projects. Hundreds of demonstrators were inspired by Presidential Executive Order 11246, which required contractors on federally assisted construction projects to not only cease discriminating against blacks, but take "affirmative action" to increase African American participation. At that time, Blacks were not getting into the construction unions nor receiving public contracts: we made up less than 2% of Union membership with no representation in certain trades like ironwork. Today, as a result of the efforts that we started, those numbers have risen to 30% nationwide.

As a consequence of these actions, a number of things occurred that changed the course of my life and expanded our mission nationally:

- I became the leader of a local organization, the United Builders Association of Chicago, which remains today as a leading African American organization in the industry.
- I was also involved in the development of the Chicago Plan, which was a prototype for integrating the construction industry that was emulated across the nation.
- I joined with the National Association of Minority Contractors, started in San Francisco, became a regional officer and vice-president, and was later inducted into the organization's Hall of Fame.
- I was invited to participate in Parren Mitchell's [D-MD] Black Business Braintrust. Congressman Mitchell chaired the House of Representatives Minority Business Subcommittee. Here I had an opportunity to contribute, learn and share ideas with black business leaders from around the country in various industries, like Earl Graves, the founder of **Black Enterprise,** etc. Through this channel, I was able to help formulate the

first legislation regarding mandatory percentage goals in the utilization of minority contractors on federal contracts, and I later led the effort to change the Small Business Association's maximum annual revenues that a minority small business can earn from $17 million to $27.5 million dollars, which was beneficial to all small minority businesses. [**Public Works Act of 1976; PL95-507 (SBA)**] During these years, I logged more than 250,000 miles to more than 40 cities and 24 states presenting the plight of minority contractors.

As we have pointed out--because of the rampant discrimination in the industry and the society at large, we are essentially seeing the first generation of African American construction firms operating in the commercial sector in Chicago. But what is involved in developing a healthy construction company and how long does it take? You cannot make up for hundreds of years of discrimination in the 20 or 30 years that we have had M/WBE programs in Chicago. If each of these successful firms got their start through trade experience, architecture or engineering, and these fields have only been significantly open to blacks for less than 30 years, how do you catch up?

Generally, the avenue to becoming a skilled craftsman is to be sponsored by a contractor, complete a recognized training program, perform on-the-job training, be admitted into a union as a journeyman, and then selected (highly subjective) to work by a contractor. Becoming a contractor, requires knowledge of a trade, and/or architectural/engineering training, or college business preparation. *Prior to affirmative action, each of these doors had been slammed in the faces of blacks with the only open avenues being along the dead-end streets of unemployment and economic exclusion.* If blacks are not exposed through education and are ignored by employment trainers, then you don't develop skilled black construction workers, and by extension- no black contractors. Ten years ago, there was still a paucity of African Americans in civil engineering curricula at the top schools -- the University of Illinois at Urbana and IIT had only three graduates, and MIT, one.

At the time of the shutdowns in 1969, I was a painting contractor, but in 1975, I, along with two partners, founded **UBM, Inc.,** a construction firm that grew to become the largest African American construction company in the State of Illinois, with over 100 employees, and was cited by **Black Enterprise** Magazine for its thirty-year history as a leading Black-owned construction firm nationally. UBM is the recipient of four **American Institute of Architecture** Awards for the Conversion and Historic Renovation of **The Reliance Building** at Washington and State Street in Chicago; the Historic Preservation of the Chicago **BEE** newspaper building and its conversion to a public library; and the construction of the new **Chavez** Public School. At that time we specialized in professional services, general contracting and self-performed concrete. Currently, our firm continues to focus on professional services including program management, construction management, owner representative services, and selected general contracting assignments. UBM is a partner in the $1 billion Terminal Six Project at O'Hare International Airport, the largest public works contract in the history of the City of Chicago.

UBM has been a model of corporate citizenship as an ongoing supporter of educational programs and organizations that advance economic and social justice. We developed two award-winning, nationally-recognized programs for college and high-school interns and prisoner re-entry training and placement that resulted in "graduates" being hired as UBM employees. The firm also funded **Project PRIDE**, which provided tutoring for African American applicants to apprenticeship programs to prepare them to pass exams and enter the world of work. Many of these trainees are now actively working in the trades. This successful project has been adopted by the City of Chicago and elsewhere.

Our successes have been applauded but they have also attracted assaults from detractors and enemies of black economic progress. The average age of a union construction worker is over 44 years old. There are 150,000 constructions jobs that go unmanned each year. Discrimination has not been eliminated in the training and certification process of construction work. Nonetheless, our efforts to push more African Americans through apprenticeship programs has both expanded the minority labor supply and created a pool of construction workers who went on to acquire the skills to become contractors. *This process has taken an entire generation to bear real fruit.* Black contractors and black workers should be utilized in filling this gap so that the goal can be realized. Yet we have some Blacks and others who are so fearful of losing their jobs that they won't do anything that could be controversial, such as assisting Blacks. In fact some of these public agencies, even when led by Blacks, put black vendors out of business because of their failure to make timely payments. At the same time, there are instances where in one trade alone in the Chicago area, 95% of the union members are Hispanic. They come from Mexican towns over 1200 miles from Chicago. Why are Black people going unemployed while these $20+ per/hour jobs are going to other groups?

Then there is the BAGC lawsuit that was recently decided by Judge Moran. This lawsuit is all about the protection of a culture of white privilege in the construction industry. The BAGC's actions are a reactionary attempt to turn back the clock on the effort to construct a society based on equal economic opportunities for everyone. In order to address this issue, let's look at how the construction process works. The bidding process breaks down into two major areas of activity: *Public and Private Sector* contracts, each of which has different procedures. In the Private Sector, contractors are *invited* to bid. Credentials matter, and previous experience with the client is a huge factor. In fact, Private sector clients routinely circumvent the bidding process altogether by giving contracts to majority construction firms through negotiation rather than an open bid process. For example, a pattern seen repeatedly in Chicago, is one in which the city's major colleges and universities use the same construction firms over and over again. African American firms receive virtually none of this work, even though many of these institutions may be located in the African American community, have substantial minority enrollments, and/or are receiving major grants and contracts from the federal government.

Contractors seeking public sector projects must be *pre-qualified* in order to submit a bid. Pre-qualification is based on the following criteria: financial, insurance, surety bonds, and experienced personnel. Obviously, with respect to the latter category, one must ask where the experience is supposed to come from if African Americans have been denied access to the requisite education and training? This is the first major hurdle that must be overcome. The other criteria require resources and experience as well: banks don't loan millions of dollars to owners who are not personally solvent, nor do insurance and bonding companies support firms without a proven track record and a sizable net worth—it's a case of the proverbial vicious cycle—and in this case, that cycle begins with racial exclusion. That is why whether we're talking about Iraq or Katrina we see no-bid "sole-source" contracts being handed to the same firms, like Halliburton and Bechtel over and over again because they get all of the major reconstruction contracts due to their "experience." Even when they mess up, as Halliburton has done in Iraq, they still get new contracts on the same preferential basis. In the case of Katrina, we see Davis-Bacon wage guidelines and other requirements being set aside, but yet we don't see a priority being given to hiring local minority residents, resulting in many of the employees being illegal workers from Mexico and Central America.

II. **Closing Points**
 - Our communities are crying for Black Business Leadership; therefore, those of us in influential positions in corporate America must do one of four things:
    1) Investigate levers of power within your company – where purchasing is done and link Black Business with those areas – may be overt / covert.
    2) Consider going into business after you have gained leadership skills and partner with someone having complementary skills and interests.
    3) Join or create a Black Business Advisory Group – where your skills can be offered to emerging and existing Black Businesses
    4) Establish linkages with political and community organizations. - Newly elected Alphas like Todd Stroger; Marlo Colvin; Kwame Kilpatrick; and older Alphas like Danny Davis need business ideas. - People like Barack Obama and Emil Jones need volunteers. - Organizations like Urban Prep Academy (See December 2006 Ebony Issue); and United Way's initiatives on Black Boys - Creation of Black businesses that function within chapters.
       • The success and the major influences I have had, as well as the close friends I have are Alphas. This year, my line will celebrate 50 years. My personal accountant, my son's Godfather, my closest business advisor is from that line.
       • We can organize for change today in any area of life we choose if we have the passion, commitment, determination, leadership, drive, humility and refusal to give up.
       • I know you can do it because I have done it in the face of great obstacles.
       • Creating a statewide and eventual national movement, which fosters "learning from leaders" towards a school of Public Policy is a process that we must institutionalize. It can start here at Governors State and in four years be a curriculum or course at several colleges and universities, and become a routine part of all Alpha conferences local, regional and nationally.

GENERATION Q:

It's Time to Shift to Alpha Activism

Commentary by
Paul King

Brother Paul King is the founder and chairman of UBM, Inc., which in 2004, was Illinois' largest Black-owned construction firm before closing. Currently, he is a construction consultant and principal industrial and commercial developer. He and his Theta line Brothers celebrated their 50th Anniversary on Nov 17, 2007. He is currently an active member of Xi Lambda Chapter. Brother King's work for Blacks in construction has earned him the title of "The man who put firm in Affirmative Action" by one major newspaper.

THE MAINSTREAM MEDIA has branded the latest group of young people coming of age with at least three different tag lines: The Echo Boomers, Generation V and The Millennium Generation.

For those in that age group who are African American, particularly for those in that group who are Alpha men, I'd like to add one more tag line, Generation Q...the Q is for quiet. We're not hearing enough from your generation. There is no outrage, let alone activism from our college brothers regarding the many assaults on Black people.

Its not supposed to be this way. As an Alpha, you've inherited a long and proud legacy to shape a history, not just witness it. The tradition of Alpha Activism is the tradition of creating great change for Black people. It's a tradition of taking steps to make sure the generation that follows, won't face the same roadblocks that were there to impede your progress.

There is not enough time or space in this magazine to list all the roadblocks, potholes and detours that exist today, obstructing the progress of our people. Our men overcrowd state and federal prisons. The nuclear family for us is now only one in four. Now in our communities, jobs are hard to come by and street corner gatherings are easy to find.

Black America can't afford to have you remain quiet. You can't afford it either. The challenges are too enormous, expansive and exhausting for you to just go to your classroom or office, then home to the comfort of your TV, or lap top. If that's all you are into, you are an Alpha fraud.

Can those of you who do not "serve the least of these my brothers" at least monthly, look in the mirror and honestly say that by getting a passing grade, having a nice lady, a good job--while separating yourself from the plight of our Black people, that you are a real Alpha man?

There is a call for you to embrace your heritage as an Alpha Activist. Shift from being stuck in the standby mode. For your computer-savvy generation, I'll call the new program: AA 2.06. I'm calling on your generation to design new and improved methods of Alpha Activism to take our people to the next level of integration in future America.

While you consider how you're going to answer my call, allow me to establish the parameters. Activism is   tantamount to service, for it benefits the larger number of people. It focuses on bringing about change.

As a college Alpha, I was a hotshot. I was President of the Outstanding Undergraduate Chapter (Theta). I gave the undergraduate speech at the convention dinner. I was elected a National Officer. As a chemistry major at the University of Chicago, I earned an Alpha Scholarship. Back then my mentors were many and great: They included Adam Clayton Powell, Thurgood Marshall, Martin Luther King, Jr., Myles Paige, William Hale, Sternson Broaddus, J. Herbert King, Lionel Newsom, Lewis Caldwell, Dutch Morial, Belford Lawson, Lawrence Young, Sidney Jones, and Charles Wesley among others.

I had a private meeting with both Thurgood Marshall land Adam Clayton Powell: Bro. Powell said, "Don't show me your degrees," he admonished. "Don't tell me about the money you'll make. Don't show me how many big words you can use. Don't show me your Brooks Brothers suits. Show me how many pickets have you carried in the heat of the day"!

"Damn right, " Marshall said to me when I told him about Powell's advice.

This was the single most important lesson I learned from Alpha Phi Alpha. It put all of the ritual, history and sacrifice we had been taught, into a clearly defined perspective, Money, celebrity, doctorate degrees, books published, mean little or nothing if you haven't reached out to the least of these. If you haven't sought to counsel young brothers, and if you haven't given service to help change the position of Black people through ACTIVISM, what you think you've achieved is pure fantasy.

Forty-three years after the emancipation proclamation when Lincoln freed our enslaved ancestors, the seven Jewels founded Alpha Phi Alpha. The Jewels' parents and relatives had firsthand knowledge of slavery. This was not done on a whim. There was great hostility in the land over the fact that Blacks were free. What happened to our forefathers back then and for decades to come makes the Jena 6 episode look like a house party. The Ku Klux Klan's influence reigned from Texas to New Jersey. Blacks were being systematically lynched up North in Indiana as well as down in the Deep South. South of Cornell University, whites had family picnics while watching lynchings, New York's newest immigrants, the Irish, resented unskilled country bred, southern Blacks for migrating to Manhattan.

What did Henry A. Callis and his companions do in this hostile environment? They took action! Rather than beg, protest or petition to enter white organizations, they formed their own fraternity. These young activists founded Alpha Phi Alpha on the principles of Black Pride, Education, Christian Values and Exemplary behavior. These Black men started an activist tradition that has lasted for more than 100 years. Their rock solid values and ability to problem-solve laid the foundation for finding remedies for those who needed help. They developed means of prioritizing, organizing and publicizing that whites found non-threatening. Their tactics minimized the violent white resistance to these efforts and, in some cases inspired some whites to offer support in the movement.

The Jewels established Activism, Service and Excellence as our principles. And one generation of Alphas after the next, have passed down their cause. In the 1950's, Thurgood Marshall, whom I've already cited as one of my Alpha mentors, was relentless in seeking to get equal education for Blacks. His activism led to the Supreme Courts Brown versus the Board of Education decision which ultimately led to the end of legal segregation and paved the way for your generation to go to the best schools and compete for the highest paying jobs.

In the 1960's, another great Alpha man, Martin Luther King Jr., led the civil rights movement, which culminated in the Voting Rights Act of 1984 and the dynamic political progress that led to Harold Washington becoming the mayor of Chicago, Deval Patrick becoming the governor of Massachusetts and U.S. Sen. Barack Obama, a serious contender for Democratic Party's nomination for the president of the United States.

In the 1970's, I was an activist using affirmative action as a means of getting Blacks in the construction industry. My Alpha Brothers, Rep, Powell and Dr. King had paved the way, by pushing President Lyndon B, Johnson so hard on the race issues, that he said in 1965, before signing executive order 11246, that it is not enough to just not discriminate but we must take affirmative action to repair the damages of past discrimination.

Construction, one of the largest industries in the U.S., was in need of repair for past and current discrimination, In 1970, one dime out of every dollar spent in the country was spent on the construction of roads, schools, bridges, skyscrapers, airports, and housing--you get the idea. And the Black community wasn't even getting the crumbs, At the time, Blacks were 13 percent of Chicago's population, but comprised less than one percent of the members in the construction union, There were no Black contractors of size, in addition to not counting all the wealth that was not going into the Black community Our movement to dismantle discrimination in the construction industry was unique, because it was the first time a major industry was called into account from top to bottom.

We challenged the industry to hire more Blacks and to cut more Black contractors in on the action. We were able to do this because Marshall and King's activism before us made it possible. Their actions changed the paradigm of the federal government and practically all major construction has federal funds involved.

We also took to the streets. With the support of more than 600 community residents, we shut down construction projects with contracts worth more than $60 million, We warned all white workers that "you can work In Chicago, but not without us."

We exported activism to other cities. Alpha man Joe Debro organized the National Association of Minority Contractors (NAMC) in California. This organization still exists today.

I worked with the late congressman Parren Mitchell (D-MD) and created the first Black congressional caucus Business Brain Trust. This Brain Trust led to the first law in history that required the use of Black Contractors in Public Construction. As a result of our activism, unions are now 35 percent non-white.

Alpha Activist John Wilks, who was Asst. Secretary of Labor when we were out to change ground rules, he quietly but efficiently guided us through the perils of that time. Because he was the head of the Office of Federal Contractors Compliance, his commitment to our struggle was incalculable. So significant was the contribution, the white contractors tried to move him out of the Department of Labor. Although, he's long since retired, the white contractors continue their fight to keep us out. They funded public policies such as Bakke, Defunis and California Proposition 209, which changed college admission procedures in the name of reverse discrimination, which in turn to shut out many Blacks.

The challenges facing Black people today are different, but in many ways are as grave as they were during slavery. Back then, the white power structure kept us in bondage, murdered us without remorse, disallowed our learning to read, write and learn arithmetic and separated our families, so that our children grew up not knowing who their fathers were. Today the white structure keeps us in prisons in record numbers, while we do much of their old horrors to ourselves. We murder each other without remorse; we fail to get a good education, we don't bother to marry, or raise or care for our children,

What many of us do, I believe, is your challenge as Alpha men to help undo. You and your generation can help create an understanding as to why our younger brothers are reaching manhood with little vision of what to do next and how to go about doing it. They have no goals and less drive. They're paralyzed by hopelessness.

Jim Montgomery (a great attorney who's not an Alpha, but could and should be) and I have started a movement called "Toward a School of Public Policy: Lessons from our Leaders." This is a dialogue between those of who have accomplished certain goals in their careers and linking them to younger brothers and sisters. The idea is to pass the body of knowledge we have with those younger people who want to know, but may not have access to answers. Our dialogues are Q and A's, not lectures.

You and your generation can address the inequities in the criminal justice system and develop an ongoing dialogue on what to do with the 100,000 plus ex-offenders who will return to our neighborhoods, year-in and year-out, once they've done their time,

I am working with my Brother, Danny Davis on "Operation Second Chance." This is legislation the congressman is sponsoring that will restore voting rights and also allow ex-offenders to take jobs they were previously denied. In my own business, I hired five ex-offenders. One came out of prison with drafting skills. He worked three years for me; he was never late, and he presented no problems. He also had a counselor who was available to talk with him daily.

I also launched Project Pride. We gave a city college $10,000, to teach tour ex-offenders how to enter the work world: how to hear and receive a demanding request without feeling demoralized; how to ask a question and not feel stupid; how to be on time and to call in when you're going to he late; and generally how to succeed on the job front.

You and your generation must work to stem the epidemic of Black on Black crime. It has reached the point of where we can no longer be silent. We have too many innocent children being killed. We have old women being afraid to identity crooks because they will get their houses burned.

I am meeting with Harold Saffold, co-founder of the African American Patrolman's league; Gary Slutkin of Cease Fire; founders of Gangs from the 60's, and police commanders and young men from troubled neighborhoods, to find out what can be done to stop this.

I am not asking you to do anything that I and greater Alphas have not done. You know the history and the heritage. You have much greater chances for success, because you can use our victories and mistakes as your roadmap towards making greater change. You know the score. You've been schooled in organizational management, team building and the agility of the Internet. You have our knowledge to draw on and your state-of-the-art knowledge to wield.

Now it's time for you to MAN UP!

Once committed, I'm sure Generation AA2.06 will take the tradition of Alpha Activism back to the future.

Here are some actions today's Alpha Brothers can take:

Each chapter, district and region, as well as individual Brothers, should understand these issues and take one or more of the following actions:

1. Mentor young Black boys. You and other Brothers can adopt a school.
2. Monitor and challenge racism in media--through Black radio, the Black press and online blogs.
3. Construct bridges between our generations so that there can be knowledge sharing.
4. Stimulate partnerships between health institutions, so our young people can prevent the current health crisis in the Black Community.
5. Discuss and develop an alternate approach to affirmative action in education, business and jobs.
6. Develop concepts and programs for returning ex-offenders to the Black community in a positive and constructive role.

I am not asking you to do anything I haven't done.

Reprinted, courtesy of ©**The Sphinx** Magazine, Fall/Winter, 2008.

CONCLUSION

The preceding pages represent a 30-year journey. The essential quest was to achieve parity for Blacks in the construction industry. Dual in nature, the effort was to get Blacks into all of the trades and to remove obstacles and develop Black contractors. At the contractor level, the emphasis was to increase the number of African American specialty firms and to create Black general contractors.

The resistance by white people and their institutions and their continuing influence was and remains unbelievably strong. Thirty years ago, white union members--100 deep--stated that the buildings would fall down if Blacks did the work. This is not 1950 Mississippi—this is 1970 Chicago! In one case, a Black tradesman seeking to get into the iron workers union had to have U.S. Marshals guard him because of threats to push him off a girder over a 2nd floor landing.

Today, there are more white females and Hispanics in many unions than Black men. At the contractor level, the triple challenge of banking, bonding, and management competency continue to challenge subcontractor growth and development. In the past we had technical assistance centers and strong vocal contractor associations arguing at the national level. We had Parren Mitchell leading the fight. Locally, we had champions like Earl Neal, Clark Burrus, and currently Ed Smith and Toni Preckwinkle.

At this writing, there are no Black general contractors **based** in Chicago that can **independently** perform beyond a minimal volume level.

What caused the current crisis? The white resistance has always been more to eliminate competition, though sometimes peppered with racism. Companies that grow so strong so as to independently beat white firms are systematically eliminated by the three evils of slow pay; incompetent public sector staff who create problems for Black firms; and the necessity to spend outrageous costs on lawyers.

Thus the view from the bridge is wiser, though disappointing. Until Blacks become angry enough and public officials sensitive enough, our situation in construction is going in reverse.

EPILOGUE

THIS BOOK IS an acknowledgement of 40 years of continuous activism. The outcome has been sporadic in its achievements. This collection documents those years, and represents a journey filled with determination, which often involved combat that resulted in both victories and setbacks. The common thread crucial to all of these experiences was unselfish organization, and unyielding principles in an unending effort to promote and elevate the role of Blacks in the Construction Industry through the use of affirmative action. If one were to link this quest for Black Contractor creation and inclusion to the Civil Rights Movement, it is clearly the first economic or effort to integrate a large industry.

As these programs became successful, resistance to them rose at a rapid clip. Who would have ever thought that what we did on July 23, 1969 would reach the Supreme Court under the guise of "reverse discrimination?" Who would have believed that the "affirmative action" programs that helped to increase an exclusively white workforce become integrated, and provided opportunity to Black firms around the country would be challenged so vigorously that the presidential candidates in the 2008 election cycle didn't even use the word?

Today, there are more **"minorities"** in the unions; but the number of African-Americans (the group that started it all) is often less than other ethnic groups and white women. The opponents of affirmative action have so poisoned the phrase that the laws and the courts, which were once our champions, are now our enemies. Black contractors have been put out of business not only by the laws, but also by the nefarious practices of public agencies who refuse to pay in a timely manner; banks who will not lend; and some public employees who conspire to apply rules unevenly resulting in the destruction of many black businesses.

But in the midst of this milieu, an historic event occurred that is a new source of inspiration, which I was privileged to witness. I attended the Swearing In of my friend, Barack Obama as President of the United States. This can portend only good things for Black Business. His Stimulus Package is just one example of the hopeful possibilities that many of us experienced through Parren Mitchell's minority contractor amendment to the **Public Works Act of 1976.** The Pride of the Obama victory, however, must be joined at the hip with **Patience.** He has inherited two wars, a politicized Justice Department, and a teetering economy highlighted by an unregulated financial sector in free fall. Therefore, in the meantime, we must go back to basics by doing the following:

1. **Challenge** our local, county and national governments to create capacity-building programs to fill the void created by the dearth of Black Contractors.

2. **Educate** elected and appointed officials as to the issues they must support in demanding change and hold them accountable by not voting for them if they fail to advocate on our behalf.

3. **Resume Activism.** Young Black people, as well as older ones who are out of work must recognize that it is in their self interest to organize, protest, lobby, educate, and agitate to achieve fairness, parity and balance with respect to Black inclusion, in private and public sector procurement programs. The light at the end of the tunnel is that if we do our part, we can be confident that the President of the United States and the Attorney General will work with us to help us succeed.

Finally, I would share with the reader one of the greatest lessons that I have learned on this journey, which is that friendships, relationships, and trust are not transferable. These things have passed the test of time, and their most important litmus test is to do what one promises.

Paul King
Chicago, June 2009

ABOUT THE AUTHOR
Yesterday

Paul J. King, executive director of United Builders Association of Chicago, has been active with the Congressional Black Caucus Brainstorming Group, the Cost of Living Council, the National Association of Minority Contractors and a Small Business Administration task force on government-funded construction programs. Active in construction affairs involving minority builders across the country, King is a speaker and lecturer on construction and related topics at universities, conventions and builder's groups.

259

> *"I like the idea that when my son came home from Georgetown University, he was reading Marcus Garvey in one hand and the Wall Street Journal in the other hand. I like that combination."*

Paul King

In 1968 there was an organization called the West Side Builders, a black group of contractors that was being helped by Brenetta Howell and Garland Guice, who were with the Chicago Economic Development Corporation (CEDCO). I was always interested in organizations and people, which is why I am active in Alpha Phi Alpha fraternity, which has been one of the best experiences of my life. In 1968, Garland and Brenetta were able to get a grant from the Department of Commerce, and they wanted to have somebody that was a contractor and had a college degree run the program. I was a member of the group, and I had graduated from Roosevelt University, so I won by default. At that time you got $10,000 a year for being full-time director, and they allowed me to continue my contracting business with the stipulation that if I got over a certain threshold I would make them aware.

This group had come together with the intention of focusing on certain issues affecting black people. Through some fortunate circumstances they chose the construction trade unions. In 1969 it was recognized that the white unions were ignoring Executive Order 11246 which required that contractors doing federal work must not discriminate [and] must take affirmative action.

In 1969, Blacks were the heaviest minority. Our focus was on shutting down work in order to force contractors to comply with the law and take more Blacks into their shops. Now, the contractors made the point they had union bargaining agreements, and they were not the problem the unions were the problem.

What we did was physically go shut down job [sites]. We had at that time the involvement of the Disciples, the Vice Lords, the Black Stone Rangers and Breadbasket, which at that time was led by Jesse Jackson. {It] was a very interesting group of people. I have never seen a group black people organized so effectively, especially considering we had these powerful egos.

The guys who were members of the gangs would turn up 300 to 400 strong in the morning and attack a construction site—nonviolently. The first demonstration took place on July 23, 1969. It was on Douglas Boulevard on the West Side, where some urban renewal work was going on. There were no black contractors and very few black workers on the particular project. It was enough to make anybody cringe. Here you are in the middle of a black neighborhood, and a white contractor is doing the work. I think they had one black sub-contractor. That gave me an opportunity to picket that job, to shut the job down, and we ran all the people home.

When the TV and the press came, they found me, because I was the head of West Side Builders. I had some words ready for them right away. That's what got me started. Emotion and true sensitivity got me started, [along with thinking about] the arrogance of somebody who builds and does not give any work to the sub-contractors who are black. The fact is that we did have the leverage of the law, and black workers were being excluded. That was the first demonstration.

And I have to admit flat out, through all the aggravation that has been attributed to the gangs, in this particular context they were meeting at seven in the morning until seven at night, sometimes all the way until two in the morning. They had representatives or one of their leaders at every meeting. They actually put the troops out in the field. They were the ones who gave us the numbers when we went to demonstrate. As for the Urban League and the NAACP and the other civil rights groups, they were out to lunch. I suspect they weren't with us. It was a demonstration where numbers and bodies counted. At that time the guys from the gangs were youngsters, teens. Some of them wanted jobs that were supposed to come out of these demonstrations. I think there is a message that I would draw from it: there is a positive force in all people. If you identify and work with it, it will contribute to what you are trying to do. There was an accord that was struck with those people that may not be possible today. I think this is one of the things that black people in Chicago must be very careful about: not to write off a group of our own people as being hopeless just because they don't demonstrate the behavior or qualities that we want to see or are comfortable around. There is something in all people that could be a positive force.

I think you have to separate the person and his opportunities from the person and his emotions and the person and his philosophy. You have to remember that with all the education you might have, with all the advantages, you are still black in a white nation. There is a portion of me that was fortunate enough to be born into a family that is still together, cohesive and supportive. I was fortunate enough to have a father who tenacity.

My father is in the wholesale produce business. His is the oldest **black-owned** distribution business, run continuously over the last 35 years. I have got the firm 8A certified--that's a program under the Small Business Administration which allows firms that are deemed socially and economically disadvantaged to get contracts without bidding. If I am successful he will be able to get government contracts to supply produce to Army bases, Veterans Administration hospitals, the Department of Agriculture and other agencies that buy fresh fruits and vegetables. I'm also in some negotiating to get P. King Produce into a position where it will have space for trade at the international port and space for local distribution at South Water Market.

My father gets up at three in the morning to go and take care of his business. He gave me the example of concern for his wife and children. My mother gave me an example of what to look for in a wife by being much concerned for her children. My mother didn't have an education past the high school level, but she saw that I learned how to play the piano and understood opera before I was 12 years old.

I say all that to make the point that one is fortunate to have all of these things. But education and family background are supposed to pre pare you to do something more with it. I became kind of a rough character when I acknowledged the racial discrimination that I saw in certain areas once I got involved. It was just so blatant that I started raising hell.

You live in Chicago; you know Chicago. We can talk about many things that are a source of irritation.

I was in the construction industry. I worked for my uncle while I was... at DeLaSalle High School. When I got to college I wanted to make some money. I remember I made my first $100 in one day by getting four painters that were out of work to do some work that I had contracted. I made $100 more than I had to pay out, so I was hooked. So I went into the painting business a year after I was out of college. I was 23 years old. I fumbled around making and losing money. I had too much freedom, not being tied down to a job [while] rearing my first kid after being married at the age of 22.

I have been speaking to college kids lately, at Florida A & M University and in Atlanta. I think there is hope for some young people. But I am seriously disturbed with the people that are my age and a little younger. I just don't see that potential mobilization that was there in 1968 and

1969. Of course the solutions are much more obscure. When you look at this economy—inflation, recession, falling of the dollar, energy and all that stuff—it is basically a political, moral kind of a deal.

My oldest boy goes to Georgetown University—he's a freshman. So I gave him some going away advice. I told him to be cool with the concept of God, cool with his family, and then study business and finance. Be cool means to be right. Understand it, get a grip on it and handle it. These are three of the most powerful forces in your life.

Most people are hopeless or oblivious or otherwise out of it and don't understand what's happening to black people. I don't know, maybe the train has left the station, and it isn't going to come back. I had some ideas on how to reach the people in places like Robert Taylor Homes, before the train left, but now it's gone. If you have a ratio of three kids per apartment in some of the projects, where are these people going to live when they become teenagers and out of the jurisdiction of their parents? Where are they going to work? I don't know, unless somebody establishes a reservation somewhere in some suburb that will accept them [and] provide a method and an incentive to go out there and live. There's a bedroom shortage in Chicago—you almost have to go to Oak Park to look for housing. If you've got kids, what's going to happen? Especially when the job market is so strict in terms of being service-oriented or high-technology-oriented. Neither area has been geared to those people in those projects. The Hispanic-Cubans and Puerto Ricans--and the Vietnamese are taking up the service jobs that used to be available. The goddam Arabs are taking over your business in the black neighborhoods.

Some black people don't recognize the serious threats that we are under: the re-emerging of the Ku Klux Klan; Blacks getting shot in Buffalo and Utah. I am talking about alcoholism being the third biggest killer among Blacks-- the kids are on Dope--the destruction of families. I think our race is under severe attack. If the people don't realize that, they are at a different level, and we don't have anything to talk about.

But I am big on Chicago. I am the first generation born here—the rest came from New Orleans. I like Chicago. I've got a nice house. I understand Chicago. I think Chicago's racism is clear. First of all, I think as a city it will prevail. The black private sector idea may be in motion by that time.

I like the idea that when my son came home from Georgetown, he was reading Marcus Garvey in one hand and the Wall Street **Journal** in the other hand. I like that combination.

I think there will be some positive action going on with the kids calling their own shots. I think also that there will be a much larger black underclass. That group of Blacks is in serious trouble, and that group will be much larger. I cannot see the miseducation that's occurring in those public schools not having an impact. This impact will be visible when they will be in decision situations.

In this period we are seeing a group of people seriously being manipulated by the media, You will find the people divided up into two groups: the ones that read books and the ones that do not. We're getting an indication of what they plan to do in the future, to try to separate us on the basis of the so-called class distinction. There is one class being black and being discriminated against. Within that class of Blacks, you have differences in perception, differences in opportunities and differences in lifestyle. But I don't think basically that a black person who doesn't have any serious bad habits such as addiction to drugs or alcohol--his taste and my taste are not fundamentally very different. I think there are some basic characteristics which do not change regardless of your education and economic conditions. I believe that that community of interest is stronger than any other thing that can separate us.

I got a lot of press on one notion: I said black leaders have failed. Look at the current headlines and you can see some credence in that remark.

I think in the concept of leadership you have to develop a few things. We have to have a black private sector--businessmen with money supporting black private institutions so that we can train leaders. We have no training from generations of black leaders. The black private sector should support an ideology that will generate black leaders. We've got to have an independent source of money to promote an idea.

I don't think there is anyone as a black leader who can encompass the aspirations and interests of all black people. I think that day has gone. My sister marched with Dr. Martin Luther King Jr. At that time he was speaking of a broad moral issue which all of us could be represented on.

Now it is very different. We take very different views about issues that once might have been accepted by most Blacks. Like "symbolic" busing to get black kids an education is all right with me, but on the real side I don't to get along with the race that is in the majority.

As far as education is concerned, that can be provided in a black school. Both of my boys went to Howalton Day School at 47th and Dearborn. Both of them tested right into St. Ignatius, a Catholic high school with a strong academic program. Competition for entrance to the school is keen, and students must take a rigorous examination to be accepted. My oldest boy left St. Ignatius and got a scholarship to Georgetown University. But his basis was a black private school right there on 47th and Dearborn.

The point I am making is that we are diversified in our thinking, and we are diversified in our interests. You take Dearborn Park, an expensive "new town" being built next to the Loop. That means something very threatening to you and me, from an ethnocentric point of view. We think we see a trend to mix that neighborhood in such a way that a ring spreads that will keep Blacks from controlling that land. To others, it might mean improving land values on housing to the south, where Blacks are still living. But we see things differently.

We can't have one person leading us because we have too many different interests. There should be a black leader in business, surrounded by black leaders in special business groups. We can take a look at the white models: you don't have one leader getting into another leader's specialty. They recognize special interest groups and organize around them. I think it is possible to achieve that once people are able to see some advantage in coming together. That's a very difficult thing to deal with: coming together.

When you talk about leadership, I think of the Blacks who serve on corporate boards. What kind of feedback do you get about what they are doing?

I think your question is very good, but I will go one step farther and include those black elected and appointed officials who sit on prestigious and influential boards. I see no tangible positive influence, unless they give some symbolism for grammar school children who might be impressed by that.

Let me give an example. Our family has a currency exchange on 55th Street at Prairie and the El. Two blocks over, on 55th and Michigan, is a currency exchange owned by a Jewish man. They mail state checks to the currency exchanges so the people can pick them up instead of being ripped off in the mailbox. The currency exchange benefits, because the people will cash their checks and the exchange will get a fee. At my mother-in-law's exchange she may get five checks a month, whereas the white owner gets hundreds.

I took this problem to the black man who signs the checks. He referred me to another black man who is head of the agency that disburses the checks. Both of these men are my friends. Both are my fraternity brothers. But they couldn't do one damn thing about helping me make some money.

I went to DeLaSalle High School. All the mayors of Chicago prior to Jane Byrne went to DeLaSalle High School except maybe Cermak. I knew the late mayor (Richard Daley) on an intimate basis. I knew his kids. They helped me to make money, based on our 25-year-old relationship at the school, and I helped them to make money also. The Catholics I knew were on a basis of friendship. They helped you make money and you helped them make money.

This is not so with our Blacks in these elected positions. I won't say that about every one of them, but about 99 per cent of them. What's wrong with us is that we can't create any leverage to make somebody else some money. Something is wrong when our people get on these boards in those positions and then don't help other people to make it. We've got three Blacks on the Chicago Housing Authority board. I am cordial with two, but so far as stroking a path to help make some money, I have not seen it yet. I am talking about getting legal contracts.

Corporate boards could be positive for Blacks, if those memberships meant doing more business with Blacks or implementing some policies to move Blacks into higher ranks.

But I'm tired of Blacks getting positions where they don't handle the money. We don't have any Blacks in charge of the Department of Public Works or the Department of Streets and Sanitation. We usually get jobs like Human Services director or superintendent of schools—some body else handles the money.

There is a tremendous void in Chicago, period, in terms of leadership or movement-type people. We have so much in common between us. Why can't we get together to make some money? Stepping aside, the same applies to the whole leadership concept.

People don't have anything really to say. I don't honestly know that many black people who have anything going on that's really all that conversation worthy. If you have got a group of people who don't recognize the plight that we are in, you are talking from two different levels.

From Dempsey Travis, *The Autobiography of Black Chicago*, 1981.

ABOUT THE AUTHOR TODAY

PAUL KING, FORMER chairman of the Chicago Business Council, is a pioneer in the struggle to promote Black inclusion in the construction industry; and instrumental in securing government support for minority contractor assistance programs in Chicago and nationally, having logged more than 250,000 miles to over forty cities and twenty-four states in this effort. After spearheading the initial demonstrations that led to construction shutdowns in Chicago in 1969, he and other activists negotiated the first **Chicago Plan,** and he became the founding executive director of the United Builders Association of Chicago.

Mr. King attended the De La Salle Institute, the University of Chicago and Roosevelt University. He is a much sought-after speaker and the author of numerous articles and editorials, including *amicu*s **briefs** in the Fullilove vs. Klutznick Supreme Court Case. His many honors include national recognition as one of the "Men Who Made Marks in Construction" by Engineering News Record in 1973; induction into the National Association of Minority Contractors' Hall of Fame; Minority Contractor of the Year (2001, Arizona State University); Affirmative Action Leader of the Century (Coalition for United Community Action, 1999); the United Builders Association of Chicago's Lifetime Achievement Award; and the John A. McDermott Award for Extraordinary Leadership in the Marketplace from Business Leaders for Excellence, Ethics, and Justice. He was also a member of the Black Business Braintrust for Congressman Parren Mitchell's [Dem-MD], who secured passage of the first legislation requiring mandatory percentage goals for minority contractor utilization on federal contracts.

King was the chairman and principal founder of UBM, Inc., the largest African-American owned Construction Company in Illinois in 2003-2004, with over 100 employees, when it was cited by **Black Enterprise** Magazine for its thirty-year history as a leading Black construction firm nationally. UBM, the recipient of four **American Institute of Architecture Awards,** was a partner in the $1 billion dollar Terminal Six Project at O'Hare International Airport, the largest public works contract in Chicago history.

Mr. King is also the Chairman and Founder of the O'Hare Development Group joint venture project

Paul King has an abiding concern for the well being of young people and UBM was a model of corporate citizenship and strong supporter of educational programs that advanced economic and social justice. The firm developed two award-winning, nationally recognized programs for African American college and high-school interns and prisoner re-entry training and placement that resulted in "graduates" launching professional construction careers, including some being hired as UBM employees. The firm also funded **Project PRIDE**, which tutored African American construction apprenticeship program applicants. Chicago, as well as other municipalities, adopted this successful project.

WORDS OF PRAISE

Paul is "a tireless worker and a friend I hope never not to have."

*Rev. C. T. Vivian, veteran civil rights leader and
lieutenant of Dr. Martin Luther King, Jr.*

"When Harold Washington was elected Chicago's first Black Mayor, I was his Corporation Counsel--another black first. Within the first 100 days, Paul had breakfast with Harold...[and] advanced the case that the Mayor should issue an Executive Order requiring all city contracts have a Minority Business Utilization Requirement. Paul's petition was successful and today after two Mayors, the Ordinance is Law...Paul and I have worked as a team to create a School of Public Policy where we who have achieved could teach young people and community residents how to create change, how to challenge the system and learn lessons from our successes and mistakes."

*James D. Montgomery, Esq., cited by Chicago Magazine
as one of the city's 30 Toughest Lawyers.*

"A pioneer in the Affirmative Action movement...a leader and fighter for full participation for minorities and minority companies in the construction field."

Alpha Phi Alpha Fraternity, Xi Lambda Chapter

"Affirmative Action Leader of the Century...for distinguished leadership and dedicated service in the struggle for Affirmative Action and economic justice."

Coalition for United Community Action, 1999

"You have been a strong advocate for and a reservoir of innovative ways [for] economic development programs for African American construction firms."

Black Contractors United

"Paul King—the man who put the "firm" in Affirmative Action."

N'Digo Magapaper

"Paul King was at the forefront of the struggle to push Blacks to enter the construction industry...His passion is for today's youth--our leader's of tomorrow. King is determined to pass on his legacy of success by proving that hard work and commitment is definitely a winning formula."

National Association of Minority Contractors

The publishers and editors of *Engineering News Record* [ENR] cite "Paul King…[as one of the] men who serve the best interests of the construction industry."

February 20, 1974; **ENR, a Division of McGraw Hill Publishing Co., Inc.**

"Not everyone agrees that minority set asides are a good idea. When the Cook County Board voted to make its 30% "goal" a legal requirement, suburban Republicans howled about "mandatory quotas"….Maybe someday, when there are a lot of Paul Kings out there, we won't need them anymore."

John McCarron, Chicago **Tribune**; October 24, 1993.

LaVergne, TN USA
27 October 2009

162142LV00003B/1/P